The Great European Stage Directors

Volume 6

The Great European Stage Directors
Series Editor: Simon Shepherd

Volume 1
Antoine, Stanislavski, Saint-Denis
Edited by Peta Tait

Volume 2
Meyerhold, Piscator, Brecht
Edited by David Barnett

Volume 3
Copeau, Komisarjevsky, Guthrie
Edited by Jonathan Pitches

Volume 4
Reinhardt, Jessner, Barker
Edited by Michael Patterson

Volume 5
Grotowski, Brook, Barba
Edited by Paul Allain

Volume 6
Littlewood, Strehler, Planchon
Edited by Clare Finburgh Delijani and Peter M. Boenisch

Volume 7
Barrault, Mnouchkine, Stein
Edited by Felicia Hardison Londré

Volume 8
Bausch, Castellucci, Fabre
Edited by Luk Van den Dries and Timmy De Laet

The Great European Stage Directors

Volume 6

Littlewood, Strehler, Planchon

Edited by Clare Finburgh Delijani and Peter M. Boenisch
Series Editor: Simon Shepherd

methuen | drama
LONDON • NEW YORK • OXFORD • NEW DELHI • SYDNEY

METHUEN DRAMA
Bloomsbury Publishing Plc
50 Bedford Square, London, WC1B 3DP, UK
1385 Broadway, New York, NY 10018, USA
29 Earlsfort Terrace, Dublin 2, Ireland

BLOOMSBURY, METHUEN DRAMA and the Methuen Drama logo are trademarks of Bloomsbury Publishing Plc

First published in hardback in Great Britain 2019
This paperback edition 2024

Cover design: Adriana Brioso

A catalogue record for this book is available from the British Library.

A catalog record for this book is available from the Library of Congress.

ISBN: HB: 978-1-4742-5399-4
HB Pack: 978-1-4742-5416-8
PB: 978-1-3504-4582-6
PB Set: 978-1-3504-4599-4
ePDF: 978-1-4742-5994-1
eBook: 978-1-3504-6193-2

Series: Great Stage Directors

Typeset by Integra Software Services Pvt. Ltd.
Printed and bound in Great Britain

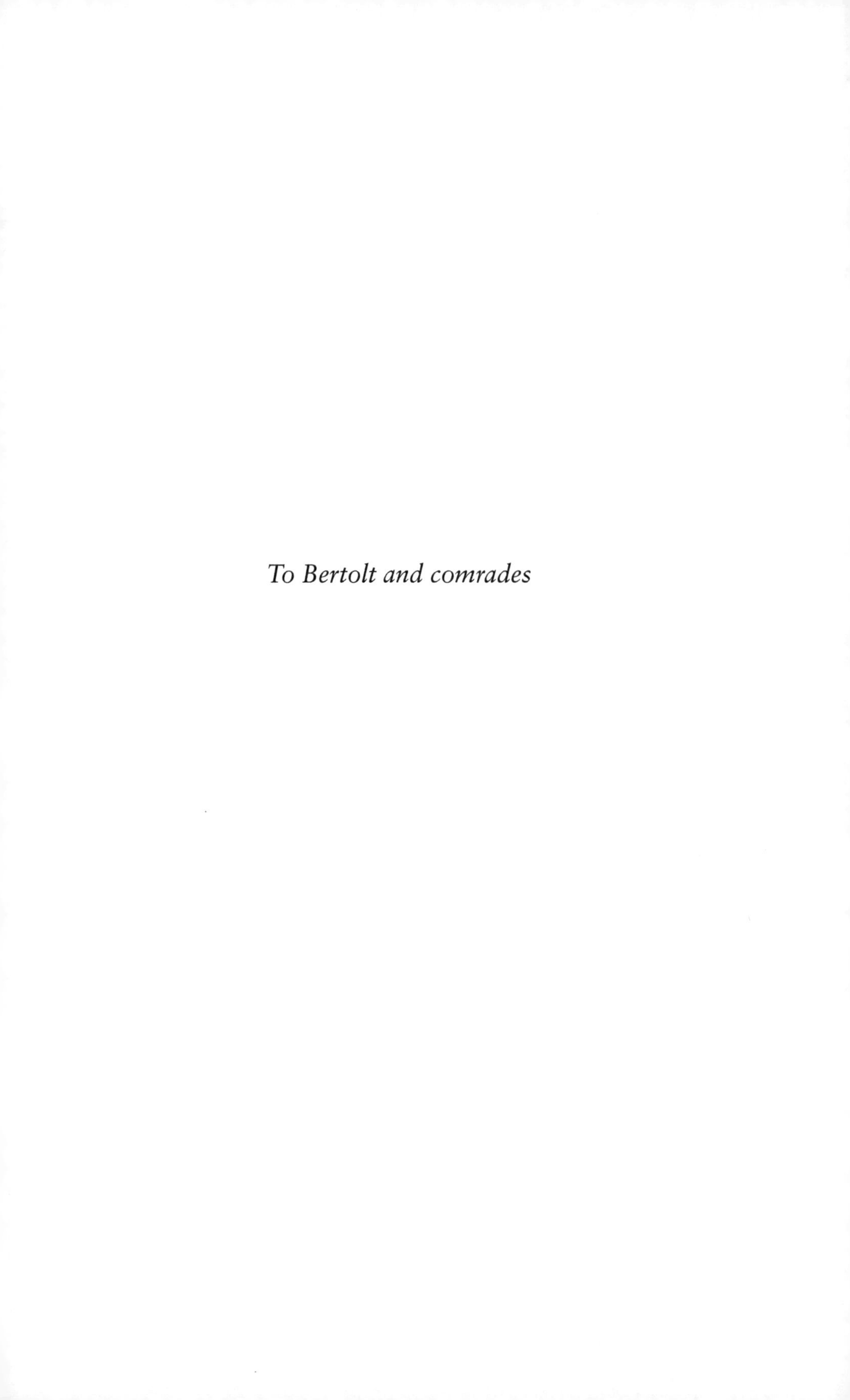

To Bertolt and comrades

CONTENTS

LIST OF FIGURES

NOTES ON CONTRIBUTORS

Michel Bataillon worked very closely with Roger Planchon for many decades (1949–86) and was an instrumental influence in the programming of the Théâtre National Populaire de Villeurbanne, which they set up together. As a theatre practitioner, notably an actor, Bataillon first began work in the Paris suburbs with the actor and director Gabriel Garran, whom he helped to found the Théâtre de la Commune d'Aubervilliers in a working-class district on the outskirts of Paris. Subsequently, along with Roger Planchon, Patrice Chéreau and Georges Lavaudant, Bataillon was at the forefront of France's project to decentralize theatre, helping to relocate the Théâtre National Populaire to Villeurbanne, a suburb of Lyon. He is also a Germanist, and has translated a range of German theatre texts into French, and worked as a dramaturg on productions of German plays. He is currently president of the Maison Antoine Vitez, the international centre for theatre translation.

Peter M. Boenisch is Professor of Dramaturgy at Aarhus University, Denmark. His primary interest is in the intersections between aesthetics and politics in contemporary theatre. His research areas are the fields of directing, dramaturgy and contemporary dance, with a particular focus on German- and Dutch-speaking European countries. His books include *Directing Scenes and Senses: The Thinking of Regie* (2015) and *The Theatre of Thomas Ostermeier*, which he co-authored with the German theatre director (2016). With Rachel Fensham, he is co-editor of the series *New World Choreographies*.

Clare Finburgh Delijani is researcher and teacher in the Department of Theatre and Performance at Goldsmiths, University of London, UK. She has published widely on modern and contemporary European theatre. Co-authored and co-edited volumes include *Jean Genet* (2012), *Contemporary French Theatre and Performance* (2011) and *Jean Genet: Performance and Politics* (2006). More recently her research reflects two of the most pressing political and social issues of the modern world: the ecological crisis and global conflict. She has co-edited a volume of eco-critical essays, *Rethinking the Theatre of the Absurd: Ecology, the Environment and the Greening of the Modern Stage* (2015) and written a monograph on representations of war in recent British theatre, *Watching War: Spectacles of Conflict on the*

Twenty-First-Century Stage (2017). Clare has also translated several plays from French into English, notably by Noëlle Renaude.

Bent Holm was Associate Professor at Copenhagen University until 2014. His main areas of research include theatre historiography, theatricality, rituality, cognition and dramaturgy. He has also worked as a dramaturg and translator of, among others, Goldoni, De Filippo and Fo. He has been visiting lecturer at various international academic and artistic institutions, most recently at Cologne, Tokyo and Verona. He has published interdisciplinary studies in Danish, Italian, French, English and Polish. Recent books include *Religion, Ritual, Theatre* (2008), *The Taming of the Turk: Ottomans on the Danish Stage 1596–1896* (2014), *L'arte dell'attore nel settecento: accuse e apologie* (2015) and *Ludvig Holberg: A Danish Playwright on the European Stage* (2018). He received the Holberg Award in 2000.

Pia Kleber has been a Professor of Drama and Comparative Literature at the University of Toronto, Canada, since 1988. Her career accomplishments include twenty years as the Director of the University College Drama Program, being named the first Helen and Paul Phelan Chair in Drama in 1999; numerous publications on Bertolt Brecht, Roger Planchon, Giorgio Strehler, Robert Wilson and Robert Lepage, and two awards of the Federal Cross of Merit of the Federal Republic of Germany (in 2002 and 2015). Having worked extensively on cultural approaches to human security, she is currently researching intersections between the Arts and Artificial Intelligence.

Margherita Laera is a Senior Lecturer in Drama and Theatre at the University of Kent, Canterbury, where she is co-director of the European Theatre Research Network. She has published widely on Italian theatre, theatre criticism, theatre translation and adaptation in edited collections and scholarly journals such as *Contemporary Theatre Review, Modern Drama* and *Performance Research*. She is the author of *Theatre & Translation* (2019) and *Reaching Athens: Community, Democracy and Other Mythologies in Adaptations of Greek Tragedy* (2013), and the editor of *Theatre and Adaptation: Return, Rewrite, Repeat* (2014). She is the Online Editor for *Theatre Journal* and *Theatre Topics*.

Robert Leach has been Reader in Drama and Theatre Arts at the University of Birmingham, UK, and Senior Lecturer in English Literature at Edinburgh University. He has acted professionally in Britain and the United States, and directed plays in Russia as well as Britain. His *Theatre Workshop: Joan Littlewood and the Making of Modern British Theatre* was shortlisted for Theatre Book of the Year in 2006. Other books include *Makers of Modern Theatre* (2004), *Vsevolod Meyerhold* (1989), *Revolutionary Theatre* (1994) and *Stanislavsky and Meyerhold* (2003). In 2018, his *Illustrated History of British Theatre* and *Russian Futurist Theatre: Theory and Practice* was published.

Danielle Mérahi studied English literature at Nanterre University from 1968. She worked as a drama teacher in partnership with various theatres, and was a founder member of and performer for the Theatre Company Théâtre du Mantois. She was also in charge of the cultural and artistic activities of La Comédie des Mantes, a community theatre in Mantes-la-Jolie. She translated Martin Crimp's early plays and texts (2006), and her academic publications include *Joan Littlewood, l'insoumise et le Theatre Workshop* (2010) and *Théâtres du Réel en Angleterre et en Ecosse des années 50 à nos jours* (2017). She is a member of RADAC, an interuniversity association of academic researchers on anglophone contemporary drama.

ACKNOWLEDGEMENTS

This book would not have come into existence without the inspired contributions of the chapter authors, Danielle Mérahi and Robert Leach, Margherita Laera and Bent Holm, and Pia Kleber and Michel Bataillon. We are especially grateful to the series editor, Simon Shepherd, and to Methuen Drama's theatre publisher Mark Dudgeon for patiently bearing with us while getting this volume together. Thanks also to Lara Bateman and others at Methuen Drama for supporting the production process.

We are particularly indebted to Silvia Colombo at the Archivio del Piccolo Teatro in Milan for her generous support of the book's section on Giorgio Strehler, to Karen Fisher and Murray Melvin at the Theatre Royal Stratford East Archive and, further, to Pia Kleber for not only providing us with a written chapter but also with access to some of the previously unpublished treasures of her personal collection of photographs and other sources on Roger Planchon.

Pia Kleber would like to thank Rajak and Vartan Ohanian and Dominique Grard from the Archives municipals/Le Rize, Ville de Villeurbanne, for providing some photographs for publication. She would also like to thank Michel Bataillon.

Danielle Mérahi would like to include a special dedication in memoriam of Clive Barker, theatre coach and academic.

Introduction to the Series

Simon Shepherd

The beginnings of directing

Directors have become some of the celebrities of contemporary theatre. Yet for most of its life, and across a range of practices, theatre has managed perfectly well without directors, celebrated or otherwise.

This is not to say that it has lacked direction, so to speak. Some form of directing, by actors, prompters, stage managers, designers, has always featured as an activity within theatre's processes. What was new was the concept that directing should be done by a role specifically dedicated to that purpose. Emerging around the 1890s after many centuries of theatre, it was both a historical novelty and geographically limited, to Europe and North America.

What these cultures had in common, at the start of the twentieth century, were the ideas and practices which we now call Modernism. In the arts it is associated with particular sorts of innovation made by short-lived movements such as Constructivism, Dada, Expressionism and Surrealism. But modernist thinking also influenced industrial innovation. This is seen in the creation of what F.W. Taylor called 'scientific' management, the systematization and hence separation of the role of a manager who bears responsibility for planning and oversight of the production process. As I have argued before,[1] the concept of director comes to be formulated at the same time as a managerial class is becoming defined. The value put upon the activity of management might be said to create the conditions for, and justify, the creation of a separable role of director.

This was apparent to Barker in 1911 when he observed that in Germany it was precisely the proliferation of management duties that made it impossible to combine the role of manager with that of actor. But German practice was perhaps in advance of the rest of Europe. Many of those now regarded as the founders of directing appeared to work in very similar ways to those who are not categorized as directors. Antoine ran his own company, selected the repertoire, took acting roles and directed plays, as did Stanislavski and Copeau. In this respect their practice differed little from, say, Henry Irving or Herbert Beerbohm Tree, both regarded as actor-managers.

Where the practice of the early directors seems consistently distinct throughout Europe is in its cultural, and sometimes political, positioning. Antoine, Copeau, Barker, Piscator, among others, positioned themselves against a dominant theatrical culture which they aimed to challenge and change. This positioning was an ideological project and hence brought with it an assumption of, or claim to, enlightened vision, artistic mission, the spirit of innovation. Adopting this rhetoric Antoine declared that directors had never existed before – that he was the first of a kind. When P.P. Howe wrote his 1910 book on that new organizational phenomenon the repertory theatre he distinguished the new director from the old stage manager on the grounds that, while the stage manager was adept at controlling the 'mechanical' aspects of the stage, the director was the guardian of the 'vision'.[2] This aesthetic formulation is, though, wholly cognate with management as industrially understood, as Alexander Dean makes clear. In 1926 he recommended that each company should have one person in the role of overall director because the director is not only responsible for each production but also, crucially, is 'the great connecting link between all parts of the organization'. Furthermore: 'Every organization needs a leader who has a vision; who sees a great achievement ahead.'[3] The non-mechanical visionary is also the Taylorist planner.

But some, it seems, were more visionary than others. You will have noted that none of the directors so far mentioned is North American. Yet while Antoine, Copeau and others were founding their theatres outside the mainstream, the same was happening in the United States. The Little Theatres of Chicago and New York started in 1912, the Neighbourhood Playhouse (New York), Portmanteau Theatre and Washington Square Players followed in 1915–16. Contemporary commentators such as Constance D'Arcy Mackay (1917) saw both the European and the American experiments as part of the same 'little theatre' movement.[4] Their practices look similar: founding theatres, against the dominant; culturally selecting audiences, possibly by a membership scheme; working with amateurs; performing explicitly naturalist dramatists, such as Ibsen. But while Antoine and Copeau have entered the canon of great directors, Winthrop Ames and Alice and Irene Lewisohn have not.

Reflecting on the contrast between North American and European practices, William Lyon Phelps suggested in 1920 that the United States lacked a public discourse that would take theatre as seriously as cars. His argument built on Moderwell (1914) and was taken up by Dean (1926).[5] Both saw little theatres as the mechanism for developing a larger theatre-going public, and hence were primarily interested in their success as organizational and economic entities, being much less interested in directors as artists. In Britain similar arguments proposed repertory theatre and the amateur movement as the mechanisms for building both democracy and a dramatic renaissance. Theatre, Barker argued in 1910, is a 'sociable' art. Thus North American and British discussions proposed that theatre could develop the cultural accomplishments of civil society. European discourses, meanwhile, were more interested in, and driven by, avant-gardist movements and experiment. For instance, Antoine positioned himself within an already existing public discourse about art, allying himself with the naturalist, and anti-racist, Zola; staging censored playwrights; distributing Strindberg's polemical preface to *Fröken Julie* (*Miss Julie*) – and making sure to invite reviewers to his theatre. For Piscator and Brecht the energizing link was to activists and ideas within both the political and the artistic avant-garde. The European director thus acquired the status of artistic activist, linked to and recognizable by existing networks of activists and makers, with their own mechanisms for dissemination and publicity. The European avant-garde, long celebrated as the supposed origins of performance art, was perhaps more clearly the originating moment of the theatre director.

The discursive position of European directors was consolidated by their own pronouncements and publications. Each of the early directors was adept in an established theatre craft, as were actor-managers. But when Barker, Meyerhold or Saint-Denis lectured on and wrote about the crafts of theatre, and even more when directors established regimes of training, they were showing themselves to be not just practitioners but theorists of a craft, not so much mechanics as visionaries. The early directors, and indeed directors since, claimed to understand how theatre works as an art form, and to have proposals for its future developments. In this sense they show themselves to be not only guardians of the vision of the play but also guardians of a vision of how theatre itself can and should work. The success of the claim to be visionary is evidence that what the director manages is not just the company or production but also the discourse about them.

Taken together new ideas about management, avant-garde practices and theories of theatre enabled the formulation of, and justified, a separated role of director. The role could then be seen as providing a specialism, missing hitherto, which is necessary to ensure the artistic seriousness and importance of theatre.

While the mechanism that formulated the role of director may have been discursive, its consequences were much more than that. Properly to carry out the guardianship of the vision meant taking responsibility for ensuring the aims and coherence of the processes of theatre-making. The artistic visionary slides into place as Dean's industrial manager. The discursive formulation results in actual power over other theatre workers. The director's control can determine not just that which is staged but also the hiring, if not firing, of those who stage it.

With the invention of directors a new power structure emerges. Yet it had been, and is, perfectly possible to make theatre without that role and its power structure. So there is a potential tension between the effectiveness and productivity of the crafts necessary for theatre and the new, but not demonstrably necessary, power structure that came to claim organizational authority over those crafts. This tension has made the role of director important and yet unstable, treated as celebrity and yet, after only a century, subject to questions as to whether it is actually necessary.

Those questions have been asked not least by directors themselves. Tangled up with the other issues summarized above they run through the volumes of this series. For the directors here have been selected not only because they are generally taken to be important, indeed 'great', but also because they reflect in interesting ways on the role of directing itself. Of course there are other important names, and interesting reflections, which have not made it into the selection list. Decisions such as these are usually difficult and almost always never satisfactory to everybody. But more stories are told than those of big names. The featured directors are not important because they possess some solitary essence of greatness but because they offer ways into, and are symptomatic of, a range of different practices and ideas. The discussion of each featured director frequently involves other directors, as well as designers, writers and actors with whom they worked and by whom they were influenced. For example, the authors of Volume 3 insist that we move our focus outwards from the featured male directors to attend to the women with whom they collaborated and on whom they depended.

The series begins with some of the earliest examples of the practice, but the only other chronological principle governing the distribution of directors is the decision to create two groups of volumes falling roughly either side of the midpoint of the twentieth century. What this arrangement highlights is the extent to which the practice of directing generates a system of self-reference as it rapidly developed an extensive discourse of its own very new art. Thus, for example, Volume 6 features directors who engage with, and perpetuate, the practices and legacy of Brecht.

Rather than suggesting a chronologically seamless evolution of practices the distribution of the directors across the series seeks to call attention to debate. Volume 1 deals with Naturalism, Volume 2 with critiques of Naturalism. The aim is to provoke thinking not so much about the director as an individual as about the art of directing in its different approaches and concerns. The vision of which the director is guardian and the assumptions as to what constitutes the art of directing are revealed as diverse and provisional. For some directors their creative work mainly involves the staging of their ideas about the world, for others creativity comes in the design of processes and the management of people, for yet others creativity has to do with the design and management of theatres. While Brook's philosophy of life may have constructed powerful and influential stagings, Guthrie's philosophy of life more or less invented the equally powerful, and perhaps more influential, concept of the role of artistic director.

If Volumes 1 and 2 display contrasted aesthetic approaches, Volume 3 has us focus on directors as founders and managers of companies and theatres. That topic of company formation and management returns again, in the context of the latter part of the twentieth century, in Volume 7. In a similar way Volume 4 brings together directors who may be seen as auteurs working within a modernist climate while Volume 5 gives us auteurs emerging from a post-Second World War Europe. In Volume 8, the directors are also auteurs, perhaps most powerfully so in that there is often no dramatist's text. But at the same time here the role of director begins to wobble, blurring into that of choreographer or visual artist.

In exploring the various directors, it becomes clear that, as noted above, some directors are major contributors to the discourses about directing, both reflecting on practices in general and foregrounding their own work in particular. This has an effect on their apparent status within the field. The existence of texts authored by directors often facilitates the study of those directors by others, which in turn generates more texts and elevates their apparent status, as a sort of greatness-construction machine. But there are other directors who are less textually established, perhaps because the director actively refuses to document their work, as did Planchon, or perhaps because there are cultural or geographical boundaries that English-speaking academics tend not to cross, as is the case of Strehler. Or it may be that directors have simply fallen out of theatrical or academic fashion, as, say, for Saint-Denis. That they are no longer, or ever were, serviced by the contemporary greatness-construction machine does not make these directors any less significant. Celebrity is not in itself necessarily relevant to being important.

Introduction to Volume 6: A Popular Theatre for All: Western European Theatre Direction in the Mid-Twentieth Century

Peter M. Boenisch and Clare Finburgh Delijani

In 1957 in the industrial working-class suburb of Lyon in France, the great stage director Roger Planchon established a theatre which he referred to as a *théâtre populaire*. In an interview at the time, Planchon insisted that *théâtre populaire* did not involve making the most popular or populist theatre possible. Rather, it committed to making quality theatre for 'the people'. Planchon, like the other directors treated in this volume – Joan Littlewood and Giorgio Strehler – thus applied what Bertolt Brecht termed as the 'plebeian' tradition of theatre: a commitment to making theatre for as wide and diverse an audience as possible, while encouraging audience members to reflect critically on the societies they lived in.

This volume explores the work and legacy of these three 'Great Stage Directors' whose pivotal work was created during the middle decades of the last century, in a period bracketed by two fundamental landmarks in the history of twentieth-century Europe: at one end, the atrocities and barbarisms of the Second World War, and, at the other end, the political protests of the late 1960s, most notably the key moment of the May 1968 protests in France, the fiftieth anniversary of which has been marked during the year of this book's publication. Both of these seismic events not only caused major ruptures in the political, societal and cultural fabric of Western societies at large but, in various ways, also impacted on the artists discussed in this book: British alternative stage director Joan Littlewood (1914–2002), Italian pioneer of 'director's theatre' Giorgio Strehler (1921–97) and French innovator of popular stage aesthetics Roger Planchon (1931–2009). Born in three different decades of the early twentieth century, all three directors created their major works during the 1950s, 1960s and 1970s, as Europe emerged from the traumatic years of two world wars and embarked on decades of new and unprecedented prosperity fostered by the economic revival and the social reforms of the post-war European 'welfare states', yet against the backdrop of the fragile stability of the 'Cold War' between the international superpowers, the USA in the West and the Soviet Union in the East. Perhaps even more than for other generations, the theatre of these three directors was shaped and influenced by the specific historical moment in which they created their work.

This historical moment, with its deep impact on every single member of society, also called for a change in theatre. Theatre, and the realm of art and culture more widely, became the prime location on which to rebuild a new ethical foundation for society, to unite people, to bring them together and to span across nations, borders and ethnicities, in order to prevent once and for all the warfare and horrific atrocities committed between European neighbours. Therefore, the work of Littlewood, Strehler and Planchon is significant, over and above its aesthetic innovation, thanks to the manner in which it approached the canon of classic plays or the ways in which it integrated various historical and modern forms of alternative theatres. Most of all, these three directors' œuvres reveal a new outlook on the role and function of theatre in contemporary society, one with which they aimed to reach out to 'the people' – a general audience, far beyond the middle classes who had been the traditional patrons of the arts since the nineteenth century. With their company ensembles, Littlewood, Strehler and Planchon worked in new contexts beyond the established temples of bourgeois culture and also mainly outside the central capitals of their respective countries. Each of them founded, from scratch, their own company and created influential new theatre institutions, which redefined the theatre landscapes in which they operated. After co-founding Theatre Union in Manchester in 1936 and touring mainly industrial working-class towns in the north of England, Joan Littlewood, one of the first and still one of the few twentieth-century women to have been legitimized by the male-dominated history of stage direction, worked, between 1953 and 1975, with her celebrated Theatre Workshop at the Theatre Royal Stratford East – in the capital city London, but specifically in its working-class East End district of Stratford. Giorgio Strehler founded his 'Piccolo Teatro della Città di Milano' in 1947, based in the affluent, elegant northern Italian manufacturing and banking city of Milan, as the first permanent, stable theatre company in the history of Italian theatre. A decade later, in 1957, Roger Planchon set up his Théâtre de la Cité in Lyon's industrial suburb of Villeurbanne, resisting numerous calls to move to the capital, Paris, and to head major companies including the Comédie-Française. Instead, he presided over this regional, popular theatre onto which the epithet Théâtre National Populaire was eventually bestowed.[1]

Directing plays from the established canon of classics – Molière, Calderón, Goldoni and, above all, Shakespeare – and equally promoting contemporary playwriting by authors including Arthur Adamov, Brecht, Shelagh Delaney, Eugène Ionesco and Luigi Pirandello, all three directors pursued the aim of opening up the institution of theatre to wider audience constituencies beyond the middle-brow cultural elite. At a time when, from radio to television, new mass media emerged that addressed the entire population regardless of their class, background and geography, these three directors envisioned theatre as a similarly inclusive, accessible, popular and open cultural institution. Directing canonical classics for them no longer signified a devotional worshipping of the refined 'eternal achievements' of Western (white, bourgeois) art. Theatre no longer had to stand as a marker of education and erudition, set apart from the mundane and banal concerns of everyday life, not least social, economic and political life. Above all, theatre was no longer to be distinct from any 'popular' entertainment 'for the masses'. Littlewood, exemplarily, envisaged theatre that would 'bridge the gulf between creative art and the lives of ordinary people': it would not only be accessible in major cultural centres but all over the country, especially in such 'places where the people have been starved of good theatre'.[2] Strehler and Planchon stood for a like-minded popular approach to theatre. They, too, sought to bring, through the medium of the stage, culture to the people – 'culture' no longer with a capital C, but as a societal bond that celebrated the popular and the inclusive.

Theatre for these three directors offered an almost utopian space to unite people of different nations and backgrounds, and to attempt to heal the many wounds that the battlefields, the concentration camps and displacement had left in almost every European citizen after 1945. At the same time, the theatre of Littlewood, Strehler and Planchon served as a critical tool with which to interrogate not least the restoration of conservative values in post-war society. Thus, theatre asserted its position as a central medium within the new democratic 'public sphere' of post-war Europe, to use the term suggested by the prominent German philosopher of this period, Jürgen Habermas.[3] Theatre became a vital site of public discourse, a key platform of exchange in which to practise the shared responsibility of being citizens of democratic European societies. Hence, Littlewood, Strehler and Planchon embodied in their artistic work an ethical attitude, a form of committed humanism, along with an engaged internationalism (or rather, 'Europeanism'), which sought to cross borders between classes as well as between the continent's neighbouring nations that had been at war with each other only a few years earlier. Such an idea of theatre as an instrument to reach out to people of all classes and nations, to bring them together across borders, and hence to function as an antidote to the warmongering nationalism of previous decades, underpinned these directors' reinvigoration of expressly 'popular' traditions, from Littlewood's revue-format in her showpiece *Oh What a Lovely War* (1963) to Strehler's reanimation of the popular Italian *commedia dell'arte* tradition in a contemporary context and Planchon's pronounced theatrical playfulness exemplified by the slapstick and other physical performance traditions he integrated into his collectively created pieces. Their vision of a contemporary 'popular theatre', based on classic works and traditions, sought to reinvigorate the legacy of Western Enlightenment, and its key values of liberty, equality and solidarity. This legacy seemed to have come to an abrupt halt in the violence of two world wars, which stood as the veritable counter-climax of that supposed Enlightenment. While putting on classics, their audiences encountered 'real' and recognizable human beings on stage who told *their* stories, with their bodies and their voices. They did not seek to transport audiences into a different fictional world, but instead sought to meet spectators in their own familiar worlds that they knew all too well. Their theatre also reached out to its audiences not as a homogenized mass of consumers and customers to be entertained, but as individuals and equally responsible subjects to be engaged in a shared responsibility to restore and better communal life, for the equal benefit of everyone. Of course, theatre cannot rectify political catastrophes and economic failures; as the work of Joan Littlewood, Giorgio Strehler and Roger Planchon may teach us, it can, however, engage, reach, activate and address people's minds, and their hearts.

To each of these three theatre directors, this collection devotes two essays written by leading international experts on their work. They will introduce and contextualize each director in turn and outline their directorial practices. At the same time, they will reflect specifically on selected aspects of the three stage directors' careers, such as their engagement with political theatre traditions and their dedication to an internationalist outlook and to cultural exchange across national (and other) borders. The essays by Danielle Mérahi and Robert Leach on Joan Littlewood's work, by Bent Holm and Margherita Laera on Giorgio Strehler, and by Michel Bataillon and Pia Kleber on Roger Planchon, offer astute analysis and, for Strehler and Planchon, draw on Italian and French archival sources that have previously been inaccessible to Anglophone readerships. All our contributors draw on their own experience of having been an audience member at a number of productions, of having interviewed some of their respective director's creative team and, in the case of Michel Bataillon, of having worked alongside the director for many decades. To preface their analyses, in the remaining sections of this Introduction, we first outline the historical context of post-war Europe between these bookends of 1945 and 1968, paying particular attention to key ideas and the intellectual history of this period, by making reference to crucial philosophical works that might enhance the study of the three directors portrayed here and the wider context within which they lived and worked. We then provide brief introductions to these three directors and their respective artistic contexts, and to the approaches taken by our authors' contributions. We will try to highlight the links within their work and their approaches, and to connect their central directorial principles with wider aesthetic and artistic tendencies of the period, in particular with the French tradition of the *théâtre populaire* on the one hand and Bertolt Brecht's 'plebeian' tradition of theatre on the other. Brecht, whose own directorial legacy is extensively considered in Volume 2 of this series, indeed served as a major inspiration, reference point and ally for all three of the theatre-makers discussed here. His work and ideas provide a nexus that draws together the very individual ways in which these directors renegotiated the European dramatic canon and envisaged the theatre institution as an active agent within a democratic society. We hope that the legacy of Joan Littlewood, Giorgio Strehler and Roger Planchon, which we celebrate in this volume, will enable us to raise (still) urgent questions about the role and the potential of the theatre institution within our own twenty-first-century culture and society.

From poverty to prosperity: Western Europe 1945–70

Death, destruction, devastation: The Second World War and its aftermath

On 8 May 1945 the German Reich declared its 'unconditional surrender'. Six years of appalling warfare across Europe, that had eventually spread across the rest of the globe, came to an end as the twelve-year rule of the National Socialist regime under Adolf Hitler, who himself had committed suicide ten days previously, finally collapsed. Of his key allies within the fascist axis of the so-called 'anti-communist international', Italy had already been liberated by the Allied forces (and its leader Benito Mussolini executed), while Japan still continued to fight on its own in the Pacific until the two atomic bombs, dropped by the United States on Hiroshima and Nagasaki in August 1945, led to Japan's capitulation in early September.[4] In Europe alone, it is estimated that nearly 37 million people (the equivalent of the population of France in 1939) died between 1939 and 1945, of which at least 19 million, more than half, were civilians.[5] More than 20 million of these casualties were suffered by the people of the Soviet Union, whose army lost 78,000 soldiers in the final weeks of the battle for Berlin in spring 1945 alone. These figures include more than 6 million Jews and other minorities deemed by the Nazi regime to be 'unworthy of living' and exterminated in concentration camps such as Auschwitz and Buchenwald, in the systematic, industrially administered mass killings of the Holocaust. In some countries, especially in the devastated Soviet Union and Yugoslavia, the entire male population of some villages had vanished. These barbaric events, the universal horrors, brutality and destruction, exceeded any imagination. The universal war caused universal trauma for those who had been lucky enough to survive at all, victims and perpetrators alike.

Thus, the Second World War resulted in a fundamental rupture in the history, culture and self-understanding of Western Europe, while also reshaping the geographical map of the Continent as well as its demographic make-up. Crisis had of course already visited Europe earlier in the century, when from 1914 the nations of Europe had engaged in their first industrially organized battles of the (First) World War, the 'Great War', fought with new mechanical tanks and chemical weapons that no longer differentiated between soldiers and civilians. The war, the Russian Revolution of October 1917, the defeat of Germany in 1918 and the aftermath of these events, resulted in the politically extremely volatile interwar-period of the 1920s that was eventually aggravated by the worldwide economic crisis following the stock market collapse of 1929. Wide sectors of society were susceptible to radical, anti-establishment as well as anti-democratic and nationalist populist leaders. In Germany, Adolf Hitler's National Socialist German Workers Party (NSDAP) was elected to power in January 1933, and there were other fascist leaders across Europe, such as Mussolini in Italy (already in power since 1922) and General Francisco Franco in Spain. Under Oswald Mosley, even in the UK dictatorial movements had sympathizers. After Hitler eventually declared formal war on Poland in September 1939 (having already annexed several European sovereign states including Czechoslovakia and Austria to his Reich in 1937 and 1938), the Continent imploded into another, even more destructive, war.

Peace, after six years, offered little reason for optimism. While the massive air raids, the Blitz, the mass executions and the fighting eventually ceased, yet the aftermath of the war carried on for some time. Across Europe, there was barely a family which would not have claimed casualties. Many simply did not know what had happened to their husbands, brothers and other family members who were missing in action, who were perhaps held captive somewhere as prisoners of war, or who had disappeared in the chaos of the bombardments or were otherwise unaccounted for. In addition, the war had caused massive material destruction throughout Europe. Many cities were left in ruins: some cities in Germany, Poland and Russia were destroyed to such a degree that they were almost uninhabitable; some were even all but erased. Millions no longer had a home; many had lost all their possessions; around 10 million more were forced to flee their home countries as a result of the post-war demarcation lines, brokered by Stalin, Churchill and Roosevelt, the leaders of the Allied countries who fought Hitler and his fascist 'axis'. Especially in the big cities, strangers were forced to share flats for many years after the war, due to the scarcity of housing. Nearly everywhere, the supply of utilities, including fresh water, had fallen apart. Infrastructure such as roads, bridges and public transport systems was likewise destroyed, as were most factories and industrial sites. In addition, the exceptionally hard winters of 1946 and 1947 caused massive food shortages and led to further casualties due to widespread poverty and malnutrition. Consequently, disease spread rapidly through weak populations.

Destroyed buildings and maimed war victims would remain daily reminders for many years to come of the manifold scars of the war. The harrowing writings of Holocaust survivors, for instance Romanian-born German-language poet Paul Celan's poem *Death Fugue* (1948), or Italian novelist Primo Levi's *If This is a Man* (1947) and *The Drowned and the Saved* (1986), pose as a memorial to the inexpressible horror of life within the concentration and extermination camps, and a testament to this 'age of extremes', as historian Eric Hobsbawm described the events that unfolded across Europe between 1914 and 1945.[6]

Total destruction and the banality of evil: An existential crisis

After 1945, Europe was *kaputt*. Along with the millions of lives, the ethical fabric of European society seemed to have been annihilated. Its population felt as if it were living in a dystopian vacuum, bereft of the very substance of what made up culture and civilization. Instead of hope, there was widespread *angst* and utter despair. The crisis was existential not only in Germany, where the majority of the population experienced the fall of the Nazi regime not as liberation but as defeat, but across the whole of Europe. It was almost impossible to have come through this period without being emotionally, physically or psychologically damaged. Today, in prosperous Western Europe, we can barely imagine the material and emotional hardship that this generation experienced. Any trust in human civilization had vanished.

The very foundational values of the Western Enlightenment, the triumphant progress in science, technological invention and philosophical thought that had underpinned Western civilization and its self-understanding, had directly led to mass destruction. In their magisterial study *Dialectic of Enlightenment*, written in their Los Angeles exile during the early 1940s and first published in 1947, the principal founders of the Frankfurt School of Critical Theory, Theodor W. Adorno (1903–69) and Max Horkheimer (1895–1973), investigated why Western enlightened rationality was unable to prevent, and in great parts even unwilling to resist, inhuman totalitarianism: a cold 'instrumental reason', as they called it, had replaced mythologies of earlier ages and, in fact, directly led to the excess of fascism and the extermination camps. Horkheimer and Adorno also pointed to the seamless absorption of the arts and media into a purely functional and pragmatic system of totalitarian thinking, in what they influentially termed the 'culture industry'.[7] To this end, they adopted a standard critique of the dominant media in a similar way to Brecht, who already in his 1930 *Mahagonny* essay critiqued the 'intoxication' precipitated by the illusion of reality staged in bourgeois theatre, and who in his 1949 essay 'A Short Organum for the Theatre' would accuse the 'retailers of evening entertainment of having degenerated into a branch of the bourgeois narcotics trade'.[8] Horkheimer and Adorno's critique, however, went significantly further. In the important fourth chapter of their study, they dissect the instrumental part played by the media in the 'intoxication' of the masses, in ideologically orchestrating the totalitarian Nazi regime, and not least the Holocaust, via propaganda. They demonstrate that the arts, culture and mass media had in fact helped to disseminate and firmly establish a new, fascist mythology: a mindset based on anti-Semitism and the hatred of anything 'foreign' and 'un-German', where any ethical objection was interpreted as a sign of weakness.

In her 1951 study *The Origins of Totalitarianism*, another influential German philosopher who had been living in exile in the United States since 1933, Hannah Arendt (1906–75), similarly interrogated the history of ideas that had given rise to the racism, anti-Semitism and imperialism that enabled the advent of fascism and equally of Stalinism in the Soviet Union.[9] In 1961 she reported for the *New Yorker* magazine on the Jerusalem trial of Nazi manager Adolf Eichmann, one of the many unknown 'behind the scenes' administrators of the *Endlösung,* the 'final solution' of exterminating all Jews. Arendt's essays describe Eichmann as the embodiment of the purely 'instrumental reason' discussed by Adorno and Horkheimer. He was, according to Arendt, no perverted monster but a shockingly normal, dutiful servant to his masters, who in court remained unable to comprehend his crime, given that for him he was simply following orders. Arendt famously spoke of the 'banality of evil'.[10] This insight called into doubt the simplistic duality of master (the omnipotent and violent demon) and servant (the passive, seduced and exploited victim, incapable of resistance). Instead, the unchallenged conformity and obedience to rules and duties has become the excuse to absolve one's self from taking any responsibility for one's actions. For Arendt, and many thinkers who followed her approach, the twentieth century demonstrated this new 'banal' form of evil, no longer perpetrated by singular extraordinary monstrous villains (from *Richard III* to Hitler) but by indifferent, obedient, nameless followers such as Eichmann. This approach was then developed further in the influential analysis of the micro-structures of power, governmentality and docility by the French cultural theorist Michel Foucault (1926–84) who, like Arendt, was hugely influenced by the writings of the German philosophers Friedrich Nietzsche and Martin Heidegger.[11]

It seemed futile to try and comprehend the atrocities of the Second World War; they appeared devoid of any 'meaning'. Equally, what meaning could life still have after, and in the shadow of, these events? The attitude that captured this shattered post-war European mindset was existentialism, as exemplarily articulated by the French writers Jean-Paul Sartre (1905–80) and Albert Camus (1913–60). The latter, who was engaged in the French

Resistance movement during the Second World War, had in 1942 already expressed the feeling of utter loss that resulted from these events, in his momentous essay *The Myth of Sisyphus*:

> A world that can be explained by reasoning, however faulty, is a familiar world. But in a universe that is suddenly deprived of illusions and of light, man [*sic*] feels a stranger. His is an irremediable exile, because he is deprived of memories of a lost homeland as much as he lacks the hope of a promised land to come. This divorce between man and his life, the actor and his setting, truly constitutes the feeling of Absurdity.[12]

The feeling of the pointlessness of human existence that had been articulated towards the end of the nineteenth century by nihilist philosophers such as Schopenhauer, Kierkegaard and Nietzsche now found a fitting home after the momentous events of the 1930s and 1940s. In theatre, this fundamental pessimism and sentiment of futility were encapsulated by the new approach to playwriting illustrated by authors such as Samuel Beckett and Eugène Ionesco, which critic Martin Esslin termed the 'Theatre of the Absurd'.[13]

The 'Cold War': A rift through the heart of Europe

While the victory of the Allied forces over the fascist axis and above all over Hitler's Nazi Reich had restored freedom in Europe, the political consequences of the world wars would continue to define the political landscape, as well as everyday life, for decades to come. The fight against a common enemy had united the United States and the Soviet Union; however, after the war the irreconcilable antagonism between Western democracy and the one-party system under the leadership of the Communist Party in the East soon rose to the surface again. Both nations had, as main drivers behind the victory over Germany and its allies, become the dominant global forces, substituting the earlier European colonial empires of France and Britain within global politics, and thus shifting the geopolitical balance away from its centuries-old European focus. After 1945, these two superpowers, and their two ideological systems, began to compete for influence, hegemony and expansion. The direct frontier between their territorial spheres of influence ran right through the heart of Europe. In their respective territories on the Continent, the leaders in Washington and Moscow set up systems according to their own values. The Western nations, and in particular the western sectors of Germany that were initially under British, French and American military administration, became democratic states. The countries in Central and Eastern Europe, including the Soviet sector of Eastern Germany, were turned into communist states modelled on the Soviet Union. Germany, in addition to losing its entire eastern territory east of the River Oder, was thus split into two separate states which were both formally founded in 1949, and in 1961 physically divided by the 1,300 kilometre-long fortified wall, of which the famous 'Berlin Wall' was only a small section, that separated the democratic Federal Republic (FDR) in the west from the socialist German Democratic Republic (GDR) in the east. It would be the most potent symbol of this bipolar post-war separation of the world.

From the Second World War the world thus stumbled more or less directly into the era of the 'Cold War': the confrontation between the two irreconcilable ideological systems of capitalism and communism. It would define the history of Europe (and indeed the rest of the world) over the decades to come, until the fall of the Wall in 1989 and the dissolution of the Soviet Union in 1991. Between the late 1940s and the 1980s, this conflict erupted more than once into 'hot wars'. However, these were now fought outside the territories of the superpowers, in the 'third world', most ostensibly in Korea and Vietnam during the 1950s and 1960s, and later in the form of the so-called 'dirty wars' of the 1970s and 1980s, where the United States financed undemocratic, fascist dictators to overthrow democratically elected left-wing governments, in Latin America, for instance in El Salvador, Chile, Argentina and Brazil; in Africa; and in Afghanistan, where the United States supported the Islamist Taliban against Soviet occupation in the early 1980s. The 'Cold War' formally began as US president Harry S. Truman declared his 'Truman doctrine' in 1947, assuring the direct military support of the United States and its allies to any country invaded by the Soviet Union. Its immediate trigger had been a civil war in Greece, where the East (and in particular the Yugoslav leader Tito) had supported the communist side. In the context of this policy, Truman's government also announced a plan for massive financial and economic grants. Foreign secretary George C. Marshall's five-year 'European Recovery Program', also known as the 'Marshall Plan', offered much-needed food and other resources to seventeen Western European states, alongside loans to revive their destroyed economies and industries. Its major intention was to prevent people in Europe from sympathizing with communism as a reaction to their poverty and deprivation, thereby attempting to contain any further extension of the communist sphere of influence and equally to bind European states to the United States and its 'way of life'.

Galvanized by the victorious communist revolution under Mao Zedong in China in 1949, the United States then began to engage in the Cold War with more aggressive rhetorics that spoke of actively 'rolling back communism'. At home, it set about purging any vaguely communist engagement, in the infamous 'McCarthy hearings', orchestrated by the 'House Committee on Un-American Activities'. Notably, the American folk singer Pete Seeger and playwright Arthur Miller were accused: the latter fictionalized the McCarthy communist witch-hunt in his play *The Crucible* (1953). The Committee also investigated numerous exiled Europeans including Bertolt Brecht, his composer friend Hanns Eisler and Nobel Prize-winning German author Thomas Mann, as well as the British actor Charlie Chaplin. Similarly, in the UK Joan Littlewood and her then partner and collaborator Ewan

MacColl, both members of the Communist Party, and the activities of their Theatre Workshop, were observed and reported on by MI5.[14] In contrast to their ally France and other Western states, the United States and the UK no longer tolerated the existence of communist parties on their territory, with Germany following suit in 1956, when the country made membership of the Communist Party a justifiable reason for not being considered appointable for a job, most specifically in public services. For decades, politicians of all parties painted the image of an imminent communist invasion whenever it suited their aims.

Meanwhile, the United States invested vast sums in arms and in the early 1950s developed an arsenal of new hydrogen bombs, each of which had a destructive capacity of 800 times the Hiroshima atomic bomb. Thus, the country generated what US president Dwight D. Eisenhower described as the 'military-industrial complex': a close alliance between the state, its armed forces and commercial arms manufacturers. As the Soviet Union had developed its own atomic weapons in the late 1940s and hydrogen bombs by the mid-1950s, an absurd arms race began, especially after the development of long-range missiles that made it possible to reach US territory from the Soviet Union and vice versa. Both the United States and the Soviet Union were eventually armed to the hilt, despite both sides being well aware that any actual deployment even of a single bomb would cause an immediate counterstrike, thereby meaning certain suicide and, possibly, the destruction of the entire planet. The United States formally threatened any communist expansion with what they termed 'massive retaliation'. Meanwhile, the Soviet Union did not tolerate any deviance from communism: it cracked down repeatedly and heavy-handedly on uprisings in its Eastern Bloc satellite states, for instance in East Berlin in 1953, Budapest in 1956, and Prague in 1968. The Cuban revolution of 1959 under Fidel Castro and Ernesto 'Che' Guevara heated up this confrontation after the Soviet Union supported the new Cuban government, and in return was permitted to station nuclear arms on the island, right on the doorstep of the United States. For several weeks in the autumn of 1962, the world was on the brink of a war between the two superpowers, a tense situation which was eventually resolved by an agreement between Soviet leader Nikita Khruschev and US president John F. Kennedy.

For most of the Cold War period, however, an awkward 'balance of power' existed, where even major disputes such as the 'Cuba crisis' were settled diplomatically and without armed confrontation, except in the case of the 'proxy wars' battled out in third world countries. Looking back at the period from a North American and Western European perspective (and even more so considering the perceived threat posed by global terrorism, the lawlessness of counter-terrorist wars and newly emerging right-wing anti-democratic movements at the start of the twenty-first century), the decades between 1945 and 1989 might appear almost like an idyll of peace and stability. Fictionalizations of the notorious secretive operations of Moscow's

KGB and Washington's CIA by authors such as John Le Carré and Ian Fleming, as well as numerous television shows and movies, have further bestowed on the Cold War an air of genteel quaintness. Yet, the eventual fall of state communism after 1989 should not make us forget that this outcome was in no way determined from the outset and in fact came as much of a surprise to Western states, politicians and populations. For everyone living through the Cold War, and in particular on the European frontline of this conflict, the prospect of a nuclear apocalypse seemed a far more real and likely outcome than imagining anything such as the Fall of the Berlin Wall in one's lifetime. Especially in the early decades following the Second World War, and certainly around the time of the Cuban Missile Crisis of 1962 and the failed 'Prague Spring' of 1968 – and hence notably in the very period in which Littlewood, Strehler and Planchon were creating their major works – the playing field was rather level, and the eventual victory for capitalism and Western democracy seemed by no means a clear, foreseeable outcome. It was Stalin's Soviet Union that had contributed the major effort towards defeating Hitler's Nazi Reich, whether during the Battle of Stalingrad in the winter of 1943 or on the streets of Berlin in spring 1945. And as many Western European cities, even major capitals, lay in ruins and disrepair until the Marshall Plan was implemented from 1950, with food shortages and rationing characterizing daily life for many years in the UK, Germany, France and other Western European countries, the apparent economic progress in the Eastern European countries seemed only too beguiling. For a period after the war, the communist bloc had indeed taken an economic lead in its industrial productivity. Technologically as well, the Soviet Union initially presented itself as a competitive contender: the Soviets were the first to travel to space, and they were able to present major breakthroughs in modern science and research. Meanwhile, a number of revolutions in former colonial countries in the southern hemisphere, where the European imperial powers were gradually losing the last vestiges of their influence, were staged in the name of communism. Even theatre history gives testimony to this: Coventry's Belgrade Theatre, the first theatre to be built in the UK after the war, in 1958, was a gift to the largely destroyed British city by the capital of Yugoslavia, Belgrade. Thus, the West had to respond with its own economic and social reforms in order to ensure that communism did not become too attractive an alternative for its own population.

The tense atmosphere of the Cold War thus dominated and directly influenced almost every aspect of daily life and also of culture. As mentioned, most notably, it felt as if the Cold War could mutate into a Third World War at any moment. Those who had lived through the 1920s and 1930s remembered the sense of impending disaster and of inevitability that the outcome of the Great War in 1918 could only eventually be another war; since they had been right then, the present Cold War period felt even more like a repeat of the earlier interwar episode. In Europe, and especially in Germany, the massive presence of (mostly US) army personnel and their regular exercises in the countryside were a further everyday reality of living in the age of the Cold War. While no longer under military government and eventually prospering as sovereign states, the Allied forces had negotiated their permanent presence in countries such as Germany and Austria, the closest frontline states in the Cold War. Equally, civilian life on the European continent was characterized by regular (quite likely pretty futile) evacuation drills in case of a nuclear attack, or an attack with the biological and chemical weapons that were equally developed on both sides. Every school pupil learnt basic civil defence, and any household would keep its cellars stocked with non-perishable food and drink in case of an attack.

From gloom to boom: Economic prosperity after 1950

The doom and gloom of the Cold War situation was made bearable, though, by a daily life whose standards, for large parts of society, began to improve dramatically. The economic directives of the Marshall Plan eventually bore fruits in the early 1950s, the beginning of what in French history is referred to as the 'trente glorieuses', the thirty glorious years of post-war prosperity. Even Germany recovered during this period, termed the era of 'Wirtschaftswunder', the 'economic miracle', that saw the country swing from unemployment of more than 12 per cent in 1949 to full employment by 1957. The country's economy grew by almost 200 per cent within this period. In the UK, the Conservative prime minister Harold Macmillan famously remarked in a 1957 speech, 'most of our people have never had it so good'.

At the beginning of this period of new prosperity, the former arch enemies France and Germany began to cooperate and thereby to emancipate themselves from the dominant influence of the United States and its close ally Britain. In 1952, French exterior minister Robert Schuman and German chancellor Konrad Adenauer signed a treaty establishing the 'European Coal and Steel Community', which in 1957 was extended, in the Treaty of Rome, to become the 'European Economic Community' (EEC) of initially six countries, thereby laying the ground for today's European Union (EU) with its current twenty-seven member states. Cooperating economically and politically, while still maintaining their individual national sovereignty (whereas the United States had repeatedly tried to suggest the integration of European countries into a United Europe, following the model of the United States), the countries established a European voice in the not always smooth dialogue between the United States and the Soviet Union. Internally, the cooperation was intended to guarantee peace and to prevent future wars between neighbouring European nations, and also to boost further economic and social stability after the post-war years of poverty and deprivation, not least by lifting trade restrictions and tariffs. Not only were the social unrest following the economic crisis of the late 1920s and the national hubris stoked by fascism still fresh in the minds of Europeans, but the more urgently present context of the Cold War also meant that social prosperity made people accept the capitalist order of the West rather than looking for any alternative system beyond the Wall or elsewhere.

The EEC's economic policy was, therefore, further complemented across Europe by a new social policy. New systems of free general health care, education (including new widened access to higher education), state pensions as well as access to culture, including the theatre, became key aspects of the 'welfare states' that characterized Europe during these 'glorious years'. The key economic imperative was not the reduction of costs and state involvement, but full employment and widespread prosperity, security and satisfaction. Most workers were organized in trade unions which negotiated regular pay rises and improvements to working conditions. Even a working-class youth could in theory now aspire to a decent level of education, even to a university degree, and go on to a satisfying job earning money and feeding an entire family from one single income. In this period of full employment, many European countries actively recruited migrants – from their former colonies as well as from the less prosperous and less industrialized countries in the south of Europe such as Turkey, Greece, Spain, Portugal and (southern) Italy. These migrant workers and their families, who in Germany up until 2003 were categorized as *Gastarbeiter* (guest workers) without citizenship status, would soon fill the manual, low-skilled jobs in factories and perform other less desirable work.

For the average European family, the standard of living they arrived at within only a decade after the devastation of 1945 was extraordinary and in excess of anything even imaginable before. Everyday life had changed beyond recognition and, for some of the older pre-war generation, beyond comprehension. Wealth was no longer restricted to a small elite but became potentially available to the majority of the population; even among the working class, full employment created at least modest affluence and disposable income. What had historically been an excessive luxury for the privileged few, such as holidays on beaches in the Mediterranean or even further afield, and the purchase of 'gadgets' merely as status symbols or for their novelty rather than as indispensable goods now became the norm. Soon, almost every household would have its own television set, its own private washing machine and refrigerator, and even its own car (if not several), all of which would be considered everyday necessities for most members of the middle class and even the working class. Many of these new commodities resulted from the massive technological and industrial developments made in the context of the military efforts of the Second World War – from synthetic plastics to magnetic tape, the transistor radio, battery power and, eventually, the personal computer. Meanwhile, cheap fuel not only allowed for the rise of private automobiles available to everyone, but also served the fast circulation of goods on the roads, while the new aircraft technologies simplified the connection between intercontinental consumer markets as well as overseas travelling. Furthermore, the telephone spread from use in offices, into every household. In tandem with the TV sets and new technologies of 'live broadcast', the world gradually became connected as a 'global village', as Canadian media theorist Marshall McLuhan influentially described it, writing in the early 1960s.[15]

Large-scale mechanization, at work but equally at home via modern household appliances, created a new quality of life – and a new and previously unheard-of time of leisure outside work that could now be dedicated to 'consuming' and enjoying life. Everyone was now united in being a 'consumer', whose new purchasing power would further energize the economy. Families would regularly 'go shopping' for fashionable clothes, make-up, entertainment devices and other goods for sale on the new 'mass market' of everyday commodities. New technologies in agriculture and food production, meanwhile, led from a period of post-war scarcity to abundance and even over-production, with the West now exporting food to other parts of the world on a large scale. And there was spare time to go to museums, theatres and cinemas, and to participate regularly in the arts.

Critical voices: The protests of the late 1960s

This fundamental change both to economic productivity and to the amenities available in everyday life was a significant qualitative step, comparable to the arrival of the industrial revolution in the nineteenth century. It had, by the 1960s, restored confidence and optimism, the belief in progress and, for some, belief even in the superiority of the West and its mode of capitalist production. Amidst economic growth and the triumph of the consumer society, politics and political engagement – so prevalent among the working and middle classes from the nineteenth century to the 1930s – gradually took a step back. Not only did it seem more attractive but, most of all, the now largely depoliticized majority could actually afford to indulge in shopping rather than engage in party assemblies and political struggle. Those who remained politically engaged took part in new social movements that were mainly liberal and social democratic, while, on the left, a new kind of 'Western left' emerged that distanced itself from the Soviet Union and Eastern communism, especially after the Soviet military crackdown against the people's protests of East Berlin in 1953 and Hungary in 1956. Of particular influence was the critical theory of the 'Frankfurt School' and their principal thinkers Horkheimer and Adorno, whom we have already introduced. Another influential voice to emerge from their circle was that of Herbert Marcuse (1898–1979). A student of Husserl and Heidegger, Marcuse had emigrated to the United States with Adorno and Horkheimer and was initially associated with their exiled Institute for Social Research before taking up appointments at Columbia University, Harvard and the University of California. His 1964 study *The One-Dimensional*

Man was a particularly important contribution to critical thinking at the time, because it did not entangle itself in biased and simplistic Cold War bipolarity.[16] Marcuse presented national socialism, Soviet communism and US-style capitalism as mere variations of a totalitarianism that he saw as characteristic of developed modernity at large. Whereas fascism based its totalitarian authority on brute terror, capitalism, in Marcuse's view, secured the conformity of people as 'one-dimensional men' by the lure and convenience of a world of commodities, media, advertising, business management and political ideology. The working class, once envisaged by traditional Marxism as the agent of revolution against the system, has thus turned, for Marcuse, into consumers and hence become a fully integrated pillar of society. Where all thinking has become affirmative, no true opposition, from within the system, remains possible. In an argument that became important both for the protests of the 1960s and for much political philosophy thereafter, the only remaining agents of change are those excluded from participating in the system. Therefore, the only alternative, for Marcuse, is based on disruptive negation and what he termed, following the French philosopher Maurice Blanchot, 'the great refusal'.

At the same time, the new modes of thinking proposed by structuralism, shaped by the French anthropologist Claude Lévi-Strauss (1908–2009), turned research across the humanities away from the positivist cataloguing of knowledge and findings towards a critical practice. Lévi-Strauss had spent the war with many other exiled European intellectuals at the New York New School for Social Research, where he met the mastermind of structuralist linguistics, Roman Jakobson. Lévi-Strauss applied Jakobson's structuralist approach to language to his field work with Amazonian tribes in the Brazilian rainforest. His key works, above all *The Savage Mind* (1962), inspired a host of structuralist thinkers across numerous disciplines, from sociologist Pierre Bourdieu to psychoanalyst Jacques Lacan, literary scholar Roland Barthes and theatre theorist Anne Ubersfeld, along with Marxist thinkers such as, in particular, French philosopher Louis Althusser. Their various structuralist approaches have in common the fact that they seek to demonstrate structures and patterns that underlie human behaviour, from language to customs and rituals; thus, they challenge the Enlightenment notion of the Cartesian all-knowing subject who supposedly determines history. Instead, for them, history, and its patterns or structures, determine individuals. However, the structuralist period of the early 1960s was only a brief prelude to the emergence of critical post-structuralism, the work of Barthes signifying this critical shift in particular. He and philosopher Jacques Derrida soon critiqued the structuralist idea of self-contained, surveyable structures. They also challenged logocentrism, the hierarchical privilege afforded to the word above senses and experiences, which subsequently had particular influence on literary and cultural studies. While reading and writing rely on learning skills, speech was considered to be more democratic because it is at most people's disposal. In the 1970s, the work of sociologist Michel

Foucault added another important critical corpus to (post-)structuralism by extending its analysis to the social and political fields.

To the younger generation born just after the war, who now had – in the new sociocultural climate just described – widespread free access to education and university study, the post-war order seemed stiff and stifling – 'one-dimensional', to borrow the term of Marcuse, whose work was widely discussed at the time and who also lectured to the protesting students in 1968. They called for political freedom and for new personal liberties, including more liberal attitudes towards sexuality and homosexuality. On a wider scale, the protests, and the 'movement' or even 'revolution' that erupted across Europe in 1968, were prompted by a whole range of international impulses, notably the 1959 Cuban Revolution under Che Guevara which for many appeared to be a 'true' realization of communism, unlike Stalin's repressive Soviet Union. Elsewhere, the American Civil Rights Movement led by Malcolm X, Martin Luther King and Dorothy Height demanded equal rights for people of all ethnicities and backgrounds, a cause with which many in Europe showed solidarity. At the same time, feminism emerged and challenged male-dominated capitalist hierarchies in business and everyday life. New political, social and cultural phenomena surfaced everywhere, bearing the omnipresent prefixes 'pop-' and 'post-', and the key critical ideas of the pioneers of French and Francophone post-structuralist, feminist and postcolonial – Michel Foucault, Roland Barthes, Jacques Derrida, Simone de Beauvoir and Frantz Fanon – thereby found their eager application in actual political protest.

Thus there was an emerging critique by the student protesters, as well as these philosophers, of capitalist consumption, the commodification of all aspects of daily life and the male-centred logocentrism of society. In addition, Western neo-imperialist warfare in Latin America, Africa and most notably during the Vietnam War (1965–75) further fuelled their critique, and even their Marcusian 'refusal' of capitalism and a Western lifestyle. An additional central concern became their parents' refusal to speak, either in public or in private, about their involvement in the barbarities of the Second World War. In fact, for years, many of the parents' generation actually continued to boast of the 'heroic deeds' they had performed as soldiers. Thus, in the late 1960s this disavowal became a further central issue of the student protests, especially in Germany.[17] The catalysts for the uprisings were thus multiple and international, but came to a head in Paris during that month of May 1968, when workers joined protesting students for weeks of a general strike. While the UK's youth also participated in student protests and political rallies against the Vietnam War (headed most famously by student leader Tariq Ali and actress Vanessa Redgrave), there were no wider effects in British society comparable to those in France, Germany and other countries on the Continent and even further afield in the Americas and in Asia, where one speaks of a '1968 generation' that was shaped by these events and the fundamental rupture it engendered in these societies.

Not only the student protests of May 1968, but also the civil war in Congo, the Algerian War of Independence, emerging feminism and the new 'hippy' youth movement, alongside sexual liberation and experimentation with new synthetic drugs (another by-product of wartime scientific innovation that had now become more widely available), defined this generation and their new attitudes. Above all, this generation challenged the established value systems and morals of Western society that they saw and experienced as stifling and 'one-dimensional'. Furthermore, the protests of 1968 signalled a time when the massive economic boom described above had eventually begun to slow down, especially in France and Italy; emergent neo-liberal economics across the West had begun to 'rationalize' the 'non-competitive' elements of the workplace, leading to redundancies and consequently to strikes in the years leading up to 1968, and eventually prompting many workers to support the student protests. During the 1970s, the 'division of labour' was further implemented on a new global scale; industrial production was moved increasingly from the highly regulated countries of the global north to the southern hemisphere; and by the 1980s, this development had led to the huge deindustrialization of the former industrial power regions of, for instance, northern England, northern France and the Ruhr Valley in Germany.

The oil crisis of 1973 became the symbolic indicator of the end of the prosperous 'glorious decades' after 1945. The crisis itself was triggered by the emergence of new global powers on the side lines of the Cold War empires: the Arab States, in particular Saudi Arabia, had benefited, through their vast oil reserves, from the economic boom in the West. When the West supported Israel in its war against Egypt in the late 1960s, it was punished by the Arab states, who stopped the oil supply. Soon the European stock market virtually collapsed, inflation soared to breath-taking figures of around 25 per cent in Western Europe, and unemployment rose to levels not known for more than a generation, while at the same time supplies of oil and food ran short. This 1970s hiccough in Western industrial productivity opened the door for new manufacturers to enter, and then to lead, the big consumer markets, coming mainly from Japan and other East Asian countries whose new companies would become household names for cars, electronic devices and other products that used to be almost exclusively manufactured by major US and European companies. In the name of the 'free market', in other words, in order to be able to compete on the new global scale, politicians in the 1980s such as the US president Ronald Reagan, British prime minister Margaret Thatcher and German chancellor Helmut Kohl, began their neo-liberal dismantling of welfare benefits, of regulated wages, trade unions and state support. From the perspective of the UK, the rupture precipitated by Thatcher was eventually more influential than the events of the 1968 protests, which remained a Continental European (and elsewhere, a US) phenomenon that the UK watched from the sidelines. Most significantly, in 1989 the fall of the communist Wall was perceived as an offer for neo-liberal capitalism to range freely across the planet. From this point on, the political imperatives as well as the social fabric of Western societies had once again changed significantly: under the spirit of neo-liberalism, the post-war ethos of solidarity and of critical opposition, which was symbolized in the work of the three theatre directors discussed in this volume, had become a thing of the past.

European theatre in the 1950s and 1960s

Theatre gave a number of different answers to the issues of the Cold War and other pressing concerns of the time. Initially, the horrors of the war and the existential crisis of the post-war years found their expression, as we have mentioned, in the Theatre of the Absurd. The plays of Beckett, Genet, Ionesco and others presented a challenge to the complacent acceptance of Western capitalism that became ever more of an inevitability with the emergence of the economic 'glorious years'. These playwrights' challenge to the conventional tenets of theatre – linear plot, coherent characters, comprehensible dialogue – prepared the ground for experimental developments in theatre and also inspired the emerging genre of performance art that eventually transformed live performance from the 1960s onwards. Julian Beck and Judith Malina's Living Theatre in the United States, and, in Europe, Jean-Jacques Lebel and other artists influenced by the Situationist International rejected anything that was perceived to belong to tradition, technocratic civilization and consensual culture.

Littlewood, Strehler and Planchon remained on a different and, one could argue, more conventional path. Strehler's 1975 book manifesto *Towards a Human Theatre* offers a passionate response to the bleak stage worlds presented by the Absurdist authors, such as the subjugated prisoners and servants in Genet's *Deathwatch* and *The Maids* (1947) or the post-apocalyptic wastelands in Beckett's *Endgame* (1957) and *Happy Days* (1961). Strehler maintained that, instead, theatre should show its audience stories and images of happiness, love and solidarity. In the shadow of two world wars, Strehler perceived theatre, similarly to Littlewood and Planchon, as a uniting force that can bring people together. These stage directors attempted to reinvigorate the social significance of theatre as a public assembly and a communal experience. Theatre, for Strehler, is first and foremost a collaborative event 'that more than any other is made with others for others'.[18] Theirs was a theatre of, and for, 'the people'.

Jean Vilar and the tradition of *théâtre populaire*

Culture thus became a powerful instrument for rebuilding society almost from scratch and for coming to terms with recent traumatic events, precisely by connecting and reaching out to others, in particular to one's former enemies. The newly formed United Nations (UN), established immediately after the war in 1945, set up in the same year its United Nations Educational, Scientific and Cultural Organization (UNESCO), with headquarters in Paris. It supported the foundation of a new organization of theatre-makers, the International Theatre Institute (ITI). UNESCO's general secretary emphatically declared in his address to the third annual ITI congress hosted in Paris in 1947: 'We assert that theatre is the most powerful tool of culture, one of the most powerful tools for international understanding – yes, one can declare, one can dare to declare, that no human society would be worthy of this name without the theatre!'[19]

Of particular influence with regard to setting up a new internationalist theatre in this spirit across Europe was French director Jean Vilar (1912–71), who had trained with Charles Dullin (1885–1949), the former student of Jacques Copeau and collaborator of Antonin Artaud. In 1947 Vilar founded the Festival d'Avignon, which he would continue to direct until his death. The city of Avignon, which like so many other cities across Europe had been all but destroyed through air raids in the final phase of the Second World War, granted financial support to his plans as well as permission to stage performances in the courtyard of the medieval Palais des Papes. Originally planned as a one-off 'week of dramatic arts' in September 1947, the event was so successful that it was repeated the following July, and eventually became an annual tradition. Initially, Vilar's own company created all the productions for the festival; other companies, international guests and co-productions were only invited from 1965, during the final years of Vilar's tenure.

Vilar conceived of the Festival d'Avignon as a particular occasion on which to rebuild bridges with other European countries by producing dramatic works from the shared dramatic canon. In the early years, he staged, for instance, Shakespeare's *Richard II* and Georg Büchner's *Danton's Death* (see Figure I.1). At the same time, his festival – which took place in non-traditional spaces, for instance outdoors in the cloisters of ecclesiastical buildings in Avignon – was from the outset intended to reach a wider audience, and not just the educated, theatre-going middle classes. Hence, Avignon, in the Mediterranean South of France, far away from the cultural capital Paris, had been Vilar's place of choice. His aesthetics were inspired by the travelling troupes of Shakespeare's time and not by the bourgeois art temples of the metropolitan capitals and their refined productions. Vilar used barely any scenery and props: there was just a simple lighting wash with no changes, no curtain and no interval, even if the performance lasted for more than three hours, as was the case with his *Richard II*. Culture for Vilar should not be 'cultural capital', as sociologist Pierre Bourdieu would later term it, in other words a means to demonstrate or advance one's social standing.[20] Instead, culture for Vilar should be an occasion to come together as a community, to celebrate but also to reflect. French society was particularly split: the country's occupation by Nazi Germany had divided it into those who supported and collaborated with the regime and those who fought against it and risked their lives supporting the underground *Résistance* liberation

FIGURE I.1 *Jean Vilar rehearsing* Le Cid *at the Avignon Festival 1951 (Willy Rizzo/Paris Match, Getty Images).*

movement. A theatre festival such as Avignon, according to Vilar, would become a demonstration of a new united community, a fresh start under the banner of democracy.

Vilar was an advocate of a tradition that in France is known as *théâtre populaire,* literally translated as 'theatre of the people'. This was defined as:

> A spirit of theatre-making which did not separate artistic creation from social project; an era marked by utopia, by battles and by broadly-sketched dreams; a place where the people could come and reconnect with democracy of the highest order: a representation of human actions and passions that enables us better to understand History.[21]

These are the opening lines to a collection of essays on the history of the *théâtre populaire* movement between 1945 and 1958, a time during which the three directors treated in this volume were all active. In multiple and varied ways, major questions raised by this term will recur throughout our explorations of the work of Littlewood, Strehler and Planchon in this volume: how exactly can a 'theatre of the people' be defined? Above, all, who are the 'people'? According to the *Larousse* dictionary, *peuple*, or the 'people', denotes a collectivity of humans living on a specific territory or in a specific state, governed by a particular set of laws. It then provides a further definition of *peuple* as a group of citizens, notably the working classes, who are distinct from the government that rules them. French theatre offers an extensive history of the ways in which theatre has been enlisted in the entertainment and education of the 'masses', dating back to the revolutionary festivals staged during the French Revolution in 1792, which took place on a monumental scale in Paris, but equally across France's towns and villages, and which drew upon song, dance, sculpture and painting in an attempt to embody democracy, regeneration and patriotism in performance.

In France, *théâtre populaire* subsequently became more formalized during the later decades of the nineteenth century. The rise in prominence of the Marxist aspiration towards the emancipation of the working classes and the availability of secular education to an increasing proportion of the population, created the conditions in which to conceive of culture as accessible to everyone and not simply to a bourgeois elite. The idealist author and director Romain Rolland (1866–1944) was the first to implement the notion of a 'theatre for the people' in any consistent fashion, taking theatre out of Paris and to the Vosges region of eastern France. Decentralizing culture by developing theatre and other arts outside the metropolitan capital – as with Vilar's Avignon festival – has always been one of the central tenets of the *théâtre populaire*, the utopian ideal of which is to bring quality theatre to the greatest number of people, especially to new audiences. Rolland defined several key features of the *théâtre populaire*: 'the first condition of a people's theatre is to be a form of relaxation'; it also had to be a 'source of energy' and 'a shining light for intelligence'.[22] Both entertainment and education were at the heart of the project; culture was perceived as a liberating force that could precipitate nothing less than the social and political emancipation of the working classes. At the start of the twentieth century, *théâtre populaire* was then promoted by another key figure in the French theatrical tradition, Firmin Gémier (1869–1933), who was profoundly influenced by Rolland. In 1920 he founded the Théâtre National Populaire, housed inside the vast 3,000-seat Palais du Trocadéro in Paris, which was rebuilt as the Palais de Chaillot in 1935.[23] Previously, only the prestigious Comédie-Française, the Opéra and the Opéra Comique had been financed by the government. Thus, the TNP was the world's first subsidized theatre for the 'masses'. However, even though Gémier inaugurated the TNP, it did not really fulfil its criteria of entertaining and enlightening mass working-class audiences until Vilar was appointed its director in 1951, after successfully establishing the Avignon Festival.

In addition to his annual summer festival in Avignon, at which his company would perform each year, Vilar continued to develop his idea of a post-world war *théâtre populaire* in the more traditional environment of the French capital, performing partly in the working-class suburbs, and partly at the Palais de Chaillot. As in Avignon, he brought to the capital a new sense of theatre as a community event. For centuries, art had been an instrument in the service of the kings, who used it to entertain the aristocratic court; and following the revolution of 1789, the new bourgeoisie used theatre to represent their own class and its interests. In Vilar's vision, however, which followed that of Rolland and Gémier, everyone was invited to come to the theatre. In his venue, working-class visitors could find affordable food, would not encounter further charges for cloakrooms and programmes, and the performances did not start too late in the evening, so that they could return home using public transport. His TNP also hosted regular discussions and other events around the performances, thus contributing to the education of theatre-goers, especially new ones. The statistics from that period are legendary: over 5 million audience members passed through the doors of the TNP, where Vilar treated them both to the repertoire of classic plays, and to new writing. Vilar considered theatre as 'nourishment, as indispensable to life as bread and wine', and in a much quoted and influential phrase, he conceived of theatre, above anything else, as 'a public service, exactly like gas, water and electricity'.[24] He set about reaching 'the public at large', 'to share with the greatest number that which up until now had to be reserved, or so it was thought, for an elite'.

What Vilar described as 'the art of popular theatre' did not at all intend to 'dumb down' the productions or make art 'accessible' in a patronising way by simplifying its complexities. For him popular theatre could be just as nuanced as supposedly high-brow theatre; the 'difficult equilibrium [...] delicate to maintain', between artistic integrity and reaching a wide public, is precisely the precondition for 'a style that is alive'. Along these lines, the 'Manifesto of the Friends of *théâtre populaire*', which appeared in 1955, declared the *théâtre populaire* movement's intention to cultivate 'a mass audience, a highly cultured repertoire, and a stage art that is both freed, and of the highest quality'.[25] The *théâtre populaire* upheld the republican, humanist, progressive belief that, in the name of democracy, education and culture must be brought to the 'people', notably to those living in working-class suburbs and in provincial areas, who had previously been deprived of access. Theatre's civic role was central to Vilar's ethics, and theatre was seen to connect individuals with the true spirit of democracy by enabling them all, on equal terms, to enjoy, and to learn, together.[26] The *théâtre populaire* was so significant in France that the world-renowned critics and theorists Roland Barthes and Bernard Dort named their prominent theatre journal, *Théâtre Populaire*.[27]

Joan Littlewood: Agitprop, revues and the legacy of pre-war political theatre

Vilar's commitment to producing challenging art theatre for 'the general public', and to doing so outside the capital, was a great inspiration to other theatre-makers in France and equally abroad. In the UK, by the mid-1960s, a similar concern for the accessibility and availability of theatre art beyond the metropolitan centre of London was evident. The Arts Council of Great Britain (ACGB), which had been formed in 1946 to counter the dominance of commercially produced theatre entertainment, had initially focused on what its secretary general William Emrys Williams described as a concentration on 'few, but roses', mainly supporting prime institutions such as the Covent Garden Opera (with almost a third of its budget), Sadler's Wells and the Old Vic, with the Stratford Shakespeare Company as one of the few subsidized companies outside the capital.[28] This changed under the UK's first Minister for the Arts, Jennie Lee, who was appointed by the new Labour government, under prime minister Harold Wilson, some years after de Gaulle's Fifth Republic had created a similar government office in France. Lee secured increased funding for the Arts Council, which was distributed mainly to the regions, including to Scotland and Wales. Under her tenure, forty new theatres were built, including, eventually, in 1969, the National Theatre, on London's South Bank.

Still, in contrast not only to Vilar but also to Strehler and Planchon, Joan Littlewood was never supported by official government funding for arts and culture, not even under Lee's progressive tenure as minister. In fact, the Arts Council became infamous for what UK Littlewood specialist Nadine Holdsworth has described as 'its miserliness' towards Littlewood's work at the Theatre Workshop in Stratford East.[29] Even as their work in London's East End quickly gained an international reputation and the Theatre Workshop was invited to the Paris Théâtre des Nations festival of 1955, to which they would return with six more productions, and even as a number of their productions transferred to the West End, Littlewood never obtained Arts Council support. In 1955, the company even had to self-fund its journey to Paris and beg for their fares back home.

Joan Littlewood came from a different 'popular' theatre tradition from Vilar's and the French *théâtre populaire*. While she had in fact spent some time in Paris after discontinuing her studies at the Royal Academy of Dramatic Art (RADA) in 1934, she soon moved to the industrial town of Manchester. There she met her first partner Jimmy Miller (1915–89), a fellow communist who ran his own company, Theatre of Action, which Littlewood joined. As Robert Leach's chapter in this volume details, Miller, working under the stage name Ewan MacColl, was engaged in the Workers' Theatre Movement, a practice of popular theatre that had emerged after the Russian Revolution of 1917, and which also boomed during the political instability of 1920s Germany. Their Theatre of Action which, from 1936, was renamed Theatre Union, was particularly inspired by communist proletarian agitprop theatre, by Brecht and Eisler's Berlin revues (some of whose songs MacColl and Littlewood's actors performed in their productions) as well as by the great German director Erwin Piscator's living newspapers and his early political documentary theatre of the late 1920s [**see Volume 2**]. Littlewood also met the exiled German revolutionary playwright Ernst Toller, who worked in Manchester at the time. In addition to contemporary world politics (Hitler's rise to power in Germany in 1933; the Spanish Civil War from 1936 to 1939), Littlewood and MacColl addressed the widespread poverty and deprivation in 1930s Britain. After the First World War, the country had never regained economic prosperity; throughout the 1920s its production output remained below pre-war levels, unemployment never falling below 10 per cent, which was much higher than in the United States and even in Germany at the time. Consequently, Britain was hit even harder than other countries by the international financial crisis of the stock market crash of 1929 and its economic aftermath.

As Leach argues, Littlewood's practice is best contextualized within the specific British leftist tradition. He draws on theories of community developed by sociologist Zygmunt Bauman, philosopher Martin Buber and cultural anthropologist Victor Turner, to demonstrate how Littlewood and MacColl made theatre not only for working-class audiences but also in collaboration with them, as strikers, the unemployed and political groups would contribute actively to their shows. Littlewood would continue with this legacy during all three phases of her work, which Danielle Mérahi outlines in her chapter. Her contribution takes us in detail through the three main periods in Littlewood's professional life, which she portrays as defined by her key collaborators: first MacColl; later Gerry Raffles, one of the old Theatre Union collaborators with whom Littlewood regrouped after the war under the name Theatre Workshop; and then the architect Cedric Price, with whom she worked on the never to be realized 'Fun Palace' project – a late and often overlooked phase in her work to which Mérahi pays attention. Littlewood conceived this cultural space especially in order to counter the deformation of 'one-dimensional' workers, to use Marcuse's term that we have already introduced. It would seek to realize the attempts at the heart of the workers' tradition of popular theatre, whose goals Brecht expressed in his 1930 essay on his 'popular' opera *The Rise and Fall of the City Mahagonny*: 'to develop an object of instruction from the means of enjoyment, and convert certain institutions from entertainment establishments into organs of mass communication'.[30] Littlewood's proposal of participatory 'fun', that sought to break down the categories of education and pleasure in what she describes as a 'university of the streets', somewhat unsurprisingly, 'simply did not fit into the existing ACGB pigeon-holes'.[31] The commercial ferris wheel on the River Thames (now called the London Eye) was the only idea from the project ever realized in London, whereas the architects of the Paris Centre Georges Pompidou took up many of Price's ideas for a so-called 'cybernetic architecture' for the arts, as he called it.

Before they settled in 1953 in their famous home, the Theatre Royal Stratford East, Theatre Workshop initially toured the UK, mostly in the north, performing regularly at the Edinburgh Festival (launched in 1947 with similar intentions to Vilar's Avignon Festival) and travelling internationally (including a tour of Sweden and Czechoslovakia in 1948). Their productions explored, as Mérahi recounts, political issues in the aftermath of the war, the atomic bomb and the beginning of the Cold War. Both our contributors pay particular attention not only to the political engagement of Littlewood and her close collaborators but also to the unique, inventive directorial aesthetics of her work. Through workshopped improvisations with actors, Littlewood combined an emphasis on psychological characterization, gleaned from Stanislavski's careful analysis of the objectives in a playtext [**see Volume 1**], with an accentuation of the performer's body, inspired by both the Russian director Vsevolod Meyerhold's biomechanical approach to physical rhythm [**see Volume 2**] and the Austro-Hungarian dance pedagogue Rudolf von Laban. Leach ends his contribution to this book, however, by proposing that while Littlewood's workshopping and performance techniques found a strong and healthy legacy in later British devising practices, the political motivation that propelled her and her artistic collaborators' commitment to unifying society in the name of justice and equality has all but disappeared with the seemingly unstoppable and incontrovertible rise of neo-liberal economics and the collapse of community values.

Giorgio Strehler: The relation of people to their time

While Littlewood initially set up her alternative ensemble in Manchester, far from the metropolitan centre of London, and Roger Planchon launched his working-class theatre in Lyon, Italian theatre pioneer Giorgio Strehler was, to some extent, engaging in parallel tendencies. Returning to Milan from exile in Switzerland after the war, the multilingual Strehler rejoined forces with the theatre critic Paolo Grassi, who had been his friend since they both studied acting at the Milanese Accademia dei Filodrammatici. In 1947, together they founded the Piccolo Teatro, the first permanent theatre (*teatro stabile*) in Italy. They intended it to be a people's theatre, just like that of Vilar, Littlewood, and Planchon. They, too, applied a policy of affordable tickets in order to attract wider audiences to their productions of canonical classics. Writing in 1958, in retrospect Strehler describes the ideas behind the launch of the Piccolo Teatro:

> We opened our theatre with the tenacious intention to be rooted in the present in every respect. Our unremitting efforts were focused on modifying reality as it existed. We neither wanted to accept it, nor to adorn it with 'plumes of progress' in the form of abstract evolution or haphazard experiments. Instead, we wanted to develop, step by step, an exemplary system to clarify both the limitations and the future possibilities of these realities [...] The search for appropriate topics and arguments is what internally connects all our productions. At all times, we wanted to deal with people's relations to the 'society' of their time.[32]

In Strehler's vision, we again encounter the conviction that the ethical benefits of culture, and especially the collaborative nature of dialogue and exchange intrinsic to theatre-making, could reach beyond the theatre itself, in order to bring together communities. He held the idealist view that a post-war Europe would be united not by free market economics but through culture, which would promote well-being and a spirit of community among European citizens. Internationalization – or Europeanization – was central to the Piccolo's ethos as it developed the 'European' art of *mise en scène*, with the inclusion of translated plays from around Europe in its repertoire and the hosting of visiting theatre productions in their original language, from around the Continent. Margherita Laera, in her chapter in this volume, concentrates on these politics and reminds us of later trans-European initiatives proposed by Strehler, such as the Odéon-Théâtre de l'Europe in Paris, of which he became the first artistic director. Yet, her analysis also illustrates how, with the hindsight of several decades, some aspects of the Italian director's politics emerge as problematic. She questions, through the lens of Strehler's attitudes towards being a 'European' theatre-maker, theatre programmer and, for a short time, elected parliamentarian, what exactly 'European' means, and goes on to problematize Strehler's belief in Europe's rich shared cultural heritage: Strehler championed European humanist values which, argues Laera, are founded on the notion of a 'European man' – an all-knowing, 'unified and sovereign entity', customarily characterized as male and white. His recourse to the European canon was inclusive in intention but simultaneously performed significant exclusions – of female authors, of non-European cultures and their writings and of experimental approaches to writing. Notwithstanding, Laera concludes that, while the European humanism in which Strehler had so much faith might not foster diversity and inclusivity, in today's Europe in which right-wing populism and the hostility to migration from beyond Europe's borders grow apace, he is nonetheless a figure whose passionate belief in transnational kinship and unification forged through culture, might have something to teach us.

Introducing Strehler's directorial work in his chapter in this collection, Bent Holm outlines how Strehler, no less eclectically than Littlewood, drew on inspiration from Stanislavski, Copeau [**see Volume 3**] and, not least, Brecht – the three 'cities', as Strehler once described his most influential teachers. Strehler indeed became particularly noted – in addition to being celebrated for his work reviving the literary *commedia* plays of Carlo Goldoni (1707–93), whose *The Servant of Two Masters* he directed during the theatre's first season and which became the director's signature piece, and for staging the works of early twentieth-century Italian playwright Luigi Pirandello (1867–1936) – for his productions of Brecht's works. His productions of Italian classics and of Brecht's epic plays, which could be seen side by side at the Piccolo Teatro in the late 1950s, inspired an influential early essay on political theatre by Louis Althusser.[33] Overall, Strehler directed nine of Brecht's plays, some of them several times. Holm discusses in detail Strehler's productions of Brecht's *The Threepenny Opera* in 1956, which Brecht went to see in Milan, and of *The Good Person of Szechwan,* which Strehler staged in 1958, 1977, 1981 and 1996.

Yet while Strehler was notably inspired by the Brechtian commitment to highlighting the historical, political and economic reasons for social injustice, he also 'betrayed' Brecht, as the title of Holm's essay suggests, by deviating significantly from the epic approach. Holm illustrates this by drawing on Strehler's own concept of 'Chinese boxes'. The first box, as Holm explains, emphasizes the centrality to any theatre production of storytelling, plot and characters; the second emphasizes, in typical Brechtian fashion, the political and historical context behind the story and characters; the third box opens out onto broader, more universal (and, in a different way, 'epic') themes, such as life, death, love and war. Any production should display the three boxes, unified into a whole. In contrast to Brecht's material realism, Strehler offered space on his stage for a 'magic realism'. He thereby smoothed some of the former's disruptive 'epic', fragmented montage by transferring – as Holm illustrates in his analysis – the critical *Verfremdungseffekt*, or distancing devices, to other elements of his *mise en scène*. In this way, Strehler employed the poetic 'magic' of his productions in order to provide a critical distance between the stage and the audience, one that would enable spectators to reflect on political and social issues. As Holm further argues, the standard view of Strehler as interpreter of the playtexts he staged is, therefore, too short-sighted. Yet, he clearly was no 'conceptual' *auteur* of 'directors' theatre' either. Rather, Strehler calls into question the very distinction between these two categories of 'interpreter' and 'conceptual director', often used to describe directorial approaches. Holm, in this context, points us towards the great affinity that one of the most imaginative and influential directors of the later twentieth century, Robert Wilson, felt with Strehler's work. Wilson showed his productions regularly at Strehler's Piccolo Teatro and, in 2007, staged Brecht's *Threepenny Opera* for its eightieth anniversary at the site of its original production, the Schiffbauerdamm theatre in Berlin. In his production, Wilson referenced Strehler's *mise en scène*, testifying to the influence Strehler exerted on Wilson, and on a host of late twentieth-century directors.

Between popular theatre and Brechtian *scenic writing*: Roger Planchon

The director who most notably followed Jean Vilar's lead in bringing quality theatre to large and diverse audiences outside the metropolitan centre in France was Roger Planchon. He had no formal theatre training but was dedicated to amateur dramatics and set up, in 1950, a theatre company with some friends. In 1952 they founded their Théâtre de la Comédie in a former printing shop in the centre of Lyon, which seated an audience of 110. Committed to making theatre accessible to working-class audiences who might otherwise consider themselves excluded from theatrical establishments, the company fully embedded their work in the daily life of their local community, engaging in what is now termed 'outreach' activities. They went into schools, factories and shops, promoting and discussing their latest productions. Each new show became a local event that was talked about across the city, and which thereby brought the community together and offered an intellectual centre to the people of Lyon. In 1957, Planchon and his company were eventually invited to take over the new Théâtre de la Cité in Villeurbanne, an industrial community on the outskirts of Lyon. This was to become the first newly built, state-funded theatre outside central Paris. Thus, Vilar's example had clearly influenced a new cultural policy: a new Minister for Cultural Affairs was appointed in France, and the state now no longer funded the Comédie-Française and Parisian theatre alone but also subsidized other theatres in France. After Vilar's death in 1972, the title of Théâtre National Populaire (TNP) was transferred from Paris to Planchon's Villeurbanne theatre, fully validating the now decentralized French theatre landscape.[34] Planchon remained at the helm of the TNP until 2002.

It is a particular honour to include in this volume a piece by Michel Bataillon, who worked at Planchon's side all the way from 1972 to 2002. During this time, Bataillon served as Planchon's dramaturg and assisted him with programming.[35] As Bataillon's essay illustrates, Planchon was determined to welcome audiences who did not habitually frequent the theatre and, to this end, was inspired both by the popular theatre movement and equally by popular cabaret and cinema. Bataillon explains how Planchon incorporated humour into his shows, developing a physical performance style filled with wacky gags and burlesque jokes. At the same time, maintains Bataillon, Planchon brought comedy and knockabout fun into dialogue with intellectual influences, in Planchon's case Karl Marx's communist theories, Sigmund Freud's psychoanalysis and Foucault's cultural theory. Bataillon reflects on his own work with Planchon and points readers towards some valuable documentation of his productions, situating Planchon within the broader context of post-war theatre-making in France and especially Vilar's work at the Avignon Theatre Festival. Bataillon explains how Planchon applied his uniquely intellectual approach to popular theatre both to classic plays and to the range of new playwrights, including Arthur Adamov and Michel Vinaver, who accompanied him throughout his career.

Yet, there is another central impulse in Planchon's work, to which Pia Kleber dedicates her essay. Like Strehler in Italy and Littlewood in the UK, Planchon introduced Brecht's plays to his country's stages. Already in 1954, with his Lyon theatre company he had directed the French premiere of *The Good Person of Szechwan*. When the Berliner Ensemble returned to Paris for their second visit in 1955, Planchon sought the famous theatre-maker out and discussed his own approach to the play with him:

> I presented myself to Brecht with my production photographs of *The Good Woman* as my only recommendation. I spent five hours with him. He told me what he liked and what he didn't in our work, and we discussed it. From this interview, and from the productions of the Berliner Ensemble, I was seized with the conviction that here was truth and that I should not hesitate to copy boldly.[36]

Brecht's influence on Planchon's work at the time was, according to his biographer Yvonne Daoust, 'almost overpowering'.[37] Complementing Holm's discussion of Strehler's engagement with *The Good Person of Szechwan*, Pia Kleber traces in her chapter the development of Planchon's art by analysing his three successive stagings of the same play, produced between 1954 and 1958.

Not only are Planchon's productions of Brecht's own plays important but so, too, is his understanding and development of a thoroughly Brechtian notion of dramaturgy that he applied to his *mise en scène* as a result of his discussions with Brecht. Planchon believed that a play is only fully realized in performance and, importantly, that the process of creating a production is in itself a critical act. Central to Planchon's understanding of Brecht is his idea of a complex, multi-layered *langage scénique* – French theatre specialist David Bradby translates this as 'scenic writing', which he compares with the playwright's 'dramatic writing'.[38] Planchon explains his concept thus:

> The lesson which we can learn from Brecht the theoretician is that [...] stage language [...] has a *responsibility* equal to that of the written text and, finally, a movement onstage, the choice of a colour, of a set, of a costume, etc. This involves a complete responsibility. The stage language is totally responsible, in the same way as the text itself is responsible.[39]

Planchon, therefore, underlined a crucial aspect of Brecht's epic theatre practice, where the choice of a stage property, a colour and not least a gesture would not only illustrate the play but in itself contribute to its narration: 'every object placed on the stage or every absence of an object [...] has some kind of significance'.[40] Planchon thus took an important step beyond Vilar's popular theatre approach and aligned it with the Brechtian tradition, thereby paving the way for a 'directors' theatre', where the director's interpretation of the dramatic work became the central aspect of the production, as we shall discuss in more detail in the section below.[41] Importantly, though, this interpretation for Planchon was never an end in itself: the many means of the stage that he had at his disposal as a director should serve, according to him, to achieve a precise portrayal of the complexity of the world (and, in Brecht's sense, also its changeability), which he presented to his local, working-class audiences in Lyon. Overall, as both Kleber's and Bataillon's essays demonstrate, while Brecht remained a most significant influence on Planchon, in clarifying the importance of enlisting all elements of stage production in the task of storytelling his work can also be seen to have created a hybrid between Brechtian practice, Vilar's *théâtre populaire* and theatrical styles made famous by the French 'Cartel' of the interwar era – the group of influential directors that included Gaston Baty, Charles Dullin, Louis Jouvet and Georges Pitoëff who developed the art of *mise en scène* in France via their use of stylized set, costume and acting. Thus, Planchon complemented their stage poetry with his concern for political and social transformation, as the two essays in this volume illustrate.

Resonances of the 'Brechtian Revolution'

Littlewood, Strehler and Planchon mark a significant shift in European culture after the Second World War. Previously in the service of the representation of a 'national culture' as defined by middle-brow classes, theatre now affirmed its social consciousness, becoming a common ground between different peoples. Remembering the traumatic events of the war, and facing the threats of atomic destruction during the Cold War, theatre as a public assembly in which to watch a play became the space where audiences could claim an ethical attitude towards the world and our fellow human beings, not least those whom we consider to be 'others' or our 'enemies'. Littlewood's, Strehler's and Planchon's imperative to see in theatre not just art but an engaged practice that negotiates meanings and attitudes in the interests of improving our own everyday lives, is of course the most pertinent echo of Brecht's expressly political artistic practice which remained inspirational for many theatre-makers of the mid-twentieth century. From 1954, Brecht's Berliner Ensemble brought productions of his own plays such as *Mother Courage* to Paris, and in 1956, shortly after Brecht's death, his theatre came to London for the first time. Littlewood's Theatre Workshop was inspired by the Berliner Ensemble's visit to the Royal Court Theatre, yet they had already encountered Brecht in Paris in 1955 at the Théâtre des

Nations festival, where they presented their *Arden of Faversham* alongside Brecht's *Mother Courage*. In Paris, Brecht gave Littlewood permission to direct (and perform the lead in) the play's London premiere later that year.[42] We have already mentioned how Planchon watched the Berliner Ensemble's Paris performances and discussed his own staging of *The Good Person of Szechwan* with Brecht, while the German director also visited Strehler in his Milan theatre in 1956 to watch the Italian's rehearsal of *The Threepenny Opera*, following an earlier visit by Strehler to discuss his production ideas with him in Berlin, which Holm outlines in his chapter. We now turn in greater detail to this profound engagement with Brecht by all three of our 'great stage directors'.

Of course, it would be short-sighted to present these three directors solely as realizing a Brechtian vision of theatre; this would reduce them to mere imitators. In fact, one of their major achievements was to bring together the political sensibility that they shared with Brecht (and which each of their personal encounters with Brecht reinforced and gave further direction) with further aesthetic elements in their *mises en scène*. Littlewood's productions were not only politically committed but also aesthetically experimental, engaging with innovative techniques from the historical avant-garde, from lighting and set designer Adolphe Appia and stage designer Edward Gordon Craig to Piscator, Meyerhold and Laban. Strehler and Planchon, meanwhile, revived old performance traditions in their popular productions, notably Italian *commedia dell'arte* and French *théâtre de la foire*. The chapters by Leach, Holm and Kleber, in particular, critically interrogate their Brechtian influence. In his chapter, Leach carefully nuances the claims often made that Littlewood was the UK's first truly 'Brechtian' theatre director.[43] He prefers to highlight the numerous other important artistic and political traditions by which Littlewood was inspired. Drawing on terms developed by Friedrich Nietzsche in *The Birth of Tragedy*, Leach describes Littlewood's theatre as Dionysian as opposed to Apollonian, a characteristic that he attributes more to Brecht's aesthetic. In Leach's view, while Brecht encourages reflection and reasoning, Littlewood's theatre was a joyous riot of popular song, dance and laughter. For his part, Bent Holm cites Brecht, who described Strehler's work, of which he was a great admirer, as a combination of his own Brechtian 'cool', and the 'fire' of emotion and arresting imagery. And, as Kleber reveals, Planchon, too, succeeded in rendering the power of Brecht's politics by virtue of going beyond Brecht, and not treating his theories as doctrines. After all, as she remarks in her chapter, 'it was Brecht himself who had warned against too narrow an understanding of epic theatre'.

Instead of direct influences and lineages, we suggest it may be more productive for the understanding of Littlewood, Strehler, and Planchon to foreground their shared political sensibility, one that echoes Brecht's aesthetic outlook. We argue that they all stand for different manifestations of a 'theatre of the people' that, around the post-war societal rupture, revived what Brecht had outlined as the 'plebeian' tradition of theatre as pleasurable popular entertainment – theatre that would not function as mere diversion but instead would reflect on lived, everyday reality. A related characteristic of their work is these directors' commitment to their ensembles. Littlewood ran all her companies as collectives of actors, designers and technicians, where everyone would share the tasks. Planchon noted the central importance in the task of reaching out to 'new' theatre audiences, in working with a permanent ensemble, with whom the audience would establish a personal rapport beyond individual productions. From his early successes at the beginning of the 1950s until the 1970s, he continued to work with his group of actors, which included Jean Bouise and Isabelle Sadoyan. In their communion with stage performers, as Vilar had envisaged after the war, audience members would become almost an extended part of the ensemble.

The specific Brechtian legacy that we can trace to a greater or lesser extent in the works of all three directors presented in this volume, therefore, has its origins not only in a leftist political outlook or in direct activist intervention through 'political theatre' (as suggested by Brecht's practice of the 1920s and 1930s) but also in Brecht's physical and sensual-affective, as well as critical, approach to theatre; specifically, that is, in the understanding of the potential of theatre performance on which his works and writings from the 1940s onwards placed particular emphasis. According to Brecht scholar Joachim Fiebach, it is in this approach to theatre that the true 'révolution brechtienne', which the magazine *Théâtre Populaire* described in a special 1954 issue following the Berliner Ensemble's debut Paris performance, manifests itself.[44] Fiebach argues that Brecht's innovation represented a fundamental cultural rupture not only for the performing arts, but more fundamentally for Western art as it had been conceived since the nineteenth century in the bourgeois tradition. Brecht, according to Fiebach, should be seen

> as the turning point of a process in which, drawing on plebeian traditions, bourgeois art practice and the understanding of art up to this point, had been opened up. A new coordinate system of modes of perception and structures of composition and communication had been developed, in which the sensual and the imaginative could become fundamental. It is in this way that Brechtian aesthetics can be said to represent a revolutionary act.[45]

From this point of view, the political act of Brechtian theatre is not so much tied to a specific political message but to a 'sensual and imaginative' (in Brechtian terms, 'gestic') mode of presentation, which enables spectators to adopt a new, different critical perspective on the play and, by extension, on reality and life outside the theatre. This is political because the audience must decide on their own position and their own attitude towards what is being shown; the attitudes and positions are not simply spelt out by the play or the production itself. Along these lines, Strehler – who maintained close connections with the Berliner Ensemble beyond Brecht's death in 1956 – wrote:

> Revolutionary in art is everything which develops a new relationship to reality, and which is able to be articulated both humanely and artistically in such a way that people can identify with it. *To grasp!* The task of art, and in particular of the theatre, is not 'to start a revolution', but to articulate the profile of a new reality, to reveal pseudo-problems, etc.[46]

We argue that Littlewood, Strehler and Planchon all shared this core late-Brechtian understanding of theatre as the creative invention of a fictional, alternative reality with its own laws and structures, which challenges conventional wisdoms and traditional perspectives, and forces spectators constantly to re-evaluate their own attitudes and to adapt their perspectives accordingly. Based on the key strategy of *Verfremdung* [see **Volume 2**], the theatre performance is, thus, connected in complex, myriad ways with realities outside the theatre, and with events and situations from real life, presented in a Brechtian 'defamiliarized' manner, which the spectators are distanced from and, at the same time, can recognize even more clearly.

Such a political theatre no longer seeks to intervene directly in current affairs, as was characteristic of Brecht's (as well as his friend Piscator's) theatre practice of the 1920s. Having the resonances of everyday reality palpably imprinted on fictional worlds allows the audience to recognize the complex paradoxes of everyday life in a fictional setting, and thereby to imagine alternatives to their own lives and society. This is the core vision of Brecht's late theatre, which he himself described as 'dialectic theatre', thereby abandoning his earlier standard term of 'epic theatre'. Already in his 1939 lecture 'On Experimental Theatre' he stated:

> The spectators are welcomed into the theatre as those who change the world rather than accept it, who intervene in natural and social processes in order to master them. The theatre no longer seeks to intoxicate them, supply them with illusions, help them forget the world, reconcile them with fate. The theatre now spreads the world before them to grasp for their own purposes.[47]

We find a similar stance on political art in the writings of the already mentioned Frankfurt School of Critical Theory: their lines of thought seem a particularly apt context to bring into dialogue with the theatre works of the three post-war directors discussed in this volume, since both predate the rupture of post-modern deconstruction that took place from the late 1960s onwards. Concerning the arts, the writings of Adorno and, in particular, of Marcuse insist on the absolute autonomy of the aesthetic realm but not at all in order to amputate it of its political relevance. Rather, 'theatre must be permitted to remain entirely superfluous',[48] as Brecht phrased it in his 'Short Organum', so that it is not usurped by everyday utilitarianism and functional thinking, in other words by Marcusian 'one dimensionality', but instead allows for surprise and discovery and, as a result, stimulates the spectators' critical (one may say, multi-dimensional) attitude, which for Brecht is the basis of true pleasure, as opposed to any narcotic entertainment that theatre may also provide.[49] In his already mentioned central work *The One-Dimensional Man,* Marcuse further warns that we should not confuse an artwork in itself with a political act; only the latter may effect political change or constitute a meaningful 'subversive force'. Especially under the conditions of capitalism (which Marcuse described as another totalitarian system, following fascism and Stalinist communism), any subversive power is already assimilated by the hegemonic system 'in a harmonizing pluralism, where the most contradictory works and truths peacefully coexist in indifference'.[50] Therefore, the truly political potential of art does not reside in the content or in specific statements or references that it might make but, for Marcuse, in the 'tension between the actual and the possible', a conflict beyond resolution. For Marcuse, the irreconcilable gap between artistic fiction and actual everyday reality is vital in order to disclose reality and its limitations, deceptions and contradictions:

> Fiction calls the facts by their name and their reign collapses; fiction subverts everyday experience and shows it to be mutilated and false. But art has this magic power only as the power of negation. It can speak its own language only as long as the images are alive which refuse and refute the established order.[51]

Thus, Marcuse extends Brechtian *Verfremdung* to propose the centrality of negation – what he terms 'the Great Refusal – the protest against that which is'.[52]

Two central principles support further the dialectic relationship of (stage) fiction and reality in the context of late-Brechtian theatre practice, principles that can also be discerned in the works of the three directors discussed in this volume: first, the importance of historicity and, second, a realist attitude. Only if these characteristics underpin stage fiction can it resist falling back into an idealist illusion with which the spectators uncritically identify and empathize. For a Brechtian 'historicizing' critical attitude to develop, the 'objective analysis', as Strehler will term it, is crucial; in other words, the precise understanding of the play's own historical context. It is 'objective' because it avoids subjective identification and recourse to emotions. It is this thorough investigation that then informs the director's 'scenic writing', as Planchon terms it: the attempt to represent on stage, via the characters' actions and conflicts, the social configuration of the historical period from which the play emerged, and to make the audience understand these wider social conflicts and power struggles. This idea underpins what Brecht termed the 'fable'. According to a historicizing approach to analysing drama and composing 'scenic writing', the characters are, therefore, never bundles of individual psychological traits but instead they show and tell the history of their time through their actions (and only secondarily through their words) which, therefore, acquire the Brechtian 'gestic' quality; the individual is always seen as an inherently social and political being, as part of society. To unearth and render this past history to a present-day audience then becomes, as Strehler suggested, the major responsibility of the director.

Instead of conjuring a fantastical *other* world, the aim of this theatre is the representation of a (very material) reality as it presents itself to human beings at a given time and not some image or idea of, for instance, the Elizabethan world that would only result in cliché and costume drama. It is on this basis of difference that the fictional stage and the real auditorium enter into a shared world: realism here does not mean a lifelike imitation of actual reality. Repeatedly in his writings, Brecht evokes the inability of photographs to capture the processes and paradoxes that determine life in our own complex societies. The dialectic encounter of stage fiction and its defamiliarizing (or, in Marcuse's term, its 'negative') impact on our own everyday reality allow us not only to look at and recognize something real in the fiction, but also to look through and understand the underpinning laws; this is the knowledge with which the theatre of this period of the twentieth century wants to equip its spectators, so as to master and also to intervene in life, to make good again and to avoid yet another, even more catastrophic, war.

The classics as contemporaries – and adversaries

More than their artist peers before the war, Littlewood, Strehler and Planchon worked in an age of growing consumerism and not least of ever more present mass media, from radio (we may think of Brecht's early work in the medium as well as Littlewood's productions for the BBC) to the new omnipresent television, pop songs and magazines. Moreover, film became a specific inspiration for Planchon's scenic language: from the aesthetics of the French *auteur* cinema of the *nouvelle vague* experimental film from the 1960s to compositional cinematic techniques such as the use of music or of cuts, counter-shots and fades. According to Adorno and Horkheimer's critique referred to earlier in this Introduction, these mass media, produced by an 'entertainment industry', threaten to 'infect [...] everything with sameness',[53] making the viewer perceive the real world merely as a continuation of this filtered perspective or 'bubble' proffered by the mass media. If theatre only acts as a further part of this entertainment industry, it loses its claim to qualify as art.

While Littlewood, Strehler and Planchon all emphasized the social significance of the performing arts, envisaged the stage as a site for critique and reflection, and intended to address as wide a section of the population as possible, they did not forsake the legacy of 'art theatre' and the Western dramatic canon. As a further echo of Brechtian practice, and a direct extension of his historicizing and realist concept, which we have already outlined, they all drew on the major resource of Western European 'art theatre', the canon of 'great works' of the European cultural tradition, from the ancient tragedies of Aeschylus, Sophocles and Euripides, via the early modern classics of Shakespeare and his contemporaries, the French neoclassical comedies of Molière and tragedies of Corneille and Racine, and German classics by Schiller and Goethe, to the 'modern' classics by Ibsen, Strindberg and Chekhov. This repertoire had been firmly established in the European tradition of the bourgeois theatre institution from the nineteenth century onwards. What now changed, with Brecht's adaptation of classics in his oeuvre, but similarly in Littlewood's, Strehler's and Planchon's approaches to these canonical plays, was their understanding of the actual role of this canon. For them, these major plays of Western theatre history were no longer situated within an aesthetic vacuum of high art, separate from the everyday life experience of the audience and contemporary politics, society and economics. German theatre historian Günther Rühle explains this post-war attitude towards theatre as a means to critique society:

> This system of critique and innovation, of challenge and new production, of opposition and the assimilation of opposition, makes [bourgeois society] so powerful. The theatre is one of the instruments within this critical process. It bestows a visible and concrete manifestation to the necessary critique, or it seeks, in its politically activist formats [...] to reinforce the audience's critical conscience. [...]
>
> By means of restaging traditional plays, whose lasting substance is manifested by the enduring or reawakened interest in them, the theatre is the memory of this traditional foundation; by means of critically reproducing the plays, however, it also makes an attempt to find a new relation to them. [...] To realize and portray what is current in the past, and to define the tradition through the present in such a way that a position of differentiation and insight can be gained, means adopting a critical stance to the present, but also to the traditional play-text as well as to the traditional theatrical form.[54]

The starting point for theatre direction, as we encounter it in the work of our three directors discussed in this volume, was the in-depth historicization, in other words, the critical exploration of the historical contexts from which the play they were producing originated and of the theatre and its forms from which it had emerged, in order then to bring this context in relation with the immediate present, in adherence with the principle of Brechtian 'realism' that we have already outlined. In this way, the classic plays, rather than celebrating a transhistorical classical 'greatness', offer an occasion to take a step back and look at the urgent concerns of the present from a distance: through the eyes of a drama from another time and through the lessons of human life embodied in these plays.

This step represents an important development in the history of political theatre direction. It mainstreamed an attitude with which a few pioneer directors, mainly in the German theatre of the 1920s, for example Leopold Jessner [**see Volume 4**], Erwin Piscator and not least Brecht, had experimented. Piscator, for instance, spoke of the director's task as 'measuring the time that has since passed'.[55] These earlier approaches to political theatre had prepared the ground for the generation of directors treated in this book by insisting on a different function of theatre, one neither defined by aesthetic beauty nor by standing merely as distracting entertainment. Instead, theatre would directly reach out to the 'masses' and, in the turbulent times of the 1920s in which these directors worked, it would expressly take sides in a cultural battle against the totalitarianism of emerging fascism. In Littlewood and MacColl's early productions with Theatre Union we find some resounding echoes of this sentiment. They supported, for instance, the Republican cause in the Spanish Civil War that had started in 1936 by staging a version of Lope de Vega's *Fuente Ovejuna* (1612–14). Alongside this particular production, they published an ambitious manifesto:

> The Theatre must face up to the problems of its time: it cannot ignore the poverty and human suffering which increase every day. It cannot, with sincerity, close its eyes to the disasters of its time. Means Test suicides, wars, fascism and the million sordid accidents reported in the daily press. If the theatre of to-day would reach the heights achieved four thousand years ago in Greece and four hundred years ago in Elizabethan England it must face up to such problems. To those who say that such affairs are not the concern of the theatre or that the theatre should confine itself to treading in the paths of 'beauty' and 'dignity', we would say 'Read Shakespeare, Marlowe, Webster, Sophocles, Aeschylus, Aristophanes, Calderón, Molière, Lope de Vega, Schiller and the rest.'[56]

The 'truth' to which Theatre Union committed itself was that of human experiences, and not least human hardship and struggle; theatre art, they maintained, must 'face up' to these problems, rather than withdrawing into higher spheres of art or just offering distracting entertainment.

Later, Littlewood's Theatre Workshop opened their Theatre Royal Stratford East in 1953 with Shakespeare's *Twelfth Night,* and in the early seasons at this new permanent venue the company excavated numerous forgotten early modern plays such as the then rarely performed works of Ben Jonson or the anonymous *Arden of Faversham*, with which Littlewood's company was invited in 1955, as we have already mentioned, for the first of several visits to the Théâtre des Nations festival in Paris. Staging classics in sparse sets (mainly designed by John Bury), dispensing with the historical costumes and scenographic splendour to which audiences were used to in the commercial theatre, Theatre Workshop (not too dissimilar to Vilar's work at Avignon) opened a new perspective on the works of Shakespeare and his contemporaries – one that emphasized Shakespeare's link to the popular tradition.[57]

Against the notion of classic drama, and in particular Shakespeare, as an emblem of erudition and a timeless manifestation of Western civilization which might warrant reverential treatment on stage, Littlewood maintained that the classics belong to everyone. Her productions emphasized the contemporary and in particular the political resonances of the plays. She edited play versions and put actors in modern dress. Defending the Theatre Workshop's *Macbeth* against its critics, she argued:

> If Shakespeare has any significance today, a production of his work must not be regarded as a historical reconstruction, but as an instrument still sharp enough to provoke thought, to extend man's [*sic*] awareness of his problems, and to strengthen his belief in his kind.[58]

The Western cultural tradition, for Littlewood, was thus not a dead archive in which to store some great artistic achievements of the past but, instead, an active repertoire of cultural memory.[59] It should be available to everyone and invite us actively to interrogate and challenge not just the play but also, through the medium of the play, our own times and our personal lives, opinions, behaviour and attitudes.

In parallel, Strehler's work focused equally on engaging with plays from the classic canon, not least the Italian tradition of Goldoni, and of course Shakespeare, often restaging and further developing his productions several times. Strehler equally approached what he considered to be 'true classics' as if they were 'contemporary, because they have a dialectical relationship with our present that one has to carve out, renouncing their glorification as everlasting, or their codification as cultural capital'.[60] In the same interview, Strehler emphasizes that this attitude cannot simply be achieved by putting actors in modern dress or by playing with easily decodable allusions to current people or situations. Instead, the currency and immediate urgency for the present of a classic play can only be understood on the basis of an 'objective analysis' of the play, which Strehler considered, in fact, as one of the principal responsibilities of the director. One has to understand how a play, far beyond telling a story, embodies certain social constellations and conflicts of its time; these can then become the basis for relating them to the present moment. In *Towards a Human Theatre,* Strehler describes how a thorough understanding of a play's meaning in its time forms the basis for discovering its potential for today:

> When we concentrated on the pivotal moments of theatre history (Shakespeare, Molière, Goldoni) [...] we wanted to project here too the themes of these playwrights onto the level, on which they, as contemporaries of their time, attempted to individualize the reality of the society they lived in, and then test, how this may become meaningful for us; test, how their contemporary reality is related to our own.[61]

The work of Littlewood, Strehler and Planchon, thereby made significant contributions to post-war twentieth-century theatre and laid important foundations for the shape of European *Regie*, or directors' theatre, that have endured to the present day. Their approaches to directing plays from the Western literary canon, often paired with aesthetic experimentation, were at the time perceived as innovative, even radical, and in part highly controversial.

Following Patrice Pavis's account of 'the three ages of *mise en scène*', all three directors, however, still sit firmly within the modernist period of stage direction – somewhat completing and fulfilling it, before the advent of performance art, deconstruction and post-modern bricolage called in the new period of the director as *auteur*. Consequently, from today's perspective, the work of these three directors appears rather remote from our own early twenty-first-century times and tastes, including our prevailing ideas about modern stage direction: these directors tend to be eclipsed by the innovations of the 'performative turn' and its alternative approaches and institutions that emerged from the late 1960s onwards. Thus, today they have largely vanished from theatre studies curricula and – with the exception of Littlewood – only a limited amount of recent academic research has been dedicated to their directorial practices and to their respective visions of a European popular culture as embodied by their theatre. Even just slightly younger directors than Littlewood, Strehler and Planchon, who produced some of their work at the same time and often in the same geographical vicinity, for instance Peter Brook [**see Volume** 5], Ariane Mnouchkine [**see Volume** 7] and Robert Wilson, seem to sit more comfortably with us today. This gap has arisen not least through that other cultural caesura of the twentieth century, the political and cultural revolution during the late 1960s, symbolized by the student and worker protests in the streets of Paris in May 1968 that we have already discussed in our historical survey.

The political protests of the time coincided, and interacted, with the emergence of new modes of performance art that would also transform the conventions and expectations of theatre and of stage direction. A new, expressly 'alternative' avant-garde definitively cut the last ties with the history and legacy of Western bourgeois theatre, its traditions and its canon, that were associated with the 'parent' generation from which the protesting youth sought to emancipate itself. At the same time, new post-structuralist, post-modern and, increasingly, postcolonial intellectual theories introduced further challenges to the established Western canon and its unacknowledged logocentrism and hierarchical privilege afforded to Western, white, straight, male and middle-class audience members. While, a decade earlier, for Littlewood, Strehler and Planchon it was no contradiction to tackle the problems of the day through classic plays, precisely this engagement of the canon with bourgeois 'high art' now made this canon suspicious to the younger generation. Where Vilar had once declared that, 'if you deprive the public of Molière, Corneille and Shakespeare [...] then without doubt a certain quality of spirit within it will be weakened',[62] the new avant-garde of the 1960s and 1970s argued that if you continue to give the public the classics of a European (and Eurocentric) high art canon, theatre will remain the institution where a cultured elite talks to itself. Both the supposedly democratic approach of 'pop art' (exemplified in the visual arts by Americans such as Andy Warhol and Roy Lichtenstein or elsewhere by other pop artists like Yayoi Kusama) and the radical provocations of new performance art and live art (from Joseph Beuys to Marina Abramović) sought to challenge and break down the hierarchies of culture in far more radical ways than the earlier 'popular' theatre movements. Furthermore, Antonin Artaud's cry, 'No more masterpieces!', from his 1938 *Theatre and its Double*, was rediscovered in the late 1950s when Paule Thévenin edited a collection of his writings. Artaud's obscure texts and experiments gained cult status as provocations for the new approaches of body art and physical performance. Contemporary performance art would now set out to celebrate the present moment, physicality and emotions instead of history, historicity and the 'logic' of realism; and it would renounce classic as much as contemporary dramatic texts in favour of physical immediacy and visceral experiences for performers and audiences alike.

By 1968, the site of advanced experimentation in theatre was, therefore, no longer the interpretation and production of classic and contemporary dramatic plays performed by actors. The watershed of the 'performative turn' dismantled the hegemony of 'literary' theatre that had been established in the nineteenth century, and also discredited the post-war attempts of directors such as Littlewood, Strehler and Planchon to revive and innovate earlier popular theatrical traditions. They were now considered as passé and part of the very establishment they themselves had set out to fight a decade earlier; they became symbols of what Brook described as 'deadly theatre'. Following a period of reconstruction in which cities, societies and a new democratic order in Western Europe were rebuilt, and during which a new welfare state allowed new groups of young people access to universities for the first time, this very 'progress' – embodied in the protesting students – eventually turned against the efforts of the critical post-war generation that had made it possible. Even Jean Vilar became a victim of his own success, accused of serving up the same shows with the same star actors that he knew would guarantee him packed audiences and easily won approbation at the TNP and Avignon. The 'entertainment' aspect to the *théâtre populaire* ethos had, according to his critics, eclipsed the political obligation of theatre to critique, interrogate and ultimately transform society.[63] Therefore, it was no surprise that Vilar became one of the targets for the protesters of 1968 in France. In Avignon, the US performance art pioneers The Living Theatre – former Piscator students Judith Malina and Julian Beck – clashed with Vilar and eventually left the Festival. They decried his way of running the Festival as 'reactionary' and encouraged audiences not to pay for tickets, and themselves took their performance of their piece *Paradise Now* into the streets of the city. 'Vilar Béjart Salazar' was one of the slogans chanted on the streets that summer, equating Vilar and choreographer Maurice Béjart, whose company Ballets du XXe Siècle had been attached to the festival the year before for its twentieth anniversary, with the Portuguese dictator António de Oliveira Salazar.

Along with other directors of France's major theatrical institutions, Vilar was accused of pressing culture into the service of the state apparatus and/or of commerce, rather than rendering it available to the 'people'. Confronted with slogans such as 'No to culture supermarkets' and 'No to the consumer society', theatre directors understood the urgent need to reappraise precisely what was meant by a 'theatre of the people'. Shortly after May 1968, the director Patrice Chéreau (1944–2013), then a young man, openly criticized the *théâtre populaire* movement that had promised to be a public service like hospitals or schools but that, according to him, had no clear or coherent social objectives.[64] In addition, he condemned the movement for having abdicated its responsibilities for artistic innovation in favour of complacent, well-worn forms.[65] In fact, the critique was not really new and did not come solely from the young student protesters or emerging artists of the post-war generation such as Chéreau. Already a decade earlier, seasoned playwright Jean Genet had led some fiercely critical voices in France who challenged Vilar's and Planchon's approach to a 'popular theatre' based on the old classics. Genet specialist Carl Lavery suggests that the character of the plumber Roger, the revolutionary who castrates himself in Madame Irma's brothel towards the end of Genet's 1956 play *The Balcony,* makes fun of Vilar's suggestion of theatre as a public service 'like water, electricity and gas', while using Planchon's first name.[66]

In May 1968, Genet and others who had shared and supported the vision of popular theatre in the 1950s, came together at a three week-long meeting of French theatre-makers. Fittingly, given the *théâtre populaire*'s commitment to decentralization, the political events of the time and the future of the movement were debated not in Paris but in Villeurbanne, at Planchon's regional Théâtre de la Cité. Several days of debate culminated in a declaration that heralded theatre as the 'occasion to politicize oneself, to choose oneself freely over and above the feeling of disempowerment and absurdity perpetually caused by a social system in which people are almost never in a position to invent their own humanity, together'.[67] Theatre was to inscribe itself in social reality in the form of 'cultural action'.

In the words of David Bradby and John McCormick, 'the signatories admitted that by purveying high culture, they had been tacitly supporting the Gaullist regime, and that they had only succeeded in reaching those classes that were already cultured'.[68] Planchon's own theatre gave ample evidence of the defeat of the good intentions: only eight per cent of the audience at Villeurbanne were actually working class. The 'people', which all these directors aspired to reach, remained largely what the Villeurbanne declaration termed as 'non-public', in other words, 'the immensity of people composed of all those who do not yet have any access, nor have any chance in the near future of accessing, the phenomenon of culture as it appears in almost all cases'.[69] Yvonne Daoust summarizes what she describes as 'the paternalistic dilemma of those who wish to take culture to the masses':

> the difficulty which faced all directors in reaching a working-class audience was that they – even Planchon – were trying to attract them to plays consecrated by the middle class. 'Culture' is less a sum of knowledge than an attitude to new knowledge, and the working class, in France as in Britain, has its own culture.[70]

On the occasion of the Théâtre National Populaire's relocation from Paris to Planchon's Théâtre de la Cité in Villeurbanne, a minister from the Ministry for Cultural Affairs proclaimed that the TNP was the theatre for the nation. Tellingly, he did not declare that it was the theatre for the 'people'.[71] At the time, students also protested outside Milan's Piccolo Teatro against Strehler's allegedly autocratic rule, and Strehler indeed left the theatre for a number of years, as Laera recounts in her chapter where she quotes Strehler:

> The protest gave me a terrible lesson: one morning I found myself standing on the right, perceived as retrograde by many, while the night before I thought I was on the left and at the avant-garde. And I did not understand how such a transformation could have happened in twenty-four hours. And why.[72]

Like Strehler in Italy, whose theatre was also more frequented by the city's wealthy middle-class patrons, Planchon eventually temporarily left his theatre in Villeurbanne and embarked on nearly two years of prolonged touring.

The *théâtre populaire* project might have originated in well-intentioned ideals, but it also grew ideologically out of a set of republican myths and humanist values that deemed the masses culturally challenged, and in need of an education that meets standards considered acceptable by the dominant, governing classes. The mythical 'people' are expected to change by integrating theatre-going habits into their cultural practice. Moreover, as the Indian cultural critic Gayatri Chakravorty Spivak reminds us, the dominant classes have a tendency to lump the 'masses' into one undifferentiated block with a common, uniform consciousness, that the intellectual and artistic elite believe it can predict and understand.[73] In an article that appeared in

Le Monde newspaper two years after the 1968 movement's shock waves were felt across the globe, a distinction was made between Vilar's *théâtre populaire*, the intention of which was to 'educate the audience', and a post-1968 *théâtre populaire* that would 'submit itself to its audience'.[74] The idea of a culture designed by the dominant classes for the 'benefit' of the working classes, an extension of France's colonial 'civilizing mission', was thrown into serious question.

To this day, debates surrounding who precisely accesses culture, in particular state-subsidized culture paid for by the 'people', rage on. What should the civic, public and pedagogical roles of theatre be? Is theatre's main purpose to entertain or to educate?[75] Back in 1968, cultural institutions that did not seek actively to include less privileged sectors of society were accused of being complicit in exclusion.[76] This accusation continues to be levelled today at theatres, galleries and other subsidized institutions. When one talks of the 'people', to which 'people' is one referring? Should art attempt to cater individually for each social category, and in doing so inevitably exclude certain other ones? In view of the fact that components of mass culture, notably radio, television and, today, the internet, are such dominant media, to what extent should theatre seek to appeal to *all* 'people', thereby running the risk of inspiring none? Does striving to appeal to as wide an audience as possible contribute towards unifying people, or else lead to a consensus that precludes social and political debate and critique? In the face of history, can theatre change lives and societies? If so, how come, over a century after the first *théâtre populaire* initiatives, social inequality still exists and, in the current neo-liberal economic system, shows no signs of being addressed? Even if theatre does address the socio-economic realities of the underprivileged, are the audiences not still predominantly the educated, liberal-minded middle-class elite? So, should artists, instead, simply stick to making art? In which case, can artistically avant-garde and experimental theatre be elitist? These dilemmas, at the heart of the *théâtre populaire* project from its inception at the end of the nineteenth century, were passionately debated during the decades in which Joan Littlewood, Giorgio Strehler and Roger Planchon created their work and managed their theatres and ensembles. Examining these questions through the works of these three committed, inspirational figures of twentieth-century theatre, enables us, today, to work towards some answers.

While Littlewood, Strehler and Planchon often stand in the historiographic shadow of both the performative corporeality and immediacy inspired by Artaud and the new 1960s performance avant-garde, and of the post-modern, deconstructive approach of the 'post-dramatic' stage directors of the 1970s and 1980s, nonetheless, their work may open up another key trajectory in twentieth-century theatre that could, in fact, point us to such answers. As we have outlined in this Introduction, this trajectory leads us from the early political theatre of Piscator and Brecht, via Littlewood's, Strehler's and Planchon's work that was inspired by the spirit of the later Brecht, to go on further to a new generation of stage directors who today once more employ the dramatic canon in order to comment on contemporary politics and society: directors such as Thomas Ostermeier from Germany, Simon Stone from Australia, Ivo van Hove from the Netherlands and Carrie Cracknell from the UK. We may describe this line, adopting Brecht's late term, subsequently revived by Althusser with reference to Strehler's theatrical work, as 'materialist theatre'. Paving the way for this 'post-postdramatic' directors' theatre of the present, the 'materialist theatre' of Littlewood, Strehler and Planchon affirmed the *mise en scène* of a dramatic playtext beyond the representation of literature. From interpreting, explaining or illustrating the text as a hermeneutic aesthetic activity, directing came to be seen as a critical practice that used the occasion of the play to interrogate the word and the world: the playtext would only come to life in relation to these material contexts and actual realities, of its own time as well as of our time. Strehlerian 'objective research', in its directorial exploration and exploitation of the playtext's manifold echoes and reverberations, contrasts with a post-modern 'deconstruction' of the text as a play of signifiers and as a mere material springboard to generate ideas and associations. The materialist approach sees the actual event and presence of the performance as the occasion of an encounter between the (historic) text and the (contemporary) public, where the actors (as well as the director) act as mediators. Even before the 'performative turn' of the 1960s and 1970s, the popular performance traditions that Littlewood, Strehler and Planchon revived and appropriated for their own purposes emphasized modes of playing where the actors acknowledged the presence of the public, the reality of the situation and the everyday concerns of their time. They played with the playtext; they played to and with the audience, no longer hiding behind a fictional illusion. Thus, these directors strove to realize a theatre that in a Brechtian sense would both instruct and entertain – a theatre which, according to Brecht's phrase from his seminal essay 'On Experimental Theatre', 'turned from a place of illusions to a place of experiences'.[77]

Our own period in history no longer exists in the direct shadow cast by the 'age of extremes': the world wars and the Cold War. However, the fall of the Berlin Wall in 1989 was the beginning of a new, global future, with new-old reactionary forces re-emerging across the world. A lot separates our own digital world which is at once globally connected yet socially so disconnected, given its celebration of individualism, from the post-war decades in which these directors worked. In our era, shaped by a new neo-liberal order of capitalist markets which knows no alternative and sees profitability as the sole paradigm for any societal activity including art, theatre and culture, it appears timely to look back and remind ourselves of their ethos, which stood for a very different, inclusive and progressive 'populism' – an outward-facing, open, communicative, reflective, intelligent and engaged populism which appears as the outright opposite to the loud-mouthed, brutish, reactionary, demagogic and anti-liberal populism that has now taken hold right in the heart of democratic societies in the early part of the twenty-first century. Joan Littlewood, Giorgio Strehler and Roger Planchon may remind us of a different response to a society that feels threatened and precarious, and which is uncertain about its place in the world. They may invite us to revisit the project of European Enlightenment that has been so powerfully deconstructed by critical forces since the 1980s. Did its core values of emancipation, of 'freedom, equality and solidarity' have different meanings from the all-encompassing individualism turned chauvinistic and solipsistic egotism, where people appear to be unwilling to take on any responsibility for the wider community, welfare and society? Moreover, against an even more powerful and all-encompassing 'culture industry' that circulates affect- and emotion-driven surfaces of meaning through its global networks, the theatre work of these three directors may remind us of what true democratic commitment may mean, based on rational analysis and critical engagement. As the epilogue to Brecht's *The Good Women of Szechwan*, analyses of which reappear throughout this volume, phrases it – 'the curtain is closed, and all questions open'.

Joan Littlewood

1

Joan Littlewood, Rebel with a Cause: Opening New Directions in British Therelease

Danielle Mérahi

When Joan Littlewood (1914–2002) died quietly in her sleep in 2002, she had been absent from the stage for twenty-seven years. Erased from the public's memories, lost in oblivion, her silent death, nonetheless, revived the buried memories of an impressive career spent far away from the spotlight. Today, her statue stands on its pedestal – Joan seated on top of a heap of rubble in front of the Theatre Royal, the 'old slum', as she used to call it – in Gerry Raffles Square, Stratford East, London (see Figure 1.1). The statue is the bronze representation of a snapshot of Joan looking sideways with her quiet and pugnacious smile, confronted with the rebuilding of the derelict site all around her. As the commemorative statue by Scottish sculptor Philip Jackson was unveiled on 6 October 2015, he commented on his vision of Joan: 'Gentle and determined, sly and you know what.' His bronze figure certainly conveys the genuine dramatic power of the model. But why 'statufy' Joan, who had always had a reputation for defying classification? Indeed, her entire life, she called into question all fixed artistic forms as well as conventional political ideas, while remaining faithful to her own political and artistic principles: she always claimed to be 'a communist' and remained dedicated to collective creation in order to serve 'this knockabout art of theatre'.[1]

FIGURE 1.1 *Philip Jackson's statue of Joan Littlewood outside the Theatre Royal Stratford East (Danielle Mérahi).*

Between the 1930s and the 1960s Joan Littlewood broke all the rules of British theatre. A subversive visionary artist, she introduced specific theatrical practices currently prevailing onstage today, for instance collective creation, and improvisation. More than any artist, her personal life was closely related to her artistic work. Her tumultuous biography can accordingly be divided into three main periods, which I use to structure this chapter: I call them the 'Jimmy Miller (aka Ewan MacColl) period', the 'Gerry Raffles period' and the 'Cedric Price period'. Each of these periods represents a geographical location, a new step in her artistic choices as well as in her personal life; each led to a specific selection of plays, a complex choice of acting practices and a thoroughgoing experimentation that comprised multiple artistic innovations. In the following, I shall attempt to outline the decisive factors – influences and experiments – that determined her own theatrical practices. Since Littlewood's artistic lifespan stretches from before the Second World War until the 1970s, she lived and worked through the most eventful and tumultuous decades of the twentieth century (see, also, the introduction to this volume). Accordingly, the political, societal and economic shocks caused by the wars offered her incentive to innovate new artistic forms.

The 'MacColl years', 1934–53

Both Ewan MacColl (1915–89) and Joan Littlewood had been 'plugged into History' since childhood. Their generation had inherited a dark past: their parents' history was marked by the First World War and subsequent political, social and economic upheaval. Women had just obtained the right to vote in 1918, thanks to the suffragettes' struggles, but still ultimately lived in a man's world. Not only was Joan Littlewood a woman but also a woman from a working-class family. The fact that she was born in Stockwell, a poor part of London, and educated in a Catholic school, accounted for her at times middle-class accent, that was often peppered with profanities. She was a woman from a 'lumpen' environment, explaining why she had so much 'fight' in her.[2] In 1933, she left the Royal Academy of Dramatic Art (RADA) where she had been a student in London, and actually walked to Manchester for a radio job.[3] Back then, radio was still the most popular (and still a fairly new) means of information and entertainment in the UK. Littlewood worked for the BBC on programmes produced by a group of journalists with left-wing convictions such as the Oxford Marxist intellectual Archie Harding who was considered 'a dangerous man', 'better up in the north where he can't do so much damage'.[4] For Harding, all radio was a powerful medium for propaganda. It was while working for the BBC in Manchester that Littlewood first heard 'the Voice' – Jimmy Miller (who later became Littlewood's husband), a 'voice actor', in other words, an artist acting for radio.

For Littlewood, Miller and their producer Douglas Geoffrey Bridson (1910–80), radio was most notably a place where a diversity of different voices could be heard. As Bridson remembered, 'I also believed that radio was there to put people in touch with each other, not merely to instruct or inform or even to entertain them.'[5] Bridson and Littlewood travelled round the Yorkshire Dales and introduced different regional dialects and accents on air by inviting groups of people to Manchester for rehearsals and recordings. Borrowing *magnetophon* recording technology, which enabled magnetic tape to be cut and easily edited in a studio, in 1938 Bridson and Littlewood made recordings at the pithead and even down coalmines, where they went on shifts with the miners in order to produce a documentary programme, *Coal*. They created programmes about everyday people and their everyday lives, thereby affording the woman or man in the street importance and dignity. This commitment to 'common' people remained a constant in Littlewood's theatre.

The American folk singer Alan Lomax (1915–2002) was a further foundational figure in Littlewood's career. Collaborating as a radio producer and field recordist on one of Bridson's BBC programmes, *Transatlantic Call: People to People*, he collected traditional folk songs. The knowledge and skills that Littlewood gained from working on the radio made a lasting impact on her theatre. She learnt that sound, which can include music, testimony, scripted speech, improvisation and noise, can create atmosphere.

Moreover, sound, like images, can make associations with other sounds or words, or else collide with them. This sensitivity towards sound, in particular, influenced her theatrical innovation in later years. In addition, radio taught Littlewood how a medium could inform, entertain and communicate with mass audiences at one and the same time. This approach to the relationship to the audience also became important for her throughout her artistic career. Radio work was, therefore, a springboard for her work in many ways.

Jimmy Miller, who renamed himself Ewan MacColl, left a distinctive and lasting mark on Littlewood. MacColl was deeply involved in leftist politics and the practice of agitprop theatre (see also the chapter by Robert Leach for further detail). He was only fourteen years old when he started as a political activist. In 1934 he obtained the rights for *Newsboy*, a play that had originated from the communist New York Laboratory Theatre. This could be seen as the landmark moment that declared MacColl's political convictions. He went on to develop his skills as a director by staging classic plays that resonated with contemporary history such as Lope de Vega's *The Sheepwell*, which he adapted in 1936 in response to the Spanish Civil War, or in 1939 Jaroslav Hašek's *The Good Soldier Schweik*, which dealt with the First World War (for more detailed discussion of both, see Leach's chapter). As he explains in his autobiography *Journeyman*, he sought inspiration not only from 'Elizabethan and Jacobean [theatre] [...] the classical theatre of Greece [...] the theatre of Lope de Vega and Tirso de Molina, Molière, Commedia dell'Arte, Brecht, the expressionists, the Russians', but also from popular British traditions such as ancient rituals, mumming plays, mysteries and moralities.[6] He was also inspired by dramatic styles characteristic of popular culture such as melodrama, musical comedy, slapstick and mime. He believed in the possibility of a 'theatre for the people' akin to Ben Jonson's, Christopher Marlowe's, Shakespeare's, Molière's, George Bernard Shaw's or Sean O'Casey's.[7] All of these influences and styles he brought to his collaboration with Littlewood, and they were subsequently to be found in her stage productions.

MacColl not only adapted scripts but he was also a playwright in his own right. His characteristic poetic and political style can be found in his play *Uranium 235* that deals with the misuse of science and the atomic bomb (the play was written just after the United States had dropped hydrogen bombs on Hiroshima and Nagasaki), or his play *The Other Animals* (1948) that denounces injustice, tyranny and the use of torture. Even though these plays have all but been forgotten by contemporary theatre scholars and makers, they were enormously prescient. *Uranium* could be seen today as a reflection on the Fukushima nuclear disaster, and *The Other Animals* as an indictment of the use of torture at Guantanamo and other detention facilities. His 1945 Unity Theatre play *Johnny Noble* reads like an alarm bell against what happened once again during the recent financial crisis of 2008. He developed his own personal lyrical style that included poetic language, ballad-opera[8] and other modes, to generate an eclectic variety that solicited from actors a great range of approaches to performance. *Uranium 235*, for example, contains didactic public address, nonsense rhymes in the tradition of popular entertainment, archetypal *commedia dell'arte* characters, stand-up routines, a circus-style 'atom tamer', an 'atomic ballet', a masked chorus and characters playing Hollywood-style gangsters (see Figure 1.2).[9] With these plays and others, MacColl and his itinerant theatre made their name, and his eclectic style that combined political activism, canonical plays and popular entertainment profoundly influenced his partner, Joan Littlewood.

From the beginning of their collaboration, through their three companies with their respective manifestos (Theatre of Action 1934, Theatre Union 1936, Theatre Workshop 1945), Littlewood and MacColl considered

FIGURE 1.2 *The 'atomic ballet' from Ewan MacColl's* Uranium 235, *staged by Joan Littlewood's Theatre Workshop in May 1952 (Daily Mirror/Mirrorpix/Getty Images).*

that the *raison d'être* of any theatre company they created would be the promotion of a popular theatre for the people that focused on both political and aesthetic considerations, and was performed by committed, well-trained artists who would collaborate together as a team, evoking the great Athenian tradition of the chorus, that represented the public's voice. They would strive perpetually to create new projects, all of which would reflect their contemporary society and the political problems of their times and their generation. They had the ambition to tour to working-class audiences around the UK, notably in northern England and Scotland, where the need for the arts was more acute.[10] Littlewood and MacColl were conscious that the conservative society in which they worked was suspicious of all forms of innovation and that a real theatrical revolution would have to take place, in order for the UK to catch up with the directorial practices on the European continent. Littlewood and MacColl were tireless scholars, researchers and practitioners, and were up to the task of essentially being the only stage directors concerned with innovation and experimentation in the UK, and, moreover, artists who could not rely on the state for subsidies or support. Their theatre knowledge was, as indicated above, incredibly eclectic, and in terms of the actor-training methods that influenced them, MacColl had been aware of the Russian director Konstantin Stanislavski's system of acting [**see Volume 1**] since 1936, when an American translation had become available thanks to Stanislavski's collaborator, Elizabeth Hapgood.[11] Yet, in an interview with theatre scholar Richard Runkel, MacColl insists that his personal interest in experimental theatre had begun prior to his discovery of Stanislavski.[12] MacColl and Littlewood were further interested in Meyerhold's biomechanics [**see Volume 2**] as well as in the Russian directors' scenic constructivism. In addition, MacColl had read the Swiss stage designer Adolphe Appia's (1862–1928) conceptualizations of space, light and the actor's body. Finally, at an early stage, he had discovered Bertolt Brecht's (1898–1956) *Verfremdungseffekt*, and MacColl's theatre style, which included symbolic elements in the scenography and montage, had much in common with the documentary theatre of German director Erwin Piscator (1893–1966), who worked together with Brecht [**see Volume 2**].[13] But it was no doubt the French communist critic Léon Moussinac (1890–1964) who was the decisive figure in MacColl's and Littlewood's search for artistic innovation.[14] Littlewood had always preserved a particularly close relationship with France, and MacColl had access to Moussinac's literature thanks to an international network of communist thinkers and activists spanning from Soviet Russia to the United States. Moussinac's books, therefore, proved to be the link that had enabled them to discover Craig, Appia, Meyerhold and further theatre theoreticians and continental European practitioners. Moussinac had been one of the first critics to theorize the connection between stage aesthetic and acting style, and to propose that the playtext might be important to the production process but not the dominant element. Moreover, he introduced to readers the names of great French directors such as Firmin Gémier, Jacques Copeau and Gaston Baty, who were leading figures in the French *théâtre populaire* movement (see introduction to this volume) and who had consolidated the art of *mise en scène* by developing the skill of transferring texts from page to stage, thus foregrounding the role of the stage director.[15] Notably, Jacques Copeau's (1879–1949)[16] *tréteau nu* idea of a bare stage, uncluttered by the trappings of naturalist decor [**see Volume 3**], greatly influenced Littlewood and the designers with whom she worked. A description of the designer John Bury's set for one of her and MacColl's productions illustrates this point:

> His settings in their starkness are platforms from which her productions are launched at the audience. Their bareness is not a merit rising out of material necessity, but a merit in itself, using the whole range of the stage, vertically and horizontally, to frame the play without detracting from it by unnecessary trappings.[17]

At the same time, Littlewood felt that the stage, notably the stage surrounded by a proscenium arch, limited the potential for the performers' movement and for the audience's imagination. Therefore, she strove to bring variety to the spaces in which her actors performed. Littlewood's and MacColl's combined strength consisted in their ability to adapt and invent by selecting any relevant ideas and techniques and adjusting them to their own needs and ideologies.

Their values were reflected in their series of three manifestos, issued, as noted, on the occasion of the launch of their three theatre ensembles. Theatre Workshop's manifesto, 'For a People's Theatre', most clearly stresses their ambitions:

> The great theatres of all times have been popular theatres which reflected the dreams and struggles of the people [...] We want a theatre with a living language which is not afraid of its own voice and which will comment as fearlessly on society as did Ben Jonson and Aristophanes.[18]

As the manifesto's title highlights, Littlewood and MacColl were committed to making theatre 'for the people'. Actor and theatre academic Clive Barker, who had performed with Littlewood's Theatre Workshop from 1958 to 1963, notably in Brendan Behan's *The Hostage* (1958), proposes the important distinction between 'people's theatre', which is 'for the people', and 'popular theatre', which takes elements of people's theatre and serves them up as entertainment for the governing classes.[19] In the case of Littlewood and MacColl's collaboration, making theatre for working-class audiences was a priority. The 'living language' to which the manifesto refers would both reflect political, social and economic situations relevant to their audiences, and introduce experimental stagecraft techniques to the production's directing, sound and lighting, acting, music and song, actor-training and pedagogical practices, thereby presenting the possibility of an alternative to commercial performance and programming. Littlewood and MacColl's early productions resembled the agitprop performance[20] that, along with Living Newspapers,[21] had so influenced MacColl. Thanks to his connections with agitprop groups, as early as 1932 MacColl had received scripts from militant playwrights such as those from the Workers Theatre Movement, which were highly active working-class groups of performers created all over the United States and Europe (see also Leach's chapter in this volume). The first full-length script produced by Littlewood and MacColl's Theatre of Action was Clifford Odets' *Waiting for Lefty*, an agitprop piece sent by friends from the Laboratory Theatre, in the United States.[22]

Even though their aims coincided with those of political theatres such as the Laboratory Theatre in the United States and Workers Theatre Group and Unity Theatre in the UK, Littlewood and MacColl avoided the stage realism and overall naturalistic approach that these theatres tended to perpetuate. They felt that agitprop privileged political action over artistic creation, whereas for them both were mutually beneficial.[23] In their productions together, it was Littlewood who mainly took over stage direction. In their adaptations of other theatres' plays, they would reduce the number of characters, have actors speak text through a megaphone, and introduce rhythms, sounds and audio recordings on gramophones and typewriters. In addition, they used screen projections, for example, of market prices, showing clear influences from Russian constructivist sets, and from Piscator's theatre. The *Manchester Guardian* reviewer considered one of their earliest productions, *John Bullion* (1934), about arms sales, to be 'the nearest thing to Meyerhold the British Theatre has got'.[24]

The Gerry Raffles years, 1953–75

In 1953, for a number of reasons Ewan MacColl ended his collaboration with Joan Littlewood. As a matter of (political) principle, he objected to her choice to establish a fixed site in the south of England and in the UK capital – the Theatre Royal Stratford East – where the theatre company would rehearse and perform. Moreover, he had joined the folk group The Hootenannys, and began to devote himself more to music than to theatre.[25] Hence, Gerry Raffles (1924–75) took over the management of the Theatre Workshop, and Littlewood's association with Raffles marked the end of an era of peripatetic theatre. In 1953, they established the Theatre Royal Stratford East, Raffles becoming the theatre's artistic director and Littlewood remaining director of the stage productions. In the following years, Littlewood directed numerous texts from the European canon, though usually less often staged or forgotten plays, such as the anonymously written *Arden of Faversham*, Shakespeare's *Richard II* (1954) and Ben Jonson's *Volpone* (1955), thereby bringing a repertoire of English classic drama to the working-class East End. Littlewood and Raffles' main concerns, however, consisted in the discovery of new writers – mostly playwrights, such as Brendan Behan (1923–64) and Shelagh Delaney (1938–2011) – who responded to current political and social issues. In 1963, they staged *Oh What a Lovely War*, which became their flagship play, in which they took documentary theatre to a new level.

With Raffles, Littlewood staged a number of Theatre Workshop productions that became significant milestones in the company's history. Together with Joan as the stage director, they also developed numerous educational projects and tried to cultivate a local audience. Behan's *The Hostage* (1958), Littlewood's treatment of a contemporary playwright's work, was a perfect example of Littlewood and Raffles's collaboration. Just as in her approach to classic texts such as Shakespeare's *Richard II*, Littlewood had an irreverent attitude towards the playtexts of living writers, rewriting them and modifying them in the rehearsal room via the actors' improvisations. She said of Behan's plays, 'Take lines from what Brendan Behan said, turn them and use them in your own way, so you create Brendan Behan's lines.'[26]

Behan's writing style, which combined storytelling with song and caricatured characters, was ideally suited to Theatre Workshop. Indeed, Murray Melvin, who created the part of the young English hostage in *The Hostage*, Behan's second play for Theatre Workshop, recalled how the actors created the play in collaboration with Behan (see Figure 1.3). He explained in an interview with me how Behan was a fantastic raconteur, and had told them Irish stories and legends: 'He was in the great tradition of Irish Celtic story-telling: legends and history – the Irish uprising, the potato famine, England and Ireland. He was a museum of information [...] He was brilliant.' Littlewood and the company would listen to Behan's tales. Melvin recounted how Behan had a very detailed way of describing the characters and situations, and would use language which stimulated the actors' imagination. 'He would sit down and you would be there for two hours. He would just keep going.' Melvin continued, 'Then the company would take all the points: you had to remember every word that was important.' Littlewood would then send Behan away, to allow her actors to improvise on the characters and information Behan had given. This method of working, described by Melvin in the interview with me, was highly productive but not always straightforward:

> The flamboyant team that Littlewood and Behan formed proved to be prolific even if the writing of the play turned out to be a painful process. Brendan would never know that he didn't write it and the public would never know that he didn't write it. But he did in a way because you were only translating all his Celtic story-telling into a theatrical format [...] His objective was there, his emotion was there, his reason was there. That was Joan's brilliance – making it into a theatrical form, making it accessible to the public. You would get it down to its raw bones.[27]

FIGURE 1.3 *Joan Littlewood rehearsing Brendan Behan's* The Hostage *at Theatre Royal Stratford East, with her Theatre Workshop actors, on 13 June 1959 (J.B. Hanley/Paul Popper/Getty Images).*

The relationship between Littlewood and Behan was at times fraught, owing to the latter's alcoholism and reluctance to write, which he did with great difficulty. As the premiere of *The Hostage* was approaching and no final script was forthcoming, the situation came to a head, but Littlewood's improvisational techniques came into their own. Behan did not provide Act 3 of *The Hostage* until two days before the premiere.[28] Therefore, the only solution was to ask the actors to improvise.[29] The pianist, Kate O'Connor, proposed a moody and evocative tune in the style of a silent film. Littlewood suggested the situation of a police raid, which the actors ad-libbed. Their improvisation was then incorporated into the final version of Behan's play. The production was a great success, notably in France, where it represented Great Britain in the Festival des Nations, an international theatre festival that took place every year at the Théâtre des Nations in central Paris that today houses the Théâtre de la Ville. Yet not every playwright was happy with the way in which Littlewood intruded into their work. As I have noted, for Littlewood the text represented just one of the materials used to create theatre, along with the actor's voice and body, the scenography, lighting, sound, music and song. The text, for her, was not necessarily the major element.

Undoubtedly, Joan Littlewood and Theatre Workshop's most famous and celebrated production was *Oh What a Lovely War*. Produced on the eve of the fiftieth anniversary of the 'Great War', it combined documents and facts from the war with songs, typical British music hall and cabaret, drawing mostly on Charles Chilton's collection of war songs. The Theatre Workshop's production seemed to encapsulate all the theories and beliefs expressed in Littlewood's three manifestos, notably dealing with 'the urgent and vital problems of today' (Theatre of Action), 'getting the essence of reality' (Theatre Union) and 'the dreams and the struggles of the people' (Theatre Workshop). The production came to address the most pressing political and social issues of the 1960s, namely the threat of nuclear war during the Cold War and the possibility of all-out carnage (see also introduction to this volume). In its acting style it borrowed from *commedia dell'arte* which, along with other theatrical influences such as the ancient Greeks and Jacobean theatre, was mentioned in the manifestos. Most notably, it responded to the third manifesto, which emphasizes the organization of the company as a collective and the creation of a 'flexible theatre-art' that is to include lighting, sound and music, cinema, dance-theatre and of course improvisation. Combining documentary fact with fictitious scenes and musical theatre, *Oh What a Lovely War* was, in retrospect, a key production in the history of documentary theatre which, today, has culminated in forms like verbatim musicals such as, more recently, Alecky Blythe's *London Road* (2015).

As a result, Theatre Workshop became an increasingly important force in European theatre. Their first invitation to the Théâtre des Nations in Paris had been in 1955, with the mentioned revival of the 1592 Elizabethan drama *Arden of Faversham*. A network of volunteers had been sent at the time by the Théâtre des Nations in search of companies from around the world to represent their respective countries. Claude Planson (1914–99) the French idealist, theatre critic and founder of the international Théâtre des Nations' festival, himself visited the Theatre Royal Stratford East and recalled watching *Arden of Faversham* in front of an extremely picturesque audience who drank beer, smoked cigars and called out at the actors 'in cockney' throughout the play, thus recreating the atmosphere of an original Elizabethan theatre (see Figure 1.4). Planson was so dazzled by the show that he invited Theatre Workshop to represent Great Britain in Paris – very much to the indignation of the British Council, who had tried to block this choice in favour of more 'reputable' British theatre, and hence refused to assist with any money. Planson ignored the British Council. The play received rave reviews in Paris, famous journalist Morvan Lebesque writing, 'Dear Theatre Workshop friends, you are the pride of British theatre!'[30] From that moment on, Theatre Workshop would attend the festival every year, and the company was soon referred to as a major influence by some of France's greatest directors, including Jean Vilar (see introduction to this volume) and Ariane Mnouchkine (b. 1939 [**see Volume 7**]). The latter remarked, 'I had seen the

FIGURE 1.4 *Joan Littlewood's production of* Arden of Faversham *at Theatre Royal Stratford East in 1955 (Courtesy of Theatre Royal Stratford East Archive Collection).*

Berliner Ensemble, I had also seen Joan Littlewood in England. Suddenly things were happening that totally differed from the "Vilar style" and were more important to me.'[31] Like Littlewood, Mnouchkine went on to found, in 1964, a theatre on the outskirts of a capital city, at the Cartoucherie de Vincennes. In addition, she also seeks to appeal to a broad audience via the use of popular theatre traditions such as clowning, *commedia dell'arte* and mask work. Moreover, both female directors (and they were among the first in the profession that at the time dated back almost 100 years!) have been politically committed to contemporary issues, never disguising their political sympathies for the Left.

Of course, *Oh What a Lovely War* was also invited to represent Great Britain at the Théâtre des Nations in Paris, in 1963. In 1966, even a (highly successful) French adaptation of the production, entitled *Ah Dieu que la guerre est jolie!* was created, directed by Pierre Debauche (b. 1930) at his Théâtre des Amandiers in Nanterre, Paris.[32] Thus, for the first time Littlewood's theatre gained great acclaim among the wider French public. While international touring afforded Theatre Workshop widespread fame and acclaim, the company transferred the hugely successful piece to the West End in London. This also led to their 'mainstreaming' and to criticisms in certain circles that they were compromising their political force in favour of entertaining the audience.[33] So, was *Oh What a Lovely War* then the pinnacle of Theatre Workshop's oeuvre, or did it foreshadow their eventual demise? Ewan MacColl was brutally straightforward: 'It was the nadir of Theatre workshop, its failure. The West End tranfers: they leave the audience "nice and comfy" [...] They "play to the converted."'[34] The production's West End transfer placed far more emphasis on its entertainment value than on its hard political messages around the First World War. This eclipsing of ideology was what MacColl had feared when he had left Theatre Workshop in 1953. Despite his singularly damning indictment, though, *Oh What a Lovely War* was as much a low as a high point. Nevertheless, it was the company's most popular success. The play had rave reviews, just about everyone in the UK could hum its tunes, it gained new audiences and travelled a great deal, and has today become literature on the school syllabus. Yet, at the time, during the touring period, the production lost many of its major original performers.

The Cedric Price years, 1961–5

The original project of 'The Fun Palace' by British architect pioneer Cedric Price (1934–2002) covered most of the last phase of Joan Littlewood's active creative career. During the 1960s, Littlewood, in collaboration with Price, ran the Fun Palace educational project, between 1961 and 1965. In parallel, Littlewood developed educational activities in the Tunisian city of Hammamet, which had become a meeting place for artists from around the world, established again by Claude Planson who had previously discovered Littlewood for his Théâtre des Nations festival.[35] As a branch of his Théâtre des Nations, and with the assistance of UNESCO, he grew the Hammamet dream of an international drama school where artists from the world over would exchange ideas during workshops, situated in a stunning location directly on the Gulf of Hammamet, on a vast plot of land with a house designed by the American architect Frank Lloyd Wright, commissioned by Romanian aristocrat George Sebastian in the 1930s and used during the Nazi occupation as the headquarters of Hitler's Africa mission under Marshall Ernst Rommel. For the first festival on this new site in 1964, an impressive 1,000-seat open-air theatre was conceived by the French architect Paul Chemetov (b. 1928) in collaboration with Roger Planchon's designer René Allio (see below). In this utopian setting, Littlewood led workshops that were met with great enthusiasm. As an example, with a group of international students she created a promenade performance called *Who is Pepito?* (1966). The 'multiracial' performance, as it was billed in the terminology used back then, in Littlewood's words, 'flowed over the physical limits of (the) amphitheatre to the seashore, the dark woods or the garden'.[36] It included music and was performed by an international cast who 'tried to recreate some of the atmosphere of the mediaeval miracles and mysteries'.[37] When Planson's Hammamet was brought to a close in 1968, Littlewood actually turned her back on the stage, in order to undertake new projects in education, notably in the context of Price's Fun Palace project.

The Fun Palace was a visionary educational and political project. Littlewood had always advocated the pedagogical role of theatre and its extension to all social classes, as noted earlier. As early as 1955, Price had sketched plans for the project. In May 2001, an exhibition entitled *Les années pop* at the Centre Pompidou in Paris featured his sketches, storyboard and models for the Fun Palace, in a section of the exhibition dedicated to neo-Futurist utopian architecture. It was conceived of as an informal space designed for leisure and pleasure, with no permanent structures, where people could stroll in, learn or take an active part in the creation of programmes, or else simply rest. The Fun Palace was, therefore, not simply a theatre but, rather, designed as an innovative technological site dedicated to the *homo ludens*, which resembled a gigantic multifunctional and flexible spacemobile that could be constantly reconfigured, rather like children's Lego building blocks.[38] The reason for the construction's flexibility was that the people who used it could interact with it and modify it. This also meant that it could be dismantled in twelve hours and removed altogether in a couple of weeks. It would include all sorts of activities for children and adults, as well as an exhibition area, an enclosed and an open auditorium, projection screens, a play complex, workshops and a restaurant. Hence, it was intended to inaugurate a new policy in leisure and an interest for 'a university of the streets': it was a new cultural model that can also be contextualized in the 'popular' culture debate outlined in the introduction to this volume.

Between 1963 and 1965, Price and Littlewood proposed various locations for their Fun Palace: the Isle of Dogs, Mill Meads, Vauxhall, Camden Town, Hackney (all in London), Glasgow, Edinburgh and Liverpool. They were all considered either financially non-viable owing to a lack of funding, or rejected due to political hostility against the project. The only place that they were able to turn to for its realization was the Theatre Royal Stratford East. Its manager Gerry Raffles tried to capitalize on the redevelopment of the theatre and proposed plans for the improvement of the building that would include the construction of music studios, a children's library and a cinema. Yet it was all turned down by Newham Council, which runs the part of London where the theatre is situated. If plans were not accepted within four years, either all the procedures had to be recommenced, or the project had to be withdrawn altogether. The project was thus abandoned, and entered the annals of history as one of the utopian plans of 'the Pop Years'. It took more than half a century until, in October 2014, Littlewood's and Price's dream was finally realized to some degree, with a two-day celebration of creativity across more than 120 pop-up 'Fun Palaces' that had the intention to get more people interested in the arts and sciences.

Moving the lines: Littlewood's directorial approach

No one 'method' as such can be definitively attributed to Littlewood, as this chapter has already indicated. Her 'style' involved seizing new elements from one theorist or practitioner or another, according to the place, to the audience, and to the play that the company intended to perform. Notwithstanding, two main influences prevailed as main and enduring reference points: Stanislavski, and movement pedagogue Rudolf von Laban (1879–1958). While Stanislavski's methods assisted Littlewood with her approach to the text, Laban's theories enabled her to develop physical movement with her actors. In a BBC interview in 2004, Murray Melvin, who had started working with Littlewood as a performer in 1957, explains how Stanislavski's methods provided the Theatre Workshop with an approach to playtexts:

> Once you had broken down your script Stanislavski-way into your units and objectives which is what you did right at the beginning, we sat down on the floor and we united the whole piece. Then we roughly worked out our objectives for each unit and once we had done that we got on our feet and that was probably the last time you ever got to sit down! You would get on your feet and take a unit and you'd try and work toward your objective – it might change as you began to move[39]

The emphasis on objectives meant that Littlewood would radically cut text, as Melvin goes on to explain:

> You would pick up your scripts and have a look at the words. Very often the words fitted the movement, if the words were good enough. If they didn't then you would analyse why they didn't. Were you missing an emphasis or point of reference in those lines? It's then, when doing that, that you could sort out whether a line or lines were superfluous to the objective of that scene. Now that got rid of quite a bit of Shakespeare, quite a bit of Ben Jonson and it certainly sorted out lots of modern scripts. The 'waffle' went, the colouring went.

Littlewood would employ Stanislavski's techniques in order to ascertain, with her actors, the characters' objectives and psychological motivations. However, as Melvin further explains, she would then adapt and contort the techniques in order to develop her own unique non-naturalist directorial style:

> You would begin to physically move that scene. Throw the script away – you wouldn't touch the scripts. We roughly knew what it was about. You then moved that scene as far as the characters were concerned: who would stand next to whom? Who would keep the other side of the group? Who would interfere? This way you would get a physical relationship. That took many forms of doing. Very often to free you up she would play some ragtime. If anyone in the company could play the piano she would like them to do silent movie music. So, we would all move together in double time: 'double time' was one of Joan's favorites because it stopped you thinking. When we started putting words to it she would do double time because it stopped you pondering. We would have to deliver our lines according to the diddle-dee-dum of double time. By doing that, often out of panic, you would hit a truism and you would then have to get back and recreate.

The use of music, song, rhythm and movement would enable Littlewood to combine a psychological approach to characterization that she inherited from Stanislavski with elements from British popular performance, and also with the movement techniques developed by Laban.

Littlewood, therefore, developed the actor's use of movement thanks to her acquaintance with the theories of the performer's body developed by Laban. It was the modern dancer (and future second wife of MacColl) Jean Newlove (1923–2017), affectionately referred to as the 'Movement Lady', who introduced Laban's techniques to Littlewood's group of actors as she participated in rehearsals, via her own interpretations of Laban's movement theory for actors and dancers. Voice thus became an extension of movement and movement became the foundation for dialogue.[40] Melvin testifies to the influence that Laban's theory of movement had on Theatre Workshop and how it assisted actors in understanding and performing text:

> For actors it is such a short-hand, a quick way into discovering a character, because if you can find out what your character is physically, it shortcuts an awful lot of problems. Once you've found what he [*sic*] is physically, it helps with finding out what he is vocally [...] We would ask whether a character is in the air, grounded in earth or in the middle. Once you've got that sorted out, which is what one did with Joan, you worked on the different planes [...] Movement comes naturally and once you've put the lines on top they are there because you can move them. Movement and memory come at the same time [...] When I am learning lines, I go home and move them myself. I move their direction, not physically but mentally. Then I physicalize those mental movements [...] Once you've done a bit of Laban, you say to yourself, 'Of course it's so simple'!

This emphasis on the body would extend to the idea that discussions about characters and scenes in the rehearsal room would take place through movement, as Melvin further explains:

> When an actor would pipe up, 'Well I think it should be …', [Littlewood] would interrupt and say, 'Don't tell us! Get up and do it!' Nine times out of ten you would get up and fail miserably because your idea was wrong, but the tenth time would work and it would all be worthwhile! You have to get up and move your ideas. Remember that you played everyone else's parts. Joan only gradually cast everyone's parts but sometimes when someone did a particular movement she would say, 'You've got to do that' – and they were cast. Gradually, she would build up the casting by the way you were working. You all had to do each other's parts, nobody had an individual problem: if you had one it was the company's problem not yours individually. That pressure wasn't on you because it was taken on by everyone.

Since meaning in Littlewood's productions was thus communicated not only via the text but also via the actor's movement, choreographed by means of extensive improvisations in the rehearsal room, the actor's own participation in collective creation was key, as Melvin suggests in the above excerpts from his BBC interview.

This notion of ensemble work, along with Littlewood's synthesis of the theories of Stanislavski and Laban, formed the basis of her artistic revolution. She introduced to British theatre for the first time a degree of freedom among the performers to express themselves, experiment and improvise, that had not been seen before, except in the contexts of popular performance traditions such as carnivals and local festivities. If there is one element that can sum up her approach to theatre-making, it is play: games were an essential and integral part of her creative process. For Littlewood, games provided the opportunity to bring artists together, to question fixed ideas, to innovate, to make mistakes and also for her to pass on her skills and expertise by means of actor-training, which had always been a priority throughout her career. Most notably, Theatre Workshop performer Clive Barker (1931–2005) paid tribute to Littlewood's play in his book *Theatre Games*, stressing how games were an essential part of her practice.[41]

Finally, another hallmark of Littlewood's directorial practice was her insistence on continuous actor-training. Since every play she directed involved a different approach, the team of performers was obliged to undergo constant further development and to adapt to the ever-changing performance modes she invented and developed. Littlewood would perpetually and uncompromisingly fight routine and convention in her permanent evolution and revolution of staging practices, which she always innovated in response to the social and political realities of her time. Her production of Shakespeare's *Richard II* in 1954 provides an exemplary illustration of her directorial practice (see Figure 1.5). It is perhaps no coincidence that French director Jean Vilar had inaugurated his Avignon Theatre Festival in 1947 with the same play.[42] Theatre scholar Dennis Kennedy notices that during this time, at the outset of the Cold War, 'Shakespeare was used in Western and Central Europe as a site for recovery and the reconstruction of values that were perceived to be under threat or already lost.'[43] Staging Shakespeare after the Second World War thus constituted an occasion for theatre-makers and audiences to examine questions of power, domination and reconciliation, and to revisit and debate fundamental ethical issues via the distancing mechanism of staging a play written over three centuries previously. Littlewood's *Richard II* provided her with an opportunity to put into practice her manifold techniques and theories she had acquired from her diverse influences as well as her various previous collaborators from the time when Theatre Workshop settled at its new Stratford home. Actor Howard Goorney (1921–2007), founder member of the company alongside Littlewood, provides insights into her analysis of the characters' motivations, as well as her involvement in physical acting. Three aspects, according to Goorney, were simultaneously dealt with by Littlewood in the

FIGURE 1.5 *Shakespeare's* Richard II *in Joan Littlewood's 1954 Theatre Workshop production (Courtesy of Theatre Royal Stratford East Archive Collection).*

preparation of this production: improvisation, movement and setting.[44] She worked intensively with actors on improvisation in rehearsal. Notably, since the cast was limited to fourteen, actors had to perform two or three parts each. In rehearsals they also exchanged parts, as the earlier quotations from Murray Melvin point out, in order to have a better understanding of all the characters in Shakespeare's play. They also improvised the transitions between scenes, so that the production would move fluidly.

Littlewood played with different styles of delivery, which included clowning, speeding up the dialogue or speaking it in a sing-songy voice, which the actor Harry H. Corbett (1925–82) finally used in his performance in the title-role. Psychological characterization and emotional investment were replaced by playful stylization. Jean Newlove meanwhile choreographed movement in accordance with the Laban method. With regard to setting, Littlewood proposed physical exercises based on themes that would 'capture the feeling of the period' in which *Richard II* was set, its violence, and the fear of 'the stab in the back'.[45] The actors interacted continuously with John Bury's set, which was as expressive as their movements. Goorney recounts: 'The harsh set with its clanging metallic surfaces (including the stage floor) [...] created a specific environment with stark lines, raw unpolished materials which were enhanced by the half-lit stage.'[46]

*

After having invested all she could in theatre-making and theatre education, Littlewood left the UK for a self-imposed exile in France in 1975. Even though she had a profound effect during her lifetime on political theatre and the English approach of 'devising' (see Leach's chapter in this volume), she only really gained full recognition from her peers after her death in 2002. Therefore, it is ironic that Littlewood is now considered to be the great pioneer of experimental modern British theatre who, in her own words, sought 'to keep the English theatre alive and contemporary';[47] who introduced a real coherence between text analysis, director's practice, physical acting, devised performance, choreography and stage design – now common characteristics of contemporary theatre practice; and who was one of the first instigators of a democratic system of ensemble theatre-making. From now on, the proud statue of a triumphant, slightly ironic Joan towering in the middle of Gerry Raffles Square, will represent a strong and permanent focal point. While, as I stated at the outset, any attempt to fix and classify her eclectic, constantly evolving and protean theatrical, political and educational activities is impossible, the permanence of her statue can surely testify to her spirit of resistance as an artistic agitator and political militant.

2

Señora Littlewood's Rifles: Joan Littlewood and the Leftist Tradition in British Twentieth-Century Theatre

Robert Leach

It is frequently asserted that Joan Littlewood's work as a director was 'Brechtian', that it was somehow a bridge between Brecht and British theatre. Writing in *The Guardian* in 2013, British actor Simon Callow (b. 1949) stated that Brecht's influence was 'first felt in Joan Littlewood's productions, [and] was a formative factor in the unique populist style she forged for her Theatre Workshop'.[1] With his Drama Centre training it is surprising that Callow did not recognize Konstantin Stanislavski's influence on her work.[2] The fact that Brecht and Littlewood were both artists of the Left, both looked towards some kind of socialist or communist future to which their art could contribute, has blinded many (and Callow has company!) to the distinctly different practices espoused by these two artists. Littlewood indeed referred to Brecht in the same disparaging breath as she referred to 'Shaftesbury Avenue'.[3] Her only encounter with his work was when she played the name part in *Mother Courage and Her Children* in 1955 (see Figure 2.1). It was a disaster. This chapter will demonstrate that Littlewood, far from being 'Brechtian' in her approach, combined Stanislavski's system **[see Volume 1]** with a British leftist theatrical tradition to create a unique form of progressive theatre which was actually an alternative to Brecht.

FIGURE 2.1 *Joan Littlewood as Mother Courage in the Theatre Workshop's only production of a Brecht play in 1955 (Courtesy of Theatre Royal Stratford East Archive Collection).*

British leftist theatre of the 1930s

After an unpropitious time at the Royal Academy of Dramatic Art (RADA), Joan Littlewood tramped north in 1934, seeking work. In Manchester she met the young communist actor-writer-singer Jimmie Miller, later better known as Ewan MacColl. It was almost like the famous encounter between Stanislavski and Vladimir Nemirovich-Danchenko (1858–1943), the co-founders of the Moscow Arts Theatre, on Slavyansky Bazaar in Moscow in 1897, as they talked through the night.

> [We] told each other the story of our lives and discussed what we called *real* theatre.
>
> Our views, we found, coincided at almost every point. We were drunk with ideas, lightheaded with talk and lack of sleep and each of us jubilant at having discovered an ally. The morning was well advanced when Joan crept with me to the front door and I went off to the labour exchange. We continued our talking marathon through the next two or three nights.[4]

Littlewood joined MacColl's 'Theatre of Action', and the collaboration which was to produce the highest achievements of British leftist theatre began.

MacColl was the son of an out-of-work iron moulder and a charwoman. He had founded a workers' theatre troupe, the Red Megaphones, in his native Salford which played short, sharp agitprop pieces for strikers, the unemployed and political groups. The prime drive of this work was solidarity: unity with workers in struggle. Though still in his teens, MacColl had drilled his comrades, inserted crude dance sequences into their brief shows, and sung stirring songs, often in traditional mode, sometimes parodies of contemporary popular songs. The Red Megaphones were part of the Workers Theatre movement which had grown out of the political upheaval of the 1920s, the Wall Street crash and the subsequent removal of the pound from the gold standard, and was a significant manifestation of a British leftist theatrical tradition. This tradition stretched back before the First World War when the Co-operative movement, socialist Sunday schools, the Woodcraft Folk and other overtly political groups sponsored amateur dramatic activity.[5] By the 1920s, besides groups sponsored by the Plebs League, the National Council of Labour Colleges and other left-wing groupings, the Labour Party itself had performing drama groups, as did the Independent Labour Party under the well-known playwright and actor, Miles Malleson (1888–1969). Their theorist was Ness Edwards (1897–1968), who was influenced by Russian Bolshevik writer-revolutionary Alexander Bogdanov (1873–1928) and later became a Labour Member of Parliament. Edwards opined that, 'the regeneration of drama is entirely in the hands of the working class'. Suggesting that the workers 'will develop their own drama [...] mainly through the many amateur workers' societies doing their drama in labour halls, club rooms, hired concert halls and in the open air', he urged that 'the workers' drama be such as to make the workers glow with creative hope'.[6] It was to be class-based and to express, first and foremost, comradeship.

A 'Workers' Theatre Movement' was formed for this purpose by a group of radical Bohemians including the writer Christina Walshe and her partner, the composer Rutland Boughton, Havelock Ellis, Eden and Cedar Paul, and Huntley Carter, though it made little impression until it was taken over by the Hackney People's Players in 1928. The Hackney group's leading spirit was Tom Thomas, a stockbroker's clerk and a communist, who sought a theatre which would celebrate working-class struggle and achievement, and build solidarity, especially with workers in struggle. The ending of his dramatization of Robert Tressell's *The Ragged-Trousered Philanthropists* (*c.* 1919) thus rejected the original's pessimism and inserted instead a positive appreciation of the hero, Owen's work.

> Finally, Harlow moves a resolution that 'Socialism is the only remedy for unemployment and poverty' and turns to the audience with 'What d'you say, mates?' [...] 'Those in favour shout "Ay!" (*To audience*). 'Let it go now! One, two, three, ay!' [...] the curtain is rung down upon a tremendous shout of 'Ay!' from the audience.[7]

The audience was thus made complicit in the drama, a stratagem which was to become a crucial feature of British leftist theatre.

Solidarity, as the French sociologist Émile Durkheim (1858–1917) notes, requires an 'in-group' set against an 'out-group',[8] and Thomas's short play to be performed by workers' groups, *Their Theatre and Ours* (1932), dramatizes this very idea. Beginning with the troupe marching onto the platform stage, 'well-disciplined, singing enthusiastically and in well-marked rhythm', the play contrasts the active, committed workers' direct address to the audience about social conditions and the working-class way of life with the actions of the 'popular' actors from the commercial theatre or films, whose faces are 'ghastly with forced happiness', and who sing songs such as 'Happy days are here again' and 'I'm singing in the rain' with no reference to the actual conditions and concerns of the spectators.[9] The performance became a celebration of the active, energetic working people, the community of the working class, tellingly signalled by the piece's very title, 'their theatre and *ours*'.

The concept of 'community' was, therefore, central to British leftist political theatre, harmonizing with and augmenting solidarity and complicity. 'Community' may be rooted in geography, in age groups, in shared interests or in class. Any individual may, therefore, belong to several different communities. According to sociologist Zygmunt Bauman (1925–2017), 'Community is a "warm" place, a cosy and comfortable place. It is like a roof under which we shelter in heavy rain, like a fireplace at which we warm our hands on a frosty day.' As such it was of real use to the working class. Bauman continues, with somewhat two-edged enthusiasm:

> In a community we all understand each other well, we may trust what we hear, we are safe most of the time and hardly ever puzzled or taken aback. We are never strangers to each other. We may quarrel – but these are friendly quarrels, it is just that we are all trying to make our togetherness even better and more enjoyable than it has been so far and, while guided by the same wish to improve our life together, we may disagree how to do it best. But we never wish each other bad luck, and we may be sure that all the others around us wish us good.[10]

For the philosopher Martin Buber (1878–1965), community was something subtler and deeper: 'Community is the being no longer side by side (and, one might add, above and below) but *with* one another [...] a flowing of *I* to *Thou*.'[11] And cultural anthropologist Victor Turner went further, describing how 'community' can become '*communitas*', by giving 'recognition to an essential and generic human bond, without which there could be no society'.[12] But Turner also notes how, as with solidarity, there is a 'perennial tensed opposition between *communitas* and structure'.[13] This is a dialectical relationship in which the one cannot exist without the other, just as in industrial capitalism, workers cannot exist without bosses.

The community with which the Workers' Theatre Movement was in solidarity was the working class, or, more specifically, the Communist Party, the working class' 'vanguard'. At the time Littlewood and MacColl met, it was growing. In 1930, the Communist Party of Great Britain (CPGB) had 1,376 members; by 1939 there were 15,500. Communist writer R. Palme Dutt remarked in 1933 that communism provided 'a complete world conception covering every aspect of life, and transforming all our thinking and activity'. There were 'little Moscows' in Britain, such as Fife, Stepney and the south Wales coalfields, where the party *was* the community, and 'being Communist meant more than adopting the current party line'.[14] It was at least potentially a sort of '*communitas*', and it was what Joan Littlewood's work would always strive to express. In the mid-1930s, with the rise of fascism and Nazism, the Communist Party moved to join other progressive anti-fascist groups to form a Popular Front. 'Community' was still central, but now its focus shifted. Theatrically, the Workers' Theatre Movement, with what seemed now its crude agitprop, was abandoned, and something which could more truly respect and reflect the complexity of the developing political scene was sought. This led to the founding of the symbolically named Unity Theatre in London in 1936. Though never formally affiliated to the CPGB, Unity was a communist enclave in the commercial theatre of the 1930s. In 1937 Unity acquired its own building in Goldington Street in Camden, and other Unity Theatres in cities such as Glasgow and Aberdeen, Cardiff, Merseyside and Bristol, as well as several London suburbs (Acton, Croydon, Willesden and more) soon followed.[15] If the members of these theatres were mostly amateur, a smattering of professionals led the way. Its mixed programmes included revue, mass declamations, documentaries and plays. Its 1938 production of Brecht's *Die Gewehre der Frau Carrar* (Señora Carrar's Rifles) was most likely Britain's first experience of a Brecht play.

More typically, *Busmen* (1937) was a 'living newspaper' derived formally from the work of the American Federal Theatre Project, about the bus strike at the time of King George VI's coronation. Though somewhat crude, it threw together a montage involving a history of London passenger transport, a House of Commons debate, scenes of the busmen's lives and work, a band playing the 'Internationale', dance, choral speech and the actual words of union leader Ernest Bevin, all played in front of an abstract, almost constructivist backcloth.[16] In favour of workers' solidarity, it sought to uphold the busmen's community and engage spectators with its struggle. Then came *Crisis* (1938), created in response to Chamberlain's appeasement of Hitler, and the pantomime *Babes in the Wood*, staged by Unity at Christmas 1938. Here, the babes were Austria and Czechoslovakia, Chamberlain was their wicked uncle, Hitler and Mussolini were two robbers, while the people were Maid Marion and the Popular Front Robin Hood. *Babes in the Wood*'s energetic singing and dancing, its topicality and its satirical humour celebrated the 'in-group's' strength against the international 'out-group'.[17]

By now Unity was a community of its own. It had six full-time employees, and sponsored night classes and discussion groups. It supported strikers and anti-fascist campaigners and its banner flew in marches and demonstrations. There were parties, rambles, bazaars and workshops. There was the Unity magazine, *New Theatre*, and summer schools for 'worker-actors'. Morris Carnovsky demonstrated American 'Method' acting techniques, and there were further contacts with other American 'Method' practitioners, Elia Kazan, Harold Clurman, Stella Adler and Lee J. Cobb. Unity's two most active directors, Herbert Marshall and André van Gyseghem, had both studied Stanislavski's system in the Soviet Union. It was these features – parody, energy and laughter on the one hand, and the techniques of Stanislavski and its American derivative, the 'Method', on the other – that formed the basis of the British leftist theatre tradition.

Theatre Union: Production and training

When Theatre of Action collapsed, Joan Littlewood and Ewan MacColl moved to London from where they hoped to travel to Moscow. The plan fell through, and the Manchester branch of the pacifist Peace Pledge Union invited them to produce Hans Chlumberg's *Miracle at Verdun*. The success of this work led to the formation of Theatre Union in 1936, which may be seen as in some ways complementary to Unity Theatre in London. Its manifesto proclaimed:

> The theatre must face up to the problems of its time, it cannot ignore the poverty and human suffering which increases every day. It cannot, with sincerity, close its eyes to the disasters of its time. Means Test suicides, wars, fascism and the million sordid accidents reported in the daily press. If the theatre of today would reach the heights achieved four thousand years ago in Greece [*sic*] and four hundred years ago in Elizabethan England it must face up to such problems. To those who say that such affairs are not the concern of the theatre or that the theatre should confine itself to treading the path of 'beauty' and 'dignity' we would say 'Read Shakespeare, Marlowe, Sophocles, Aeschylus, Aristophanes, Calderón, Molière, Lope-de-Vega, Schiller and the rest.'[18]

From this list they began in 1937 with Lope de Vega's *Fuente Ovejuna* (The Sheepwell), a play which theatre historian Allardyce Nicoll considered remarkable because de Vega 'develops a dramatic form later to be associated with experiments in the "proletarian" theatre'. He singles out the scene in which Frondoso and Laurencia listen to the villagers of Fuente Ovejuna asserting their solidarity even in the face of torture as 'surprising' in its 'democratic sentiment'.[19] Littlewood and MacColl's production was one such 'experiment'.

It was of course the time of the rise of Franco in Spain, and the Spanish Civil War, and this play tells the story of one Spanish village's resistance to the tyranny of unelected power. It values above all the strength and solidarity of community. Besides this, Theatre Union's first foray into the 'classics', about which they had written so urgently, also had a rich variety of true-to-life characters, some strong crowd scenes and plenty of rapid action. It also had songs: the originals were dropped and in their place were inserted contemporary popular Spanish Republican tunes. These three elements – strong characterization, dramatic energy and political motivation – were key features in all Littlewood's subsequent work. The production of *Fuente Ovejuna* was complemented by other activities derived from the agitprop of the Workers Theatre movement, and addressing problems of community in another dimension. Thus, Theatre Union provided interludes at rallies in support of Spanish democracy, the highlights of which were often the moments when lights illuminated particular spectators, who had agreed to make personal statements in support of the Spanish people:

> We'd get Arthur X who worked as a back-tenter [editorial note: worker who cleared debris from weaving looms] in a mill in Oldham, who'd say, 'My name is Arthur X, I'm 23, I earn 4 pounds 18 shillings a week, I'm married and I've got two children,' and he'd tell his story in very simple terms as part of the thing, and then we'd give a roll-call of the dead, Arthur Jenkinson, shot on the Manzares River, Alec Armstrong, decapitated on the Aragon Front, and all the local people that everybody knew, and mixed this with people making personal statements.[20]

Thus, the audience was implicated in and complicit with the action. This was the fourth element in Littlewood's 'community' theatre.

In order to give the political discourse more immediacy, Theatre Union embarked on an astonishing programme of education and self-education. Littlewood herself reproduced a section of the extraordinary syllabus for studying the ancient Greek Dionysian theatre in an appendix to her autobiography, and to it were added similarly intense studies of medieval, Renaissance, Spanish, Elizabethan and Jacobean drama. 'It was considered mere philandering to read latter-day classics, let alone modern plays, unless you'd acquired a thorough grounding in the ancients,' she adds laconically.[21] But practically the group was not just modern, but modernist. The dancer and actor Rosalie Williams (1919–2009), for instance, was 'overwhelmed' by the training:

> The range and intensity of the training programme that Joan and Ewan had worked out, and the combination of their unique talents seemed quite

> extraordinary [...] Each night at seven o'clock we reported to a huge empty room over a furniture store in Deansgate, Manchester, and also on Sunday afternoons and evenings. We started each evening with relaxation exercises, lying on the floor. Then voice production, Stanislavski, ballet, movement and mime.[22]

The sessions usually began with relaxation – lying down, each limb relaxed, breathing rhythmically. Then perhaps 'crouching – relax', 'crouching under a cart when rambling – it's raining', 'Put your arms up in the air. Relax, letting them down,' 'Lunging forward with arm movement – and then arms circling movement for contrast,' and so on.[23] These exercises were self-devised but extraordinarily sophisticated.

They led naturally to movement exercises, based largely on *commedia dell'arte* as Littlewood and MacColl understood it, for example, from Callot's seventeenth-century engravings of *commedia dell'arte* figures, and Jacques-Dalcroze's concept of rhythm and expressive movement, Eurythmics. Littlewood used Eurythmics to devise a number of 'weight transference' exercises, such as putting the left foot forward to kneel on the right knee, putting the head on the knee, folding the arms, transferring the weight to the left knee and stretching the arms upwards. A series of exercises centred around frog movements, leaping round the room in a squatting position, then jumping like a frog onto the partner's back. This could be followed by holding the partner in a wrestling hold, struggling, till one (pre-agreed) partner jumped on the other's back. These exercises are in fact significantly close to some of Meyerhold's Biomechanical *études* (movement exercises) [see **Volume 2**], though neither Littlewood nor MacColl knew these.

Most important to them were the exercises they derived from Stanislavski. The English translation of *An Actor Prepares* was first published in 1937, and Littlewood and MacColl pounced on it. The actor Patience Collier remembered first working with Theatre Union in 1938: 'It was my introduction to Stanislavski, and it was a revelation and such a change from the mechanical approach to work I had been used to. We took exercises from his book, *An Actor Prepares*, and applied them to the parts we were playing – things like units and objectives, imagination, concentration and so on.'[24]

MacColl invented exercises for the actors, such as coming home, closing the curtains, taking off the shoes, putting a record on the gramophone, resting in a chair, looking at a book, taking the record off, and so on. How many units are there? If the main objective is 'going to bed', how does each objective, each unit, relate to that? Plays, too, were split into units and an objective found for each character in each unit. And the units were properly related to Stanislavski's 'Through Line of Action', Littlewood urging the actors to form 'an unbroken series of images, moving pictures', so strong that they would provide a stimulus for action, exactly as

Stanislavski did.[25] Joan Littlewood's notes from this period show just how precisely she attempted to work through Stanislavski's book. She told her actors:

> In the art of acting the finest moments are the moments of inspiration. At such moments it is impossible for the actor to understand how certain hidden feelings in him found expression. If you ask an actor how he feels at such moments, he perhaps cannot tell you – and yet at these moments he is in fact *living the part.*[26]

Clearly this derives from Elizabeth Hapgood's translation of Stanislavski's work: 'The very best that can happen is to have the actor completely carried away by the play. Then regardless of his own will he lives the part, not noticing *how* he feels, not thinking about *what* he does, and it all moves of its own accord, subconsciously and intuitively.'[27] Other notes Littlewood made at the time are even closer to *An Actor Prepares*. She asserts:

> First our art will teach us how to create *consciously* and *rightly* – that is the mastery of our technique – *conscious* and *right* creative moments in our role will in turn open the gates of inspiration. To play *rightly*, that is, *truly*, our acting must be logical, it must be coherent, we must think, strive, feel and act in unison with our role.[28]

Stanislavski wrote:

> Our art teaches us first of all to create consciously and rightly, because that will prepare the way for the blossoming of the subconscious, which is inspiration. The more you have of conscious creative moments in your role the more chance you will have of a flow of inspiration [...] To play truly means to be right, logical, coherent, feel and act in unison with your role.[29]

Joan Littlewood's method was developing. It attempted to fuse the workers' agitprop immediacy with Stanislavskian 'truth' in response to the needs of the community.

Bertolt Brecht: Aims and methods

Bertolt Brecht (1898–1956) came from a different tradition.[30] He entered the theatre after the First World War, when German advanced practice was dominated by Richard Wagner's idea of the *Gesamkunstwerk*, the total work of art which fused music, poetry, light, scenery, dance and more into a single overwhelming whole. Stage and auditorium were merged. And the new art, Expressionism, sought something similar. It favoured extravagant, often highly emotional acting. The expressionist actor 'played' something such as Stanislavski's superobjective – the overriding objective which ultimately motivates the actor's every action – rather than allowing the superobjective to be the underlying glue which held the units and objectives together. The aim, however, as with Wagner, was to engulf the audience. It was against this that Brecht reacted.

The leading expressionist actors in the years immediately after the Great War were Fritz Kortner (1892–1970) and Werner Krauss (1884–1959). The latter's total involvement with his role was notorious. Theatre critic Herbert Ihering described Krauss as being 'possessed by his inner experience', so that 'the word was not accompanied by gesture, not amplified by movement: the word was gesture, the word became flesh'. He concluded, 'If Expressionism ultimately is concentration, here is an Expressionist actor.' As for Kortner, before even his first entrance in director Leopold Jessner's 1919 production of *Wilhelm Tell* [**see Volume 4**], his 'driving, raging, blood-surfeited voice vibrating in wrath' could be heard, and when he arrived on stage, he 'holds us fast [...] takes our breath away [...] fills us with almost physical fear'.[31] Brecht was among the first to reject such exaggeration. His musical dramas and operas composed with Kurt Weill (1900–50) as much as his play *Mann ist Mann* (Man Equals Man, 1926) can be seen mocking such excess. Soon he was composing the austere *Lehrstücke*, or 'learning plays', which sought a wholly different form of embodiment. These didactic plays, cool and detached, as well as other works of the early 1930s such as *Die Mutter* (The Mother, 1932) and *Die Ausnahme und die Regel* (The Exception and the Rule, 1929/30) led him towards forms which sought to teach the way to understanding Marxist social and political analysis. It was in exile in the 1930s that he developed his theories, away from the stage, though he always tried to relate them to practical performance problems. His conclusions overlap to an extent with the positions Joan Littlewood was coming to occupy at the time, yet they also differed from hers in significant ways. It is useful to highlight these differences, while bearing in mind that such an apparently binary opposition is by no means a comprehensive comparison. Indeed, perhaps they agreed more than they differed.

Where Littlewood celebrated the working-class community within which she worked, Brecht sought to historicize his stage, so that the audience would view the action objectively. Patrice Pavis noted that 'to historicize is to refuse to show human beings in an individual, anecdotal light; to reveal the underlying sociohistorical infrastructure beneath the individual conflicts [...] Historicization brings out two historicities: the play in its own context, and the spectator in the circumstances of his attendance'.[32] Thus, Brecht insists on

> the simplest possible groupings [on stage], such as express the event's overall sense. No more 'casual', 'life-like', 'unforced' grouping; the stage

> no longer reflects the 'natural' disorder of things. The opposite of natural disorder is aimed at: natural order. This order is determined from a social-historical point of view.[33]

His attitude to the audience as community is starkly clear: 'A collective entity is created in the auditorium for the *duration of the entertainment*, on the basis of the "common humanity" shared by all spectators alike [...] *The Mother* is not interested in the establishment of such an entity. It divides its audience.' This is clearly far from Littlewood's idea, deriving from agitprop, of complicity, solidarity between audience and actors, members of the audience calling out their own experience, becoming part of the performance. It is the product of Brecht's requirement for *Verfremdung* in performance, for 'defamiliarization' [**see Volume 2**]. Brecht thought that 'Spectator and actor ought not to approach one another but to move apart'.[34] He described the actor Helene Weigel's performance as the servant in *Oedipus* to illustrate his ideal of acting:

> She announced the death of her mistress by calling out her 'dead, dead' in a wholly unemotional and penetrating voice, her 'Jocasta has died' without any sorrow but so firmly and definitely that the bare fact of her mistress's death carried more weight at that precise moment than could have been generated by any grief of her own. She did not abandon her voice to horror, but perhaps her face, for she used white make-up to show the impact which a death makes on all who are present at it. Her announcement that the suicide had collapsed as if before a beater was made up less of pity for this collapse than in pride at the beater's achievement so that it became plain to even the most emotionally punch-drunk spectator that here a decision had been carried out which called for his agreement.[35]

The word 'agreement' here is the retranslation of Brecht's biographer, Stephen Parker, which replaces Willett's original word, 'acquiescence'. As Parker notes, 'the key insight for Brecht was that Weigel's controlled acting style promoted the spectator's distanced intellectual appreciation of the reason for the suicide'.[36]

Brecht equally admired Weigel's performance in *The Mother*:

> In the first scene the actress stood in a particular characteristic attitude in the centre of the stage, and spoke the sentences as if they were in the third person; and so she not only refrained from pretending in fact to be or to claim to be Vlassova (the Mother), and in fact to be speaking those sentences, but actually prevented the spectator from [...] imagining himself to be the invisible eye-witness and eavesdropper of a unique intimate occasion.[37]

He commended those performers in the 1935 New York production of *The Mother* who spoke 'with the same sense of responsibility as a statement made for the record in a court of law, and because the gest stays in the memory'.[38] The 'gest', or signifying gesture or posture, is Brecht's riposte to Stanislavski's search for the character's objective.[39] A gest, also called gestus [see **Volume 2**], is a bold physical statement of a crucial idea from which consequences flow. Brecht sought not only the gestic in his actors but noted that 'not all gests are social gests', explaining how 'one's efforts to keep one's balance on a slippery surface result in a social gest as soon as falling down would mean "losing face"'.[40] It was the social gest which he wished to see on his stage. He noted how the actor Peter Lorre as Galy Gay in the 1931 staging of *Man Equals Man* whitened his face as Weigel had done in *Oedipus*, 'instead of allowing his acting to become more and more influenced by fear of death "from within himself"', and commended the way the actor divided the role into 'four phases, for which four masks are employed – the packer's face, up to the trial; the "natural" face, up to his awakening after being shot; the "blank page", up to his reassembly after the funeral speech; finally the soldier's face'.[41]

Brecht's acting exercises may also be compared with those which Littlewood and MacColl devised for their actors. *Die Strassenszene* (The Street Scene) was Brecht's 'basic model' in which he asked the actor to assume the character of a bystander who witnessed an accident, and to report the events which s/he had witnessed. The actor performed a series of detached actions; at no point was 'a stimulus for action' sought. Even when this was refined into 'exercises in temperament', Brecht asked for 'showing', not 'being': 'Situation: two women calmly folding linen. They feign a wild and jealous quarrel for the benefit of their husbands; the husbands are in the next room.'[42] In rehearsal, Brecht suggested the actor use certain 'aids' to his performance: speaking in the third person, rather than the first person; transposing the present tense into the past; and speaking the stage directions out loud.

> Using the third person and the past tense allows the actor to adopt the right attitude of detachment. In addition he will look for stage directions and remarks that comment on his lines, and speak them aloud at rehearsal ('He stood up and explained angrily, not having eaten,' or 'He had never been told so before, and didn't know if it was true or not,' or 'He smiled, and said with forced nonchalance'). Speaking the stage directions out loud in the third person results in a clash between two tones of voice, alienating the second of them, the text proper.[43]

Brecht thus sought 'a way of acting which will leave the spectator's intellect free and highly mobile'.[44]

The Good Soldier Schweik: Apollonian and Dionysian approaches

From the foregoing, it might be possible to suggest that Brecht and Littlewood were a 'duality' in the sense that the German nineteenth-century philosopher Friedrich Nietzsche, in *The Birth of Tragedy*, sees Apollo and Dionysus as a duality. Nietzsche noted the 'tremendous opposition' between 'the Apollonian art of sculpture', which might be compared to the Brechtian need for coolness and distance, and the 'nonimagistic Dionysian art of music', which has some resemblance to Littlewood's practice.[45] In this formulation, Apollo is the 'deity of light', 'the sculptor god', notable for his 'measured restraint, and freedom from the wilder emotions'[46] while 'under the charm of the Dionysian [...] the union between man and man (is) reaffirmed' and 'each one feels himself not only united, reconciled, and fused with his neighbour, but as one with him'.[47] Brecht is like Homer, 'the type of the Apollonian naïve artist', while Littlewood, who urged her actors to study 'the cult of Dionysus' in her Greek theatre syllabus, more resembles Archilochus, who 'introduced folk song into literature'.[48]

This can be illustrated by comparing dramatized versions of Jaroslav Hašek's novel, *The Good Soldier Schweik*, unfinished at the author's death in 1923 but published in a German translation in 1926 and in a bowdlerized, shortened version in English in 1930. The book was a favourite of Brecht's as well as of Littlewood and MacColl. The central character, Schweik, is a resourceful, impossibly respectful and humble orderly, who becomes caught up in the First World War, yet always manages to avoid the fighting. Brecht and the radical director Erwin Piscator [see **Volume 2**], with whom Brecht worked on a production in 1928, were interested in historicizing Schweik, in finding the gests which illuminated the social and historical circumstances in the story, and what might be learned from this. They approached the material as Apollo or Homer might have approached it. Littlewood and MacColl, on the other hand, treated it more as Dionysus or Archilochus might have treated it, as a way of celebrating the resilience of the common man and the value of community.

The signal point of Piscator's version, made with Felix Gasbarra and Bertolt Brecht, was the wretchedness of the Austro-Hungarian Empire, of which Schweik was a citizen, and the incompetence of their war effort. It was not simply a satire on something which had happened, it was a coruscating investigation of the most important factor in contemporary German politics and society. However, the fact that the novel was unfinished led to an almost intractable difficulty – the ending. Dada artist George Grosz (1893–1959), who painted the set for Piscator's production, proposed a slapstick scene with 'everything in ruins', or else skeletons drinking each other's health; writer-dramaturg Léo Lania (1896–1961) wanted Schweik to return home after the war and there to be arrested, showing nothing had changed. Piscator himself thought of an ironic ending in heaven, where the maimed and amputated war veterans parade before God, though he later modified this and ended the production with these victims simply meeting the Kaiser. He seems to have found this a more satisfactory, perhaps Apollonian, finale.

Piscator presented the story in an objective approach, with treadmills, or conveyor belts, built into the stage, rather than a more usual revolve, so that Schweik's long walk in search of the front line at Budjevice took place on the moving belt. Schweik walked and walked, but never got anywhere. It was a 'cool' view of an endless promenade. This was complemented by the use of puppets and cartoons which supplied 'the role of the environment', according to Piscator:

> These puppets were not just an 'artistic idea' of mine, but represented the ossified types which populated the political and social life of prewar Austria. We distinguished between a range of categories: semipuppets, puppetlike types, semihumans [...] Everything was done to exaggerate the single figures into clownlike symbols.[49]

Added to this were Grosz's series of cartoons which were projected onto the backcloth like a film.

The acting further reinforced the objectivity. The part of Schweik was taken by Max Pallenberg, an actor from Max Reinhardt's theatre (**see Volume 4**) who had considerably to modify his acting style. The long walk towards (or not) Budjevice took over half an hour on stage. According to *Die Welt am Abend* newspaper's review, Pallenberg's Schweik had 'something of a good, innocent, long-suffering animal who does not know, cannot know, why he must suffer so much indignity'.[50] For Brecht,

> Schweik's three-day-and-night march to a front which he oddly enough never gets to was seen from a completely historic point of view, as no less noteworthy a phenomenon than, for instance, Napoleon's Russian expedition of 1812. The performer's self-observation, an artful and artistic act of self-alienation, stopped the spectator from losing himself in the character completely, i.e. to the point of giving up his own identity, and lent a splendid remoteness to the events.[51]

The 'historicization' and the Apollonian 'restraint' were obvious.[52]

Joan Littlewood and Ewan MacColl saw pictures of this production in Léon Moussinac's (1890–1964) *The New Movement in the Theatre* which had been published in English translation in 1931. When they acquired a typescript of Piscator's stage version they determined to stage it. The typescript, however, was in German, but with the aid of the English translation of the novel, MacColl created a version not dissimilar to Piscator's. It was presented by Theatre Union at the Lesser Free Trade Hall in Manchester in

May 1939. It too used a mixture of living actors and cartoon figures, and employed ideas from Piscator's staging, including a series of projections by local artist Ernie Brooks, though treadmills built into the stage floor proved beyond them:

> For the first time we used a revolve; each turn revealing another Ern Brooks cartoon to set the scene. Cartoons and costumes were all black and white, with occasional flashes of colour for delight. No khaki. It became the most popular play we ever produced.[53]

To obtain the back projections they persuaded some technicians from the Metropolitan Vickers factory nearby to build them a projector from scratch.

Nevertheless, theirs was a much more 'Stanislavskian' approach to the material, one which evoked warmth and humanity rather than 'restraint' and learning. Their version of the ending, for example, though it originally followed Piscator's scene of the maimed and wounded reaching heaven's gates, and there meeting the Kaiser, was altered to something much more in keeping with their approach. MacColl's surviving script for the 1954 revised production has Schweik finally reach the front. Marek, his comrade, is trapped and killed on the barbed wire. Schweik carries him slowly down stage.

> **Schweik** So long, brother. Brother ... brother ... brothers. (*His voice has risen. He has revolted*) We're going home, brother. Home! Beg to report you Generals ... Beg to report all you fine gentlemen who make wars ... beg to report you've killed my mates ... killed 'em you have ... Beg to report, I'm going home. Fight your own bleeding war.
>
> (*There is a withering burst of machine-gun fire. Schweik staggers, then falls to his knees.*)
>
> **Schweik** Brothers, brothers, brothers!
>
> (*He dies. The machine-gun fire, the crash of shells, the bursting Vary-lights reach a crescendo as the curtain falls.*)[54]

The idea of *brotherhood* becomes central, reaffirming the notion of community and the Nietzschean 'union between man and man'. It is also worth noting that Joan Littlewood sought in her actors not 'an artistic act of self-alienation' or a 'splendid remoteness', but a performance rooted in Stanislavski's system. As already noted, Patience Collier recalled how, in rehearsing *Schweik*, 'we took exercises from his book, *An Actor Prepares*, and applied them to the parts we were playing – things like units and objectives, imagination, concentration and so on'.[55] Consequently George Cooper, who played Schweik in 1954, conveyed not Pallenberg's 'remoteness' but a warmth Pallenberg never aspired to. One critic said he achieved 'an angelic imbecility that hides the shrewdest common sense', while another described 'Mr Cooper, with his North Country accent and his beaming face, constantly shifting from bewilderment to resignation'.[56] Significantly, this production *unified* audience and actors, and created a sort of community: Peggy Soundy recorded how 'the locals ... loved *The Good Soldier Schweik*. I used to travel home to East Ham on the bus, and I'd be sitting there with the theatre audience. I could hear them talking about the show and they felt *Schweik* was, somehow, part of them'.[57]

A third version of *Schweik* was written by Brecht in 1943, *Schweik in the Second World War*. In this, the abbreviated plot centres on Baloun's irrepressible appetite, but its most striking innovation is a series of interludes set 'in the Higher Regions' where Hitler, Goering, Goebbels and Himmler gather round a globe. 'All are larger than life-size except Goebbels who is smaller than life-size,'[58] and they worry like flustered chickens about whether 'the Little Man' will support their grandiose schemes. Their majestic – or grotesque – presence is a telling contrast with Schweik's humble earthly existence. It is theatrically incongruous, 'defamiliarising/estranging' and 'historicizing' the action. Brecht's solution to the problem of the ending is also revealing. Schweik, now marching vainly across the windswept, snowy steppe towards Stalingrad rather than Budjevice, meets a terrified little Hitler in the storm. Hitler is lost, too, and does not know whether to go east or west, north or south. His attempts to travel in all directions at once gradually metamorphose into a wild dance, and Schweik begins to sing:

> Yes, you cannot go back and you cannot move on
> You're all rotten on top and your bottom's gone.

The chorus is picked up by all the players 'who take off their masks and step forward to the edge of the stage':

> The stones of the Moldau's bottom go shifting,
> In Prague three emperors moulder away.
> The top won't stay top for the bottom is lifting.
> The night has twelve hours and is followed by day.[59]

This is far from Littlewood and MacColl's evocation of brotherhood. The historicization here amounts to something such as didacticism. Brecht could never resist the temptation to teach. Even his greatest play, *Der kaukasische Kreidekreis* (The Caucasian Chalk Circle), ends with a six-line 'lesson': 'Bear in mind the wisdom of our fathers.'[60]

Joan Littlewood and the actor

After the Second World War, the Theatre Union group re-formed as Theatre Workshop, but their political motivation remained urgent, and their exploration of technique and devotion to training as well as performance continued. A significant dimension was a new emphasis on movement, though Rosalie Williams as well as Littlewood herself had invented movement exercises before the war. Littlewood had in fact attempted to integrate it with the Stanislavski work. One set of her movement class notes are annotated: 'Enhance each pose with some imaginative idea. Enhance it with given circumstances [...] Swat a fly in one of these poses. *Give everything a living purpose* – a live objective and real action.'[61]

This work was advanced when in 1946 she made contact with the German-Hungarian movement pedagogue and mentor of 1920s *Ausdruckstanz* (Expressionist Dance), Rudolf von Laban, who following his exile during the Nazi regime continued to work in Britain. Laban's work seemed to complement Stanislavski's approach in the sense that Laban insisted that every movement must have a purpose, or objective. In response to Littlewood's invitation, Laban sent his 'dancing star', Jean Newlove, who soon became integrated into the company. Her presence and her work gave Theatre Workshop's practice new depth. Newlove not only trained the actors rigorously, she was able to use Laban's principles to create character through movement for immediate application to particular plays. Knowledge of and continual practice with Laban's work enabled the actors greatly to increase their range, and many achieved an extremely advanced level. Newlove described how the actors' bodies

> were technically able to implement, complement their character. What they wanted to do in the character – their bodies were able to sustain it. They were able to extend their movement range. It liberated them to play different roles, and let them think in the role.[62]

Theatre workshop actor Howard Goorney remembered that, 'when Sigurd Leeder, co-director of the Jooss Ballet, came to see us, he said: "These actors move as some of the best dancers I've ever seen," and coming from him this was praise indeed.'[63] But it must be emphasized that this work was directed towards the realization of the characters' objectives. It reinforced Littlewood's Stanislavskian approach.

Littlewood now needed to find a way to integrate the various elements of the 'system' she was evolving for actors, and she found this, first, in games and improvisation. Memory games, 'Blind Man's Buff', 'Cowboys and Indians' and movement games were all grist to her mill. Actors were asked to improvise stories – a girl dreams of leaving home, dances her fantasies, seeks a job, explores the city, meets different people, etc. Street scenes, the struggles of a housewife, scenes in concentration camps, meetings between characters of different status were played with, as were more obvious explorations of stage space, such as finding one's way blindfolded across an obstacle-strewn area, and improvising scenes in different styles (naturalism, melodrama, slapstick and so on). All this led to Littlewood's mature method of creating the production, which in fact came remarkably close to

Stanislavski's 'Method of Physical Actions', though she knew nothing of this development of the original system.

Secondly, Joan Littlewood believed, as Brecht did, in the company as an ensemble. But the purpose of this was to enable the actors to trust one another, and thus to enable them to be open enough to find the truth in the moment. Of course, she knew more than most of her actors, and she was more experienced theatrically than they were, and her guiding hand was often felt. But her working method respected their integrity and their creativity. 'I do not believe in the supremacy of the director, designer, actor or even of the writer,' she said. 'It is through collaboration that this knockabout art of theatre survives and kicks.'[64] Critic Irving Wardle asserted that she was 'the only British director in the great Continental tradition: the absolute ruler of an egalitarian ensemble, for whom the creation of a fine work on stage is inseparable from the creation of a freely co-operating collective'.[65] An example of such collaborative work was Theatre Workshop's production of Ewan MacColl's *Johnny Noble* (1945) immediately after the war. For the scenes at sea, she asked each actor to suggest just one sound to express its essence. Suggestions included the slapping of the ship's halyards, the drone of the engine screw and so on, and these were used to create movement. David Scase as Johnny sat on a box, swaying slightly back and forth, while his fellow actors on stage swayed from side to side. These movements in slightly different directions created the pitch and roll of the ship. Littlewood then added a red light and a green light at each side of the stage, each also moving up and down, thus orchestrating a scene which played in near darkness and with the ship's engine quietly throbbing, was so effective that some spectators reportedly felt seasick.

Littlewood embarked on a new production with no preconceived ideas of matters such as the blocking of the actors' movements or the arrangement of 'gestic' groupings. Rather, she started with discussions, with actors researching and reporting back on aspects of the play's context and background, and invited them to contribute ideas and opinions. She recorded how in the making of *Oh What a Lovely War* (1963), the group had worked together: 'Each brought a different point of view. They hated some of those songs. They didn't want to do propaganda, so they argued their way through each scene, and you've got, in the piece, the points of view of many people.' She continued: 'There were no rehearsals as they are known. There was a collection of individuals, more of an anti-group than a group, working on ideas, on songs, on settings, on facts. And if you get a few people with a sense of humour and brains together, you'll get theatre.'[66] This was active exploration to unearth the truth beneath the text, but it was still combined with Stanislavskian textual analysis, with defining units and objectives, and thereby uncovering the play's 'final objective'. Writer Henry Livings spoke of Littlewood's 'relentless analysis of what is *really* going on',[67] and actor Murray Melvin described her 'teasing out the truth below the lines'.[68]

Stanislavski's system remained central to this. Littlewood's notes on the typescript of Ewan MacColl's 1952 play *The Travellers* indicate the units of action, each of which is given a title and the characters' intentions for virtually every line. At the beginning of the play, Enrico Goriano is waiting 'in a state of extreme nervous tension' until Kari Nielson, his girlfriend, arrives. The italicized words in brackets in the following extract represent Littlewood's annotations:

KARI'S LATENESS

Enrico [*I must not hurt her*] Kari!
Kari [*I must hold him off*] I was delayed at the passport office. They asked me so many questions.
Enrico I am going crazy thinking you are not coming.
Kari Nothing could stop me. [*They embrace again*] Oh, Enrico, are we really going! I didn't really believe it would come true.

GORIANO'S HAPPINESS

Enrico [*I will show her I am sorry for having suspected her*] But of course, I, Enrico Goriano, say we go and we go. Now we must hurry. Here, I carry your bag.
Kari [*I must hold him off*] No, I'll take it.[69]

This approach was allied with the other active ways of mining the text. One specific technique was the playing of 'parallel scenes', that is, invented situations which uncover the emotions or actions of the text but in changed circumstances and between different, invented characters. Actor Nigel Hawthorne recorded one such incident during rehearsals for *Oh What a Lovely War*:

> There was a scene in which she felt that the actresses playing French country girls were being too modern in their approach to the Tommies. They were gathering round a group of soldiers, bringing them gifts of bread and wine and flirting with them [...] The band begins to play 'Mademoiselle from Armentiers' and they pair up and, whirling round and round, totally at ease in one another's company, dance off into the distance. So Joan invented an imaginary convent, just a few chairs and a table for the altar, and with the rest of us pretending to be devout nuns chanting in the background, each girl was asked to bring a posy of flowers down the aisle of the 'chapel', shyly present her gift to the Mother Superior and receive her blessing. Then Joan made them return to the scene itself. The difference was remarkable – it made sense for the first time. It sounds simple enough, I know, and there'll be cries of 'Anyone can do that!' The painful truth is that anyone can't.[70]

Work such as this justified the Scottish poet Hugh McDiarmid's comment that Theatre Workshop displayed 'a perfect example of team work [...] it was doubtful if groupings had ever been more naturally achieved (or seemingly so)'.[71] Such a comment is a neat – if unintended – riposte to Brecht's cry for 'No more "casual", "life-like", "unforced" groupings.' A comment from Howard Goorney further illuminates this. In Littlewood's productions, he says,

> no-one was ever given a move for the purpose of getting them from one part of the stage to another, or in order to form interesting groupings. These often occurred, and Joan was highly praised for them, but they had been arrived at organically during rehearsal as a result of interaction between the characters and were not pre-determined.[72]

It also brings to mind the methods of Stanislavski's brilliant younger contemporary, Vsevolod Meyerhold (1874–1940), whose work Littlewood and Ewan MacColl had admired in Moussinac's book. Meyerhold's system of 'biomechanics' in fact resembled Stanislavski's 'Method of Physical Actions' surprisingly closely [see **Volume 2**].[73] Meyerhold's early rehearsals were also devoted to exploring the play's 'final objective', discovering the characters' relationships, the play's rhythms and so on, largely through biomechanics and improvisation, and he too asked his actors to research topics of relevance to the work and to report back to the group. He never 'blocked' a play in advance, and used improvisation and 'parallel scenes' throughout his rehearsals.

Most significantly, perhaps, neither Meyerhold's nor Littlewood's productions were ever regarded as 'finished'. Two visits to the same production by either one of these directors was unlikely to provoke precisely the same response: the second would be subtly, and sometimes radically, different. 'As soon as a production is fixed, it's dead,' Littlewood insisted.[74] Her productions changed and evolved over a series of performances, and she watched and took notes at almost every one. After the curtain came down, she gave her notes to the actors. She sought 'acting in the present tense', rather than simply recreating what had been done in the rehearsal room, thinking each performance anew, rather than simply repeating yesterday's performance. Actor Richard Harris (1930–2002) recalled her saying: 'Don't practise how to say a line – it's whatever comes out tonight' and on another occasion, 'You're getting used to that, change it.'[75] Clive Barker recalled actor Harry H. Corbett saying that 'his ambition was to give one performance in which he had only one motivation, the one which took him out of the wings and onto the stage. From that point, he wanted to play only off his reaction to the other actors.'[76] It was the same with Meyerhold, who said: 'The good actor is distinguished from the bad by the fact that on Thursday he doesn't play the same way he did on Tuesday. An actor's joy isn't in repeating what was successful, but in variations and improvisations within the limits of the composition as a whole.'[77] Elsewhere, he also stated: 'The actor must not rivet his role tightly, like a bridge builder with his metal construction. He must leave some slots open for improvising.'[78] Compare with Joan Littlewood: 'Theatre is *today* [...] The excitement I'm talking about – today and tomorrow – that is the present tense. Would you like to repeat this conversation again an hour from now?'[79]

Consequently Littlewood created some of the most profound productions in British theatre history. They were not 'learning' experiences, rather, they were Meyerholdian and celebratory. But what is also interesting about them is that they are part of a specifically British leftist theatrical tradition which focuses through agitprop-like moments on solidarity and community. Just as the Red Megaphones had created agitprop theatre in support of strikers in Lancashire, and Unity had supported striking busmen and attacked Chamberlain and appeasement in the 1930s, Theatre Workshop's post-1945 productions also aimed to intervene directly in political controversy. MacColl's *Johnny Noble*, for instance, brought on stage two 'Roaring Boys', symbols of those who were fighting energetically to take Britain back to pre-war laissez-faire capitalism:

1st Roaring Boy Time we got back to normal.

2nd Roaring Boy Time we got back to the good old days,
The happy-go-lucky production ways.

1st Roaring Boy Back to the dignified position
Of unrestricted competition.

2nd Roaring Boy Back to surplus and higher rent,
And a profit of eighty-four per cent.[80]

The 1946 production of *Uranium 235* (see Figure 1.2) confronted head-on the challenge of the atomic bomb dropped at Hiroshima, and *Landscape with Chimneys* (1951) dealt with the contemporary housing crisis. This was the subject of a notably energetic Communist Party campaign, and the play dramatized some of the anxieties and dangers of squatting in empty mansions. At the end, as the police come to evict the squatters, Hugh and Clare, the whole cast confront the audience with the old American trade unionists' song: 'Which side are you on?'[81] Thus, the production dramatized the 'in-group's' struggle against the 'out-group', and directly involved the spectator. Rather than to teach a lesson, in Brechtian style, it aimed to make the audience complicit in the struggle.

Laughter in the theatres of Bertolt Brecht and Joan Littlewood

Joan Littlewood's theatre resonated with joyous laughter, as it asserted the rights and confronted the challenges to her community. It was, said Kenneth Tynan, a 'dream of theatre as a place of communal celebration, a Left wing shrine of Dionysus dedicated to whipping the Puritan frown from off the popular image of Socialist art'.[82] For Brecht, though he had no time for 'Puritan frowning', laughter was very different. It was closer to the laughter dissected by the French philosopher Henri Bergson (1859–1941), who noted '*the absence of feeling* which usually accompanies laughter', and that 'laughter has no greater foe than emotion [...] its appeal is to intelligence, pure and simple'.[83] Nevertheless, for Bergson, as for Brecht, laughter was still a social act. 'Our laughter is always the laughter of a group,' Bergson wrote, and in language which Brecht would have recognized, he suggested that laughter, because it 'must have a *social* significance', becomes 'a kind of *social gesture*'.[84] Such laughter recognized that the human quality of adaptability had atrophied or been suspended in the person laughed at: they were displaying a mechanical rigidity. The subject did this yesterday and the day before, therefore he or she will do it again today, despite the fact that the context has changed. Yesterday's gesture, when it is isolated today, is recognized as meaningless. 'Gestures can only be imitated in their mechanical uniformity, and therefore in what is alien to our living personality.'[85] As the critic Walter Benjamin stated: '[Brecht's] Epic theatre is gestural [...] The gesture is its raw material [...] Gesture is falsifiable only up to a point; in fact, the more inconspicuous and habitual it is, the more difficult it is to falsify.'[86]

Bergson goes on to suggest that almost every 'fashion' is laughable in some respect, but we find it difficult to recognize this in contemporary fashion. He suggests that 'a sudden dissolution of continuity is needed (which will) bring it to our notice'. Again, as Benjamin noticed, 'the more frequently we interrupt someone engaged in an action, the more gestures we obtain'.[87] On one level, Bergson describes perfectly the Brechtian 'alienation effect', though he is applying it to the operation of laughter. Nevertheless, his suggestion that the purpose of laughter is above all to correct is not dissimilar to Brecht's didactic purpose: 'Laughter is, above all, a corrective [...] By laughter, society avenges itself for the liberties taken with it.'[88]

Littlewood's laughter, and her purpose, were different. Her laughter was closer to the carnivalesque, inclusive not didactic, renewing not satirical. Carnival, for the Russian scholar Mikhail Bakhtin (1895–1975), embodied the unofficial culture which coexisted with, and contradicted, official culture. That Littlewood stood for unofficial culture may be seen in the official Arts Council's disdainful treatment of her, and its extreme unwillingness to provide Theatre Workshop with any form of subsidy, while it generously funded other rival theatres, such as the Royal Court Theatre, despite her far more substantial record of achievement. It may be noted in passing that the post-war East German government was anxious to embrace Brecht's work as 'official': the Berliner Ensemble was set up in 1949 with a government subsidy of over a million East German Marks, including an annual sum of US$10,000 to employ West German actors as guests. Carnival laughter is described at length by Bakhtin, and obviously Joan Littlewood's twentieth-century theatre is not the same as the medieval festivities – or anti-festivities – which Bakhtin describes. Nevertheless, it is possible to isolate some features from Bakhtin's descriptions and suggest they are the nub of the British leftist theatre tradition, especially as it was exemplified in Joan Littlewood's work. First, Bakhtin points to 'spectacle', akin to what Littlewood staged, for example, in the 'Circus Parade' at the beginning of *Oh What a Lovely War*, or the welcome home provided to the soldiers at the opening of *Landscape with Chimneys*. In *Fings Ain't Wot They Used T'Be* (1958), 'the entire company are on stage dancing wildly to a "Hokey-Kokey"' at the start of the play, and 'a banner is stretched across the stage with the words, "WELCOME HOME FRED" written on it'.[89] Spectacle becomes conflated with theatricalization when actors play pierrots playing soldiers, or dancers appear as Energy and Mass, neutrons and protons. In *A Taste of Honey* (1958), dialogue is theatricalized into Music Hall crosstalk, while there are traditional routines such as the Music Hall hat routine (Peter: 'How do I look?') and the pantomime food routine ('*Geoffrey empties food from his pack onto the table while Helen thrusts it back. Helen finally throws the whole thing, pack and all, onto the floor*').[90]

Dance was pervasive in Littlewood's theatre. Very frequently the actors danced instead of simply walking ('*Geof dances and goes off with the bedclothes. Jo dances off. Geof dances in with the props for the next scene.*'[91]), there were 'wild Irish jigs' (*The Hostage*), elegant ballroom dancing (*Oh What a Lovely War*) and even a fight which is 'danced' (*Johnny Noble*). Music and song are equally ubiquitous: *Johnny Noble* was a ballad opera, *Fings Ain't Wot They Used T'Be* and *Make Me an Offer* (staged in 1959) were musicals, while *Oh What a Lovely War* was described as 'a musical entertainment'. The jazz trio added to *A Taste of Honey* was widely thought to be a particular triumph.

One feature of carnival which Bakhtin makes much of is religious parody, and Joan Littlewood staged a series of these. In *The Hostage* (1958), Mulleady and Miss Gilchrist 'appear on the stairs kneeling and singing their prayers' while 'Mulleady's hand strays and gooses Miss Gilchrist'. She reproves him.

> **Mulleady** I'm very sorry, Miss Gilchrist, let not the right hand know what the left hand is doing. Miss Gilchrist, can you – (*The hand strays again and strokes Miss Gilchrist's tail.*)[92]

In *Fings Ain't Wot They Used T'Be*, the marriage ceremony is parodied, as Redhot is dragooned into being a witness and Paddy into being Best Man. When the Priest asks for the ring to be produced, Redhot, a jewellery thief, 'brings out a trayful of rings' he has lifted from some shop.[93] Littlewood's most famous religious parody is the church service for the soldiers before they go into battle in *Oh What a Lovely War*. 'Onward, Christian Soldiers' becomes 'Forward, Joe Soap's Army,' and 'The Church's One Foundation' becomes 'We are Fred Karno's Army', sung while Sir Douglas Haig prays cynically for victory 'before the Americans arrive'.[94] Littlewood was also happy to resort to what the translators of Bakhtin call 'billingsgate', rudery and slang. Songs such as 'Christmas Day in the cookhouse', 'I Don't Want to be a Soldier' ('I'd rather fornicate my bleeding life away') and 'Kaiser Bill' ('We don't give a cluck for old Von Fluck') all fall into this category, as do Tosher's reference to his 'peckham rye' (his tie) in *Fings Ain't Wot They Used T'Be* and Mulleady and Miss Gilchrist's 'Our souls. Our souls. Our souls' which is slurred into 'Our souls. Are souls. Arseholes.' The Lord Chamberlain's hovering blue pencil prevented too many such profanities.

Bakhtin was keen to emphasize that carnival was an expression of a community. 'The basis of laughter which gives form to carnival rituals', he wrote, 'frees them completely from all religious and ecclesiastical dogmatism, from all mysticism and piety', that is, from the 'official culture'. 'Carnival celebrated temporary liberation from the prevailing truth and from the established order; it marked the suspension of all hierarchical rank, privileges, norms and prohibitions.'[95] Carnival laughter, he said, was 'the laughter of the people'. It was 'universal', 'the people's unofficial truth'.[96] Joan Littlewood's theatre was always concerned to be inclusive. *Landscape with Chimneys* deals with a whole community, 'the men who unload ships, the men who stoke fires, the women who clean offices, the unimportant people', who live in the street which is made up of houses, each one separated from its neighbour by a plaster wall. Each one consisting of four rooms. Here, in these little boxes, men and women sleep. Dream, love, bear their children, eat, laugh, quarrel, suffer and die. And the audience are included, too. 'You know this street too well, some of you were born here, some live here now.'[97] In *The Hostage* 'everyone is caught up in a swirling, interweaving dance' and the soldier sings:

There's no place on earth like the world,
There's no place wherever you be.[98]

And even the marginalized characters in *A Taste of Honey* are part of a community – 'There's one thing about this district, the people in it aren't rotten,' Geof says – and outside children can be heard playing and singing.

This inclusiveness also involves the audience. The characters – or the actors – talk to them directly. 'Do you hear that?' Pat asks the audience in *The Hostage*. 'It's a great thing, an Oxford University education! Me, I'm only a poor ignorant Dublin man. I wouldn't understand a word of it.' Later the soldier says to the audience, 'Now the thing is, will Theresa go to the cops? Even if old Einstein is half sozzled there's still the other two to get through. Will they shoot me? Yeah, I suppose so. Will Theresa go to the cops? No.'[99] *Oh What a Lovely War* begins with the pierrot Master of Ceremonies welcoming the audience: 'Everybody in? Come along, madam; we're just starting.'[100] Victor Spinetti, who played the Master of Ceremonies, has recorded how on the opening night he was approached by Joan Littlewood and asked to 'go out there and talk to the audience'. And so,

> for the first time in my life I just stood there and talked to friends. Joan wanted me to break the ice, to destroy the barrier between them and us. Perhaps she thought it would encourage them to participate in the show [...] So every night I would go out and talk, sometimes for a minute, sometimes for a while. If anyone joined in, as they did at Stratford, it became a feature of the show.[101]

Joan Littlewood wanted her audience to be complicit in what was happening. This explains, for instance, Helen's asides to the audience through *A Taste of Honey* – 'She'd lose her head if it was loose' – 'Wouldn't she drive you mad?' – and when Peter arrives, 'He would show up just when I've got her hanging round my neck.' Significantly, Littlewood only allowed Avis Bunnage, who played Helen, to speak thus to the audience because she had the experience, including of variety theatre, to be able to do this convincingly. Murray Melvin and Frances Cuka (Geof and Jo) were not permitted to speak directly to the audience. Thus, this was not, as Nadine Holdsworth has suggested, 'a Brechtian-style alienating device that points up the artifice of theatrical practice';[102] it was a way of making the audience complicit in the action, and, interestingly, it depended on the particular performer, Bunnage here, Spinetti in *Oh What a Lovely War*. Brecht's Mother Courage or Galileo never speak directly to the audience like this, and when Brecht uses this technique, it is either through a Narrator figure, or is carefully marked off: 'Hear what he thought and did not say.'[103]

Joan Littlewood's legacy

Joan Littlewood's theatre was based in community, politically radical and suffused with regenerative laughter. The actor was asked to dance, to sing, to improvise in rehearsal and performance and to understand and use the Stanislavski system. Near the end of her stage career, in 1961, she argued that 'each community should have a theatre' and asked, 'cannot each district afford to support a few artists who will give them back some entertainment, laughter and love of mankind?'[104] That was her purpose, but the dream was not realized, and after *Oh What a Lovely War* transferred to the West End and was then made into a film with a string of 'star' performers, Theatre Workshop as she envisaged it, and her own career, slowly petered out. But the methods which she had pioneered did not die. The best repertory theatre directors of the 1970s and 1980s, including Alan Dossor (1941–2016) at the Liverpool Everyman and Peter Cheeseman (1932–2010) at the Vic in Stoke-upon-Trent, gladly acknowledged their debt to her innovative practice. The production technique developed by Joint Stock Theatre Company under Max Stafford-Clark (b. 1941) and William Gaskill (1930–2016) was known as the 'workshop' method, derived, as the name suggests, from Littlewood. It involved a ten-week preparation period, including an initial four weeks when the actors improvised and discussed the ideas which were then moulded into a script by a writer, a process which brought to the stage such fine plays as David Hare's *Fanshen* (1975) and Caryl Churchill's *Light Shining in Buckinghamshire* (1976).

Later groups to follow somewhat similar paths in the 1990s and 2000s included Suspect Culture, who worked not from a pre-existing script but from discussions and workshops, through which the script evolved; and Forced Entertainment, who also create shows through improvisation and discussion. Indeed, such 'open' practice has become almost the norm in the twenty-first century among 'alternative' and 'progressive' theatre companies, and has become known as 'devising'. The political drive fuelling Theatre Workshop, however, did not fare so well. At first the leftist flame burned brightly. There was, for instance, the community and political theatre of John Arden (1930–2012) and Margaretta D'Arcy (b. 1934), typified by community plays and events such as *The Business of Good Government*, performed at Brent Knoll in Somerset in 1960, but also by angry presentations involving spectators as participants, as Theatre Union's Spanish Civil War presentations had done, like *The Vietnam War Carnival* in New York in 1967. *Harold Muggins Is a Martyr* (1968) was 'a Gala/Festival/Play/Celebration/Hit', for which they collaborated with Cartoon Archetypal Slogan Theatre and Bradford College of Art. In his Preface to *The Workhouse Donkey* (1963), Arden specifically called for a Dionysian theatre, noting that 'Miss Joan Littlewood has already put forward a similar and apparently highly practicable proposition.'[105]

A political theatre rooted in community solidarity, carnivalesque laughter and political challenge, rather than Brechtian 'defamiliarization' or Apollonian 'remoteness', was also developed by other alternative theatre practitioners and companies in the 1960s and 1970s, including Foco Novo, Belt and Braces, and Red Ladder. Perhaps the outstanding figure in this movement was John McGrath (1935–2002), who in 1971 founded the 7:84 company, which took its name from the fact that 7 per cent of the population owned 84 per cent of the wealth. McGrath, a playwright of some distinction for both television and theatre, and someone who thoroughly understood Brecht, had been in Paris in 1968 during the protest *événements* (see introduction to this volume), and he was working at the Liverpool Everyman when he established his touring company. By 1974 there were two 7:84 companies, one in England and the other in Scotland. The Scottish company in particular embedded themselves in the community and its left-wing and radical culture. In a series of productions, McGrath mixed the 'open' techniques described above with hard-edged leftist content. Rather than overtly 'teaching', however, 7:84 relied on ribald and regenerative laughter, song and an ability to create something genuinely of the community. In 1982, 7:84 mounted a retrospective season which implicitly acknowledged their forebears, and included presentations of the Workers Theatre agitprop piece, *U.A.B.Scotland* by Harry Trott, Glasgow Unity's *Men Should Weep* by Ena Lamont Stewart and Ewan MacColl's *Johnny Noble*. Their best productions often took the form of documentary, but with a strong emphasis on community solidarity and 'theatricalizations' reminiscent of Unity's pantomime *Babes in the* Wood or Theatre Workshop's pierrot show, *Oh What a Lovely War*. Thus, *The Cheviot, the Stag and the Black Black Oil* (1973) took the form of a ceilidh, while *The Game's a Bogey* (1975) used the urban variety show for its structuring. There was as much audience involvement in these shows as in Theatre Union's Spanish Civil War presentations, and here again the aim was to make the spectator complicit in the action rather than overtly to teach.

However, 7:84 were caught in something of a paradox: they were able to flourish because the official Arts Council subsidized them. In 1979, Mrs Thatcher came to power and that support was quickly withdrawn. The leftist 'Fringe' companies began to disappear or, in the case of 7:84, to so alter their character as to be unrecognizable from what they had been. It was ironic that the Workers Theatre movement, Unity Theatre and Theatre Workshop had never received a state subsidy, though in the case of Theatre Workshop the Arts Council did begrudgingly award them a pittance after they had stunned the Paris International Theatre Festival in 1955 with their brilliance. In the end, the suppression of the leftist theatre was another of Mrs Thatcher's destructive triumphs. It went hand in hand with the destruction of British industry, so that the future of the political Left itself in Britain became doubtful, and with the collapse of the Soviet Union, Marxism and progressive politics generally took another blow. The line from the socialist Sunday schools, through the Workers Theatre movement, Unity Theatre and Theatre Workshop to Arden and D'Arcy and 7:84 was broken.

Giorgio Strehler

3

Giorgio Strehler: The Epic Stage Director Who Betrayed Brecht

Bent Holm

Italy has made three major contributions to theatre history: the material theatre in terms of architecture, scenography and stage machinery; the masked, improvised physical comedy of the *commedia dell'arte*; and thirdly, opera. In theatre history, three specific years, separated by two centuries each, are of particular importance in this respect: 1545 saw the birth of the masked comedy, when a fraternal *compagnia* signed the first mutual contract to form a professional troupe of actors in Padua. Thus, a system was founded which was to last for centuries, characterized by the *compagnie* of strolling, improvising actors. Two hundred years later, in 1743, playwright Carlo Goldoni (1707–93), in his attempt to raise and reform the art form of the *commedia* by abandoning the masks and improvisation, presented the first comedy with a fully written text, *La donna di garbo* (*The Woman of Grace*), in Venice. Lastly, in 1947, Giorgio Strehler (1921–97), together with the theatre critic Paolo Grassi (1919–81), founded Italy's first lasting stationary and publicly subsidized stage, the Piccolo Teatro in Milan, and at the same time introduced to the Italian stage the art of stage direction as a part of modern theatrical practice.

Strehler was a complex character who combined a personal lifestyle that was somewhat disorderly with a professional life completely focused on the stage. He stands as the most significant reformer and innovator of Italian theatre in the twentieth century and at the same time as one of the era's most outstanding European stage directors. The Piccolo Teatro, his lifework, became a leading European stage in the second half of the twentieth century. Throughout his life, Strehler's vision to create a different kind of theatre remained his strongest driving force: a vision to create a new audience, a new repertoire and a new theatrical language. Overall, we can discern four main periods in his artistic career. In Italy, the initial post-war period was an era of reconstruction and reconciliation, of modernization in terms of international art and culture, and of recuperation in terms of national cultural heritage; in that respect theatre as an art form was supposed to unite people (see also the introduction to this volume). This was followed in the 1950s and 1960s, during the climate of the Cold War, by disillusionment, and on stage by a strategy of critique, and subsequently during the 1970s, by an overtly political stance, so that Strehler's theatre would again divide people. Then, in the 1980s, a philosophical dimension was added, focused on the illusion of reality and the reality of illusion, with his productions developing still more refined aesthetic registers. However, regardless of the degree of artistic transformation, some reference to reality and social circumstances always remained a constant in Strehler's work: aesthetics were never there for their own sake. Meanwhile, his growing frustration about declining and unstable support from the state became another constant. His last ever production was *L'isola degli schiavi* (*Island of Slaves*) by Pierre de Marivaux (1688–1763), which Strehler directed in 1994, three years before he died in Lugano in Switzerland on Christmas Eve 1997 at the age of seventy-six. During his long and innovative career as a stage director, in addition to plays, Strehler also directed many works for the opera stage. Overall, from 1947, he directed more than two hundred productions, and beyond the theatre, he was active as a politician for the Socialist Party.

Strehler: A European hybrid in a traditional theatre world

Giorgio Strehler was, in the fullest sense of the word, a European of conviction and practice (see also Margherita Laera's chapter in this volume): 'I have always spoken three languages, Paris is for me the front door, Vienna was the first city I visited,' he said, and added, 'I have come and gone in Europe as in my own backyard.'[1] His productions outside Italy were for the most part created in France, Germany, Austria and Switzerland, reflecting the three cultures in which he was rooted: Italian, French and German. He introduced, in Italy, a pan-European theatre conception and practice, with a specific focus on Brechtian developments. Being an eclectic artist rather than a dogmatist, Strehler still never abolished Italy's domestic tradition. In a way he Europeanized the Italian stage, and at the same time he Italianized Brechtian theatre. I begin this chapter by offering some biographical background and will chart the vital part Strehler played in Italian and indeed in European theatre, before discussing how he transferred Brechtian theory and practice to a different artistic and cultural context.

Giorgio Olimpio Guglielmo Strehler was born in Barcola in Trieste on 14 August 1921. His background was Austrian, Slavic, French and Italian; thus, four languages were spoken at home: Italian, German, Montenegrin and French. Strehler's family was also devoted to performance: his mother Alberta Lovrich was an accomplished violinist in the 1920s and 1930s; her father, Olimpio Lovrich, was a Montenegrin horn player, conductor and choirmaster and her mother, Maria Firmy, was born in Paris. His father Bruno Strehler was an impresario and venue manager, whose parents were Guglielmo Giuseppe Strehler, born in Vienna, and Natalia Jasbitz from Trieste. Strehler's father died young, when the boy was three; his mother then moved with the young Giorgio to Milan, where she continued her musical career. Strehler became a law student but soon enrolled in the Accademia dei Filodrammatici, a Milanese drama school, where he graduated in 1940 with a full honours degree. It was there that Strehler met Paolo Grassi, then a junior teacher, who later became one of his closest collaborators. Strehler's stage career began in the early 1940s, when he played minor roles in unsophisticated Italian comedies as a member of touring companies. A career as an orchestra conductor was another option that Strehler pondered recurrently. In an interview in 1997, the year of his death, he re-evoked that dream.[2] In fact, there are several testimonies that he directed theatre like a conductor.

Strehler made his debut as a theatre director in 1941 with three one-act plays by the contemporary Italian playwright and Nobel Laureate Luigi Pirandello. During the war, he refused to serve in the military for the Salò Republic (Mussolini's second attempt at forming a 'Social' Republic, following his retreat to northern Italy in 1943) and joined the Resistance. Condemned to death for his dissident activities, Strehler escaped to Switzerland, where he met other anti-fascist intellectuals, both Italian and French, and where he directed, among other plays, T.S. Eliot's *Murder in the Cathedral* and Albert Camus' *Caligula* – at first, in the detention camp Mürren, and later on, between 1944 and 1945, with a group he had founded in Geneva, the Compagnie des Masques, using the name Georges Firmy after his French grandmother. After the war he returned to a bombed-out Milan where he launched into a period of intense cultural and artistic activity. He wrote as a theatre critic, campaigned for the re-election of socialist mayor Antonio Greppi, organized theatre-themed meetings to discuss new ideas and read new international plays, and directed several successful productions based on a bold selection of newly translated texts by Eugene O'Neill, Émile Zola, Armand Salacrou, Maxwell Anderson, Maxim Gorki, Paul Claudel and Elsa Shelley. He later talked about these years as a long and hard fight against the old system of the star actor and against those commentators and performers who thought directors were useless and even damaging for the theatre.[3]

At this time, the Italian theatre structure was still dominated by the traditional model of the touring troupes (*compagnie*), led by a typically powerful and charismatic *capocomico*, who would also be the leading actor star. This traditional structure had a far longer life in Italy than in most other countries. An institution such as a national theatre did not exist in the country that was only formed in 1871, after three wars of independence. A theatre simply meant a building used by touring companies, and not the site of an ensemble. Some troupes even travelled with their own portable stages, settling at a certain place as long as it was opportune. The actors were *figli d'arte*, people who were born and had grown up in the profession, and who frequently belonged to family dynasties where skills and crafts were passed on from one generation to the next.[4] Stage practice was based on a system of character types that each actor had specialized in, since realistic or naturalistic acting approach had never really taken root. This meant that rehearsals as we understand them, aiming at a deep and faceted portrayal of a character, were not required or even desired. Less attention was paid to the visual aspect of the performance, while textual improvisation and approximation were ripe. This traditional approach is clearly illustrated in Pirandello's *Sei personaggi in cerca d'autore* (*Six Characters in Search of an Author*, 1921), where the actors under the command of the *capocomico* are unable to interpret the characters' complexities due to their conventional typology.

The backbone of this traditional system was the great actor (*mattatore*), the admired soloist who had acquired his craft through apprenticeship. A regular education for actors was only introduced in 1936 at the initiative of the influential critic and theorist Silvio D'Amico (1887–1955). The figure of the stage director was so unknown in Italy that it was necessary to invent a word for this function. At the request of D'Amico, a philologist coined the term 'regista' in 1940.[5] As Strehler put it, 'With forty years' delay, stage direction came to Italy. [The stage directors] should take the place of *i capocomici*, without being *figli d'arte*.'[6] In Milan, one of the few experimental theatre groups that was open to such directorial practices was Paolo Grassi's Palcoscenico, which Strehler joined as a performer in 1941, for the opening, at the city's Teatro dell'Arte, of *L'ultima stazione* (*The Last Station*), a play by anti-fascist intellectual and writer Beniamino Joppolo (1906–63). Reuniting after the war, Grassi produced *Piccoli borghesi* (*Petite Bourgeoisie*) by Maxim Gorki, which Strehler directed in 1946 at the city's Excelsior theatre.

They had a dream: Strehler, Grassi and their small world stage at the Piccolo Teatro

In the immediate post-war period, Milan was energized by an unusual dynamic, (leftist) intellectual and artistic environment, where the young theatre-maker and activist Dario Fo (1926–2016) also gradually began to attract attention. Paolo Grassi embraced the idea of theatre as a public service, similar to transport, the health service and education, a principle that was at the time also popularized by Jean Vilar and his Théâtre National Populaire in Paris (see the introduction to this volume), and elsewhere by the *Volksbühne* and the people's theatre movements. Politically and culturally, it was the right moment for such strategic approaches. In 1947, a positive response from the municipality allowed the birth of the Piccolo Teatro, as the first publicly funded theatre in Italy. It was opened in a derelict cinema that had previously been used for a variety of other purposes; during the fascist Salò Republic, it had even served as a site for the torture of resistance fighters. The new theatre's full name, Piccolo Teatro della Città di Milano, is significant. First, the theatre was indeed '*piccolo*', small; there were 523 seats in the beginning and 650 following the rebuilding in 1952. Secondly, it was also '*della Città di Milano*', that is, the city's and, moreover, the citizens' theatre, rather than being named after a leading actor or family in the Italian tradition. The Piccolo Teatro became the model for a number of similar so-called *teatri stabili*, permanent public theatres, across the Italian regions. Its artistic and democratic foundation resounds in its guiding principle: *Un teatro d'arte – per tutti*, 'An art theatre – for everybody'. The ambition was to make high artistic quality relevant and accessible for a broad public. The challenge was multiple; in order to create an art theatre, it was necessary to create a theatre art. In order to reach a new audience, a price policy and subscription systems were developed. 'Popular', though, never came to mean pleasing the audience.

The utopian aspect that marked the project to begin with – theatre as a celebration of popular unity – has a number of historical implications. In the general euphoria immediately following the Second World War, Strehler saw the theatre as 'profane rituality', a feast for all the people. Looking back retrospectively, he talks about

> the dream of a popular theatre, intended as a theatre of unity: a great place where the collective can gather in order to celebrate together, united, its myths, its tragedies, the dead, its joys, its worries; and this has been found in the 'secular sacredness' [...] A dream that warmed us. The dream of unity, yes, the dream of theatre as a *popular feast* for the entire united people. [...] [T]oday I realize, I have understood, that it is necessary, without interrupting that discourse, to review the problem, not anymore to view the theatre as a theatre of unity, but as a theatre of division [...] When Brecht told me while we talked about these things, 'You know, look, good theatre should divide, not unite,' I was not yet able to understand the lesson [...] The world was about to explode into a thousand pieces and we were still dreaming about 'the unity of the people.'[7]

Thus, the dream was shattered as the Cold War brought an end to the immediate enthusiasm. It became clear that 'the people', society, was split and the stage could not or should not unite, but should instead – as Brecht had phrased it – divide the public. It was a time of political criticism. The sometimes quite sophisticated manoeuvres required to secure the Piccolo Teatro's survival should be seen in the light of the ideological and political climate during the Cold War, which involved a shaky balance between a progressive critical agenda and a tactical coexistence with the increasingly reactionary public authorities. The simple fact that until 1962 a quite restrictive censorship was enforced in Italy put further limitations on the theatre's options. But even after censorship was abolished, interventions against undesired expressions concerning governmental, religious, political, moral and social conditions would occur.

One way to safeguard the theatre's position was a strategy similar to the one used by Brecht in the light of his somewhat tense relationship with the East German regime, namely to achieve international recognition. The Piccolo Teatro's global fame began in 1949 with a tour to London and Paris, showing *Il Corvo* (*The Raven*) by *commedia* playwright Carlo Gozzi (1720–1806). From 1956, the theatre cemented its international reputation by touring with Goldoni's *Arlecchino servitore di due padroni* (*The Servant of Two Masters*), first staged by Strehler in 1947, and in its various incarnations the director's iconic signature piece. The early productions of Gozzi and Goldoni can indeed be seen as an exploratory rediscovery of the Italian stage's roots in masked comedy. *The Servant of Two Masters* was in many ways illustrative of the challenge as well as the strategies of the new theatre. In the first version from 1947, the actors painted the masks on their faces (see Figure 3.1). Yet, soon Strehler began to work with actual masks for Pantalone, the Doctor, Harlequin and Brighella. This raised some problems. The physical technique of acting with masks had vanished; and the material technique for the making of leather masks was lost. To reconstruct the physical technique, French mime teacher Jacques Lecoq (1921–99) was invited to work with the Piccolo actors.[8] Apart from his work with Strehler, Lecoq also collaborated with Dario Fo on a couple of satirical shows that were performed at the Piccolo Teatro in 1953 and 1954; they had clear Brechtian implications in terms of political criticism and stylized acting. Meanwhile, the sculptor Amleto Sartori (1915–62) reinvented and reinterpreted the traditional masks. Both he and Lecoq had been attached to the university theatre in Padua that had pioneered the revival of *commedia dell'arte* in the immediate post-war period.

These experiments and experiences were essential to Piccolo Teatro's development of forms of expression which, together with the Brechtian principles of gestural and social characterization, were to make up the basis of their school for actors, founded in 1951 with (for some years) Strehler as the main teacher.[9] Reflecting Strehler's eclecticism, its pedagogy drew on a mix of Konstantin Stanislavski's (1863–1938) psychological realism [see **Volume 1**], the more poetic and expressive techniques of French actor-pedagogues Jacques Copeau (1879–1949) [see **Volume 3**] and Louis Jouvet

FIGURE 3.1 *Giorgio Strehler's original 1947 production of his signature piece, Carlo Goldoni's* The Servant of Two Masters *(Courtesy of Archivio Piccolo Teatro di Milano – Teatro d'Europa).*

(1887–1951), and Bertolt Brecht's strategies of *Verfremdung* [see **Volume 2**]. The training resulted in advanced standards of ensemble acting, and a mastery of expressive techniques that in turn made these techniques invisible. The expression was the content – passion transformed into gestural musicality, rhythmicalized embodiments of the characters' emotional developments. Performers were seen as instruments in an overall orchestration that included the visual and acoustic registers, rather than being confined to portrayals of individual characters. The more radical, avant-garde or even abstract expressionism of theatre revolutionary Antonin Artaud (1896–1948) and of the mime pioneers Étienne Decroux (1898–1991) and Jean-Louis Barrault (1910–94) [see **Volume 7**] featured as further points of departure for the development of a new stage language and the exploration of body and space, in a process described by Strehler as a movement from mysticism towards dialectics: the displacement from a metaphysical or purely aesthetic conception of art to a focus on art as a critical reflection of social or political realities.[10]

Although *The Servant of Two Masters* soon became the Piccolo's international show piece, Strehler elaborated, changed and re-staged it continuously, in ways that reflected the theatre's and the society's circumstances as well as the various phases in the director's work. He created six versions in total, which referred to the recuperation of a lost art form, then to a Brechtian meta-theatricality, thirdly to bitter disillusionment, then to dream-like play with illusions, followed by renewed optimism: these were the most central topics that were prominent in the various productions. Furthermore, new approaches to Goldoni became an essential part of Strehler's efforts. His readings broke with the prevailing image of 'il buon papá Goldoni' and instead opened the public's eyes to the complex depiction of the mental, social and material realities that make up his plays. Strehler's most important productions in this respect were *La trilogia della villeggiatura* (*The Holiday Trilogy*, 1954), *Le baruffe chiozzotte* (*The Squabbles at Chiozza*, 1964) and *Il Campiello* (1975), all of which Strehler also re-staged at various moments in close connection with his focus on Chekhov and Brecht.

During the 1950s and 1960s, the discrepancy between Strehler and Grassi's original vision of a public theatre and the actual attitude of the local authorities was growing almost desperate. Strehler's frustration and bitterness found a theatrical expression in his 1966 production of Pirandello's *Giganti della montagna* (*The Mountain Giants*): in the final scene, the theatre's safety curtain went down and crushed the cart of the poor players as a silent comment on their lack of recognition. Between 1968 and 1972, Strehler left the theatre and formed the *Gruppo Teatro e Azione*, feeling the need to start from scratch in a period of attack from the New Left that saw the *teatro stabile* system, and Strehler as part of it, as reactionary and the figure of the stage director as a despot.[11] In an ensuing polemical debate during the 1970s, Strehler accused the fashionable avant-garde of epigonism and narcissism; according to him, the 'true avant-garde' took risks and developed new forms of aesthetic expressions that could even be applied to familiar works. The total break with the past to him seemed just as pointless as the rejection of renewal.[12] About the same time, Strehler was under consideration for the artistic directorship of the Teatro Stabile di Roma, but apparent political motives prevented the socialist Strehler's appointment.[13]

When Grassi became head of Milan's Scala Opera in 1972, Strehler instead returned to the Piccolo Teatro, now as the only director, and with the promise of better operating conditions for the theatre, including a much-needed new auditorium. This had been discussed since the 1960s, when the company began performing some of their productions at the 1,500-seat Teatro Lirico. In 1986, the 400-seat Teatro Studio opened as one of the Piccolo Teatro's new stages, which Strehler inaugurated with a stage adaptation of Louis Jouvet's theatre lessons, entitled *Elvira o la passione teatrale* (*Elvira or The Passion for Theatre*), himself playing Jouvet's role. Strehler resumed his acting on a large scale in the two-part *Faust frammenti* (*Faust Fragments*, 1989–92). In 1991, the Piccolo Teatro became part of Teatro d'Europa, a network of European stages founded by French Minister of Culture Jack Lang and Strehler, which, supported by the European Commission, still exists today. Strehler eventually resigned in 1997 following further disagreements with Milan's mayor and harassment in the wake of the so-called *mani pulite*, the campaign against corruption in public administration that reached even the Piccolo Teatro. Furthermore, he was frustrated by the delay of the new theatre building and the prospect of it becoming a national theatre. Jack Lang was appointed head of the theatre in order to hold together the diffuse situation. Strehler came back once more to take charge of the Piccolo's fiftieth anniversary celebrations, but when the new theatre, with its 999 seats, was finally opened in January 1998, with his (unfinished) production of Mozart's *Così fan tutte*, he had passed away just a month earlier.

'If it turns out it does not work, then get rid of it': Strehler and Brecht

Even though his life and career thus took multiple directions, one inspiration remained crucial to Strehler throughout: the Brechtian focus on material reality. However, as I shall demonstrate, Strehler inherited from Brecht without, for that matter, becoming a dogmatist follower. His focus on Brecht was controversial, since the German was a much disputed figure in Italy for political reasons. The political reality in which Strehler and Grassi worked and to which they responded, is also reflected in Brecht's fate in Italy: they were subject to the same political trends. Brecht's work became part of the ideological battle after the Second World War, with its distinctive discord between the right and the left. Previously, fascism had blocked Brecht in Italy, as well as in his native Germany. Nevertheless, soon after its 1928 Berlin success, *Die Dreigroschenoper* (*The Threepenny Opera*) in fact had been staged by the Teatro degli Indipendenti in Rome in 1929 under the title *The Wake of the Frauds*, directed by the Futurist Anton Giulio Bragaglia (1890–1960). It was billed, though, as an adaptation of John Gay's *Beggar's Opera* (1728) rather than the work by the politically dubious German. When it was again performed in 1943 at the Teatro Argentina in Rome by the Accademia d'Arte Drammatica as Vito Pandolfi's (1917–74) graduation performance, it was once more presented as an adaptation of Gay's work, since Brecht was by now banned by the censors.[14]

After the war, translations of Brecht's works appeared in a series edited by Grassi, but they attracted little attention. Brecht remained a controversial name to put on stage. A pioneer at the time was the (Catholic) director Gianfranco De Bosio (b. 1924), the founder of the University Theatre in Padua, where in 1951 theatre critic Eric Bentley had staged *Die Ausnahme und die Regel* (*The Exception and the Rule*), which De Bosio followed in 1953 with *Mann ist Mann* (*Man Equals Man*) in collaboration with Jacques

Lecoq. Equally in 1953, a theatre festival in Bologna showed *The Exception and the Rule*, and Teatro dei Satiri in Rome presented *Mutter Courage* (*Mother Courage*). After his satirical shows from 1953 and 1954, Dario Fo had planned a Milanese adaptation of *The Threepenny Opera*, but his politically controversial theatre group was dissolved before this could take place. In 1957, De Bosio had become head of the Teatro Stabile di Torino, where in 1961 he staged *Arturo Ui*. And even after the abolition of censorship in 1962, there were problems with staging Brecht's plays. In 1963, pressure was placed on the Torino theatre to call off its plans to stage *Man equals Man*, so that it would not become a 'Trojan horse for communism in Italy'.[15] That same year, a student performance of *Die Gewehre der Frau Carrar* (*Señora Carrar's Rifles*) was banned in Venice. As late as 1970, action was taken in Genoa against *Die sieben Todsünden* (*The Seven Deadly Sins*).[16]

Yet it was Strehler's productions of Brecht's dramatic works that aroused the strongest reactions. In 1954, he directed *Die Massnahme* (*The Measures Taken*) as a graduation performance at the Piccolo's theatre school. His other Brecht productions included *The Threepenny Opera* (Piccolo Teatro, 1956 and 1973; Châtelet Opera Paris, 1986), *The Good Person of Szechwan* (Piccolo Teatro, 1958; Schauspielhaus Hamburg, 1977; Piccolo Teatro/ Lirico, 1981; and Studio, 1996), *Schweyk in the Second World War* (Piccolo Teatro, 1961), *The Exception and the Rule* (Piccolo Teatro, 1962 and 1995), *Galileo* (Piccolo Teatro, 1963), *Mahagonny* (Scala Opera, 1964), *Saint Joan of the Stockyards* (Piccolo Teatro/Lirico, 1970), *Lucullus* (Scala Opera, 1973) and *The Story of the Abandoned Doll* (after *The Caucasian Chalk Circle*. Scala Opera, 1976; Piccolo Teatro/Studio, 1995). In addition, he staged various programmes at the Piccolo Teatro with Brecht's poems and songs, such as *Milva sings Brecht* and *Milva sings a New Brecht* (1965/95) and *I, Bertolt Brecht* (in three parts, 1967–79), in which Strehler himself performed. The 1995/6 season was proclaimed as 'Brecht-season', which even at that time was still not considered uncontroversial, now owing to the fall of the Berlin Wall and the collapse of the Soviet Union, in the wake of which the Italian Communist Party was also dissolved. During this season Strehler had planned to stage a *Mother Courage of Sarajevo*, a project that was eventually completed in parts by his assistant Carlo Battistoni after Strehler's death.

The 1956 production of *The Threepenny Opera* was a particularly risky move, which required advanced tactics of the theatre-makers. In an attempt to neutralize what was perceived as political provocation, they even put on the premiere of Diego Fabbri's (1911–80) religious play *Processo a Gesù* (*Trial against Jesus*) in the same season. Before rehearsals began, Strehler had visited Brecht in Berlin, asking him twenty-seven specific questions. There are two reports of the meeting that took place on 25 October 1955: on the one hand, Strehler's account, on the other hand, the Berliner Ensemble dramaturg Hans-Joachim Bunge's notes.[17] Strehler recounts how Brecht did not remember much about the first performance in 1928. The Italian then explained the prologue he considered inserting to contextualize the play's topicality, an idea which Brecht accepted straight away, slyly adding, 'If it turns out it does not work, then get rid of it.' This was of course exactly what eventually happened. According to Bunge, Strehler wanted to understand the work in its original context and was eager to achieve a similar effect in his own context. Brecht initially responded in general terms but then Strehler's questions became more specific as to whether he would be willing to accept an updated rewriting. He would. Brecht suggested a displacement to the Italian quarter of New York around 1900 that would imply Milan without showing it directly. Strehler considered starting with a film of Milan. These stimuli contributed to the director's eventual solution that was, while not exclusively sticking to the discussion at the meeting, inspired by the exchange of ideas. Bunge's notes further record observations about the problem of an epic acting technique Strehler was struggling with (a struggle that would continue for the rest of his career). Although his solutions might seem extreme, even stylized, he refrained from outright caricature and left space for the audience's co-creativity, leaving the portrayal of the characters full of contradictions that intended to stimulate the audience's imagination and understanding.

Strehler eventually situated the plot in 1914 in the United States, though taking some liberties (see Figures 3.2 and 3.3). Brecht's stable was changed

FIGURE 3.2 *Teo Otto and Luciano Damiani's set for the prologue scene of Brecht's* The Threepenny Opera *for Giorgio Strehler's first 1956 production of the play (Courtesy of Archivio Piccolo Teatro di Milano – Teatro d'Europa).*

FIGURE 3.3 *Piccolo Teatro actors Andrea Matteuzzi, Tino Carraro and Enzo Tarascio in Giorgio Strehler's 1956 production of* The Threepenny Opera (*Photo: Bernardi/Courtesy of Archivio Piccolo Teatro di Milano – Teatro d'Europa*).

into a garage, and the wedding bed became a limousine. Later, in the 1973 version, he changed the setting to the prohibition era, while in his 1986 Paris production, he highlighted references to the mafia. A recurring element of the set design was a couple of turning, oversize 'bicycle wheels' containing lights, set against the background of a bare brick wall. From a realistic perspective, they made little sense, but they were a very evocative device and appeared completely natural. In the first production of 1956, these illuminated wheels together with other details still represented a realist fairground environment, recognizably alluding to the popular Milanese neighbourhood close to the theatre.[18] Later versions created a stage world that appeared at the same time realist and abstract.

In 1956, Brecht came to Milan to observe the final rehearsals. He laughed heartily about Strehler's solutions – so much so that the actors asked furiously who this disturbing person watching the rehearsal was. 'The playwright', was his response.[19] So the playwright was happy with the liberties the director had taken. He even wrote a new, more optimistic verse for the finale. Strehler describes how Brecht tried to reach him in the days after the premiere, but that he was totally exhausted after the efforts that had gone into staging the show. Brecht was full of understanding: 'God knows how tired he must be! Let him rest!' Strehler then states:

> One afternoon, mysteriously, a message from Brecht arrived, typewritten on an envelope. Just a few words in which Brecht informed me of his desire to entrust me with the artistic management ['tutela'] of all his works in Italy and also in Europe, if possible, in the future. Nothing else. Signed only with his initial, the letter B.[20]

Hirst confirms this account: 'Brecht loved the Milan staging, as a result of which he entrusted Strehler with the artistic direction of all his works. The request was typed on the back of an envelope which he sent to Strehler after the production had opened.'[21] The original document can be found in the Piccolo Teatro's archives. It states something slightly different, though: 'lieber Strehler, ich wollte, ich könnte Ihnen in Europa alle meine stücke überlassen, eins nach dem andern. danke bertolt brecht Milano 10.2.56'. It is handwritten, not typed, not written on an envelope, fully signed, dated the day of the premiere (which was also Brecht's birthday); it appears deliberately vague and ambiguous and certainly far from expressing any commitment: 'I wish I could leave all my pieces to you in Europe, one after the other.' Those few lines have become a tale in themselves, not least thanks to Strehler's somewhat liberal interpretation.

Brecht's enthusiasm about the performance was, nevertheless, beyond dispute. The day after the premiere, he sent a letter from Milan to the actress Ruth Berlau in Copenhagen:

> The production – brilliant in its conceit and detail and very aggressive [...] It was apparently a great success, and indeed, the piece seems very fresh. Strehler, probably the best director in Europe, had moved the play to 1914 [...] This is very good, and following the Third World War, one could move it again to 19..[22]

On his return to Berlin, he wrote to the ensemble of the Piccolo Teatro, in a letter dated 27 February 1956:

> Let me thank you once again for the excellent production of my *Three Penny Opera,* which has been staged by your great director. Fiery and cool, casual and exact – this is how this production distinguishes itself from many I have seen. You really manage to reincarnate the work [...] It would be a pleasure and honour if your theatre could show the *Three Penny Opera* in Berlin, at the Berliner Ensemble am Schiffbauerdamm's theatre, which saw the original premiere.[23]

Among the Milanese audiences, the show aroused strong reactions for its scathing depiction of the bourgeoisie in the expanding *miracolo economico,* the Italian variant of the post-war economic boom (see introduction to this volume). Anton Giuglio Bragaglia accused the 'socialists Grassi and Strehler' of 'dedicating their anti-bourgeois propaganda evening to the wealthy people who can afford to pay the high prices for these elitist ideas. It is simply a sign of bad upbringing to insult the paying public who support the theatre.'[24] A similarly fierce controversy broke out in 1963, when Strehler staged *The Life of Galileo,* which had only become possible after the abolition of censorship. As it 'brought the Pope on stage', it stood out as the most offensive of Strehler's productions of Brecht. The Vatican launched a campaign against the Piccolo, claiming that the show 'aimed to discredit the Church as an institution and turn less historically informed and critical souls among the audience against it'.[25] The theatre paid a high price as its public subsidy was subsequently cut. The production, following four months of long rehearsals, was an artistic triumph, though. It also stands out as a tactical masterpiece of Grassi's manoeuvring through the massive political complications. While Strehler put the theatre's existence at risk by insisting on staging *Galileo*, Grassi's pragmatic policies made sure it survived, artistically and economically – just one example of the division of roles between Strehler and Grassi, the artist and the strategist.

A question of allusion, not illusion: Strehler's allegorical Szechwan

Talking about Brecht, Strehler would very commonly highlight his undogmatic approach to the profession, which was very much in accordance with Strehler's own stage practice but differed from the prevailing attitude held by most declared 'Brechtians'. In 1958, two years after *The Threepenny Opera*, Strehler produced *Der gute Mensch von Sezuan* (*The Good Person of Szechwan*), Brecht's Chinese parable from 1941 which had premiered in Zürich in 1943 and eventually in Frankfurt in 1952. Already in 1948 Brecht had recommended that the Piccolo Teatro present it.[26] The play's fundamental disharmony between passion and intellect matched the complexity of 'fiery and cool' – of 'Feuer und Kühle' that Brecht had attributed to Strehler's work.[27] Strehler would stage *L'anima buona di Sezuan* four times, with a decisive shift from the first to the following versions, in a process that developed over thirty years.

In the play's prologue, the water seller Wang introduces three gods who are searching for a 'good person'. Only the prostitute Shen-Te is willing to house them, and the money she receives from the gods enables her to buy a tobacco shop. Now she gets exploited from all sides, even by the unemployed pilot Sun, whom Shen-Te has fallen in love with. Therefore, she adopts the persona of a brutal male cousin, Shui-Ta, who handles her affairs ruthlessly and develops the humble shop into a full-scale tobacco factory with a lot of employees. The plot continues as Shui-Ta is taken to court, charged with the abduction of Shen-Te who has meanwhile become pregnant with Sun's child. During the trial the gods appear as judges, and Shen-Te reveals herself to them. They refuse to intervene in earthly affairs and disappear, leaving Shen-Te to her desperate dilemma further elaborated in the epilogue. The Chinese sceneries are precisely described in Brecht's text: a street with houses; the store; a place under a bridge, where Wang seeks refuge in a sewer pipe; the city park with a willow; a side room at a suburban restaurant; the factory office with chairs and blankets; and, finally, the courtroom. Brecht endeavoured to avoid emotional involvement by inserting a number of interludes, songs, sections of lyrical language and direct appeals to the audience. He further breaks up the rhythm and creates a kind of polyphony, encouraging the actors to demonstrate the characters and the audience to observe and analyse the events rather than empathizing.

Strehler's first production from 1958 largely maintained Brechtian conventions. As the play takes place near a cement factory, the set design by Luciano Damiani (1923–2007), made of bamboo, wood and canvas, was kept in cement-grey shades. As prescribed by Brecht, when Shen-Te was disguised as her tough cousin Shui-Ta, she wore a mask. The poor people were dressed in grey, the rich in black, and only the Chinese gods appeared more colourful. German theatre critic Siegfried Melchinger produced a detailed account of Strehler's rehearsals. As he notes, while the actor according to Brecht should distance himself from his character, 'with Strehler he transcends it. He doesn't allow in any way the actor to diminish the intensity of his identification with the role; instead he forces him to express a concentration of its emotional meaning.'[28] This detailed observation suggests my overall assessment of Strehler's relationship to Brecht: that he was faithful to Brecht precisely by betraying him.

In the Hamburg production of 1977, the Chinese features were replaced. Damiani originally envisaged a car graveyard with puddles, filled with tyres, a crashed bus and other objects. He ended up putting on stage plastic-covered flooring flooded with water with walkways through heaped-up scrap such as a mangled aircraft propeller one might associate with the unemployed pilot Sun – a no man's land, with a glimpse of a volcano on the horizon. In front of the volcano was Shen-Te's cabin, something between a tent and a wagon. Shen-Te's costume was a long drab (night)dress and beret. Transcending conventions of realism, the set and costumes developed their own autonomous reality, open to interpretation and association, yet at the same time they were never abstract as the details were authentic, while the combination of these details rendered the scene and costumes incongruous with full-scale realism.[29]

The basic scenographic concept was repeated in Milan in 1981 at the Piccolo's Lirico stage, in an even more minimalist and abstract version by designer Paolo Bregni (b. 1937). Strehler had considered moving the play to the developing world but eventually changed his mind, probably because it would reduce the complexity and openness. He pruned the text, as he felt it was full of redundancies, suggesting this was the case since Brecht had never staged it himself. He cut roles, moved text from one place to another, inserted new text, simplified the composition of the scenes, reduced the number of Wang's interludes, cut Shen-Te's interrupting reflections, simplified the lyrical language, changed or removed some of Brecht's inserted scenes, all with the aim of attaining a more organic flow instead of Brecht's ruptured rhythm. In addition, the epilogue which abandons the fiction and formulates the fundamental message, was omitted. During the final rehearsals, Strehler cut the performance down from four and a quarter hours to three and a half. One particularly significant intervention concerned Shen-Te's motivation for her transformation to Shui-Ta. Strehler moved it forward so that it had more to do with the protection of her child with Sun, in other words, with passion and emotions than with economic reasons. In the fourth version from 1996, at the theatre-in-the-round Piccolo Teatro Studio, Damiani elaborated his earlier Hamburg design to include the wreckage of an entire aeroplane. Strehler now even removed the entire wedding sequence between Shen-Te and Sun – a radical intervention that again created a gap for the audience's imagination.

Over the years, Strehler thus endowed the text with a completely new structure. Considering Brecht's concept of *Episierung* ('making epic', or 'epification') – his rejection of the linear, unified 'Aristotelian' narrative technique – it is remarkable that Strehler apparently added a more classical rhythm to the story, in accordance with a conventional narrative model. The characters' emotions, the love stories (Shen-Te's love for Sun; her maternal love) were brought to the foreground. Nevertheless, the fundamental Brechtian contrast between emotional involvement and critical distance remained as a dynamic tension. Yet it is important to note that Strehler shifted defamiliarization, instead, to other theatrical registers. Most notably, it was achieved by space, costumes, choreographic, gestural and vocal ways of acting, and, first and foremost, by the use of light. Practically all of the lighting was focused on or related in some way to the cyclorama: of the 100,000 watts used for the lighting, 60,000 were placed behind the cyclorama.[30] This produced the effect that the characters were almost sculpted by the light, appearing as figures rather than individuals.

The *Verfremdungseffekt* was further achieved through drastic scenographic minimalism – no park, no houses, no restaurant and so forth. An autonomous universe was created in the shape of the cyclorama's luminous round horizon and a round floor, a revolving stage covered with plastic and filled with water (a simple concretization of the fact that it rains a great deal in Szechwan). In the third version from 1981, the minimalism was even more radical, as Shen-Te's cabin appeared almost as a scrap sculpture, surrounded by a few boards to walk on that determined the actor's movements (see Figure 3.4).[31] Small changes were added to the cabin to illustrate Shen-Te's emerging prosperity, including

FIGURE 3.4 *Andrea Jonasson as Shen-Te in Paolo Bregni's set for Strehler's 1981 production of Brecht's* The Good Person of Szechwan *(Photo: Luigi Ciminaghi/ Courtesy of Archivio Piccolo Teatro di Milano – Teatro d'Europa).*

at a certain point a TV antenna. The depiction of the factory connoted a concentration camp as a couple of watchtowers were suggested. Changes in time and space took place by means of the revolving stage. Rubber boots, raincoats and umbrellas meanwhile characterized and categorized the roles; the upper class was equipped with sunglasses and rainwear, and dressed in a masculine way. Generally, the costume style was Western, denoting the 1940s.

Strehler's perfectionism with regard to tiniest details was legendary: each tobacco box, each bottle would be specifically selected and sometimes handmade, since to him the idea of randomness was unthinkable – as if, in an unmaterialistic way, the objects had a soul. One might describe this as abstract or poetic realism, where 'realism' does not refer to the depiction of an environment through a totality of objects, but instead to the careful selection of a handful of objects that are so convincingly deployed that the audience forgets how original the solutions were compared to the playtext. Thus the water seller Wang was not a Chinese character with a carrying pole, but he instead moved around on his 1930s Italian ice-seller's bicycle, dressed in a way that was clearly referencing Brecht himself; the gods appeared first in long cleric's coats with soft hats, later as Catholic Primates – though dressed in Chinese silk decorated with dragons – and then in evening dress and opera glasses as spectators in a theatre box, following a cue in the text stating that 'We are only spectators.' Later again, they were Beckettian tramps in dustbins; and finally, when they adopted the role of judges, they appeared as Chinese deities.

The performers' gestural expressivity was in some cases stylized to the point of artificiality, however, not to the point of reducing them to dehumanized puppets – with one important exception: a puppet is in itself in some ways a living dead – dead material called to life through movement. This thematic connection was subtly exploited in the depiction of the cold and cynical Shui-Ta. As noted, Brecht prescribes the use of a mask. Strehler responded to this by transforming the character into a kind of living corpse, almost a zombie with sunglasses and gold teeth, displaying both restrained and extreme bodily expressivity, and thereby conveying the character's scary energy far more drastically than indicated by Brecht (see Figure 3.5). In terms of physical movement, he/she appeared as a puppet that became a sign, a Brechtian 'gestus'. Thus, shifting the meaning from textual to corporal registers seemed, formally, more Pina Bausch than Brecht, remarkably at a time before the big breakthrough of dance, image and performance theatre in the 1980s. The characters' physical register was ruled by a kind of synthesizing, *dansant* realism, based on the Piccolo theatre's particular style of actor-training, namely the 'epic' acting that integrates emotional and corporal movements. While the 'living dead' marionette-like stylization was reserved for Shui-Ta's performance, generally the

FIGURE 3.5 *Andrea Jonasson as Shui-Ta and Massimo Ranieri as Sun in Strehler's 1981 production of Brecht's* The Good Person of Szechwan (*Photo: Luigi Ciminaghi/Courtesy of Archivio Piccolo Teatro di Milano – Teatro d'Europa*).

de-individualization of the characters did not imply their dehumanization: even though they were not portrayed naturalistically as 'persons', they did not appear one-dimensional either. This also applied to the tonality of the actors' diction which, rather than emphasizing psychological expression, was orchestrated like musical voices, or else, conversely, remained deliberately toneless or neutral. Strehler took inspiration from the famous Brechtian exercise whereby a 'he/she said' is added after each line of the play in order to achieve an attitude of defamiliarization. The vocal registers were thus rhythmicalized and intonated in ways that were clearly artificial and not conventionally 'realist' at all, but that still distinctly expressed the characters' emotions and psychology. As for the maternal emotions of Shen-Te, Strehler even let the actress use almost melodramatic registers.

Furthermore, the performers never came into physical contact with each other, thus emphasizing Brecht's narrative tale about distance. Meaning was communicated to the audience via the actor's entire body, namely her/his way of walking, posture and choreographed rhythms. This was a further element of Strehler's *epification*, where every gesture became a sign, and the actor's expression was no longer reserved to facial expression. The cyclorama itself exposed all attempts at empathetic portrayal as vain, given that gestural, sculptural and figurative expressions reached the audience before any realistic detail and nuance. Here, then, lay the radical shift of register that released Brecht by betraying him. Strehler dissolved Brecht's more realistic conception of time and place, but never into outright abstraction; the components of the set, costumes, props, even movement and diction appeared completely organic and realistic in terms of their materiality and function, yet their combination and montage still transcended any realism because of the strategies for *Episierung* already discussed.

Thus, the performance's rhythm and appearance contrasted drastically with Strehler's dramaturgical adaptation. As noted, Strehler placed more focus on the characters' individual emotional stories, yet he staged the play in a way that conferred a distance and more generic quality to it. A tension emerged between the emphasized individual emotionality in the dramaturgical structure and the non-concrete objectivity of his *mise en scène*. Thus, Strehler moved Brecht's epic tools, most notably defamiliarization and *gestus*, into other theatrical registers: the visual and performative ones, made more powerful by simplification, and the loadedness of the visual and gestural expressions that unfolded almost musically in the encounter with the audience's perception. The stage's circular shape transformed Brecht's parable into a micro-cosmos, a *theatrum mundi*. Thanks to the revolving stage, time and space moved and at the same time were not getting anywhere. All areas of the circular stage appeared open – also to the audience's co-creativity – as did the entire dramaturgy. It was a question of allusion, not of illusion.

Strehler's eclecticism between concept and interpretation: A tale of three cities

In debates about what may or perhaps even should be done to a dramatic text, the distinction between directors as 'interpreters' and as 'conceptualists', and the dichotomy between theatre as *either* respectful 'interpretation' *or* rabid *Regietheater* and concept theatre are widespread but unhelpful clichés, as not least Strehler's case demonstrates. Within the argument, an 'interpreter' may be seen as a director who allegedly 'serves' the dramatist's text loyally, as opposed to a 'conceptualist' who deliberately inflicts stage solutions which do not correspond to the playtext's explicit or implicit stage directions. Yet, all staging inevitably involves more or less thorough and deliberate conceptualization. Casting, scenography and gesture are not present in the text in a way comparable to how music already 'is' in a score. Strehler, it is true, called himself an 'interpreter': 'I am one who practises an interpretative profession.'[32] Hirst picked up on this and described Strehler as 'first and foremost an interpreter; however striking his theatrical productions [...] may have been, they have always proved a source of illumination – and often revelation – of the dramatic text'.[33] Thereby, a certain image of Strehler had been staged that pegged him in the camp of the 'interpreter-director', contrasting him with image-focused stage directors such as Peter Brook (b. 1925 [**see Volume 5**]), Peter Stein (b. 1937 [**see Volume 7**]) or fellow Italian director Luca Ronconi (1933–2015). This categorization of Strehler as 'text-interpreter' still dominates the understanding of his work; yet it is an undue simplification of his practice. His 'conceptions' were so seamless, organic and inconspicuous that he was erroneously considered as 'mere' interpreter. Strehler's at times, in fact, radical interventions followed his artistic instinct, but he never ostentatiously exposed his directorial ideas. Of course, his point of departure was the dramatic text. He pursued what he saw as the text's reality, truth and authenticity.[34] He delved deep into the text and its cultural and material context. But, in addition, he absorbed the text in a long exploratory process during which he fully appropriated the material: he transformed it into an original theatrical work – an aspect which I find mostly ignored in discussions of his work. He himself suggested that his own 'temperament undoubtedly is more rhythmic than semantic'.[35] Therefore, his respect for the 'text' had at least as much to do with musicality, including voices, bodies, light, space, sound and rhythm, as with the words on the page. In fact, 'text', for him, really meant 'score'. From the perspective of the history of Italian theatre, his focus on 'text' should even be seen in a strategic sense: as upgrading theatre to an art form which involved a renowned artist, the author, thus removing the earlier focus on the great actor, as discussed in the beginning.[36]

Strehler's work on a production would develop over the course of several years, from the initial birth of an idea to the complex preparations for all levels of the show, including the scenography, and culminating in a frenetic period of rehearsals. It would possibly even continue beyond the premiere, in a number of new productions that would further reinterpret the same play. Strehler's approach is sometimes presented as unprepared and spontaneous, and he has even contributed to this myth himself, playing the 'intuitive artist'. However, the annotated manuscript for the staging of *The Tempest*, for example, demonstrates quite the contrary. The notes take up more space than the playtext itself. In addition, a 400-page report on the preparatory discussions about the play reveals that Strehler had analysed it in collaboration with the dramaturg Luigi Lunari, set designer Luciano Damiani, the composer Fiorenzo Carpi, the translator Agostino Lombardo, and none other than the influential Polish-American dramaturg and Shakespeare expert Jan Kott. The combination of such long preparatory processes and Strehler's spontaneous creativity – thus, a well-prepared improvisation – is a very Italian strategy indeed, echoing the *commedia dell'arte*'s approach. Strehler's incredibly meticulous thoroughness was the prerequisite for the seemingly 'easy' solutions that he found in the rehearsal room.

He had no one regular 'method' but instead aimed at an undogmatic complexity. An eclectic openness coexisted with the invention of specific models in his approach, such as that which emerged when rehearsing Chekhov's *The Cherry Orchard* in 1974: the method of 'Chinese boxes'. It was Strehler's new way of discriminating between, and addressing, the story, history and myth in a given text. The story refers to characters and emotions, covering psychology, action and the narrative/plot. History points to historical political, social and economic circumstances. Myth is about the universal dimensions, 'eternal stories', metaphorical and poetic layers. Therefore, the three boxes contain narrative, political and poetic (aesthetic) dynamics. The main box, however, is the fourth that embraces the other three in one. Strehler introduces the idea as follows:

> There are three Chinese boxes, one inside the other. The first box is the box of the 'truth' (the potentially true, which on stage is the ultimately true). The story is a human, interesting story [...] that is embedded in history; the interesting thing is that it shows us how the characters really live, and where they live. It is a 'realistic' interpretation/vision, like an excellent reconstruction one may attempt to realize in an 'atmospheric' movie.
>
> The second box is the box of history [...] which is not absent in the first box, but there it only constitutes the distant background, the almost invisible trace. Here, now, history is not just 'costume' or 'prop': it is the very purpose of the story. It is more the shifting of the classes in their dialectical interrelations that is my main interest. [...] As such, the characters are 'human beings' with precise individual characteristics, their clothes, their faces, but they represent – first and foremost – a part of history in motion [...] Here, even though objects, props, clothes

and gestures maintain their plausible character, they are also slightly 'displaced', slightly 'alienated' in the discourse and perspective of History. For sure the second box contains the first, but for that reason it is bigger. The two boxes complement each other.

Finally, the third box is the box of life, the box of human adventure, of being born, growing up, living, loving, not loving, winning, losing, understanding, not understanding, passing, dying. It is an 'eternal' parable [...] While the characters are here still seen within the truth of a narrative and within a 'political' process, they are also seen in a quasi 'metaphysical' dimension, like a parable of human fate. [...] The narrative becomes a great poetic paraphrase which still contains the story and history but where everything becomes a part of the great human adventure, of human flesh that perishes.

This last box moves the performance onto the 'symbolic and metaphysic-allusive' level [...] Each box thus has its own physiognomy and its own peril. The first carries the risk of pedantic minutiae [...] of observing the narrative through the 'key-hole' and not going further. The second box comes with the danger of isolating the characters as emblems of history, frozen into a historical thesis or theme [...] This removes true humanity from the characters and instead elevates them to a historical symbol [...]

The third box is in peril of becoming simple 'abstraction'. Merely metaphysics, as if outside time [...] Thus the entire performance becomes abstract, symbolic, universal as it comes close to losing its earthly weight [...]

A 'right' production should give us the three perspectives together on stage in unity [...] A 'right' set design should be able to vibrate like a light that moves in accordance with these three 'impulses.'[37]

It seems obvious to connect the boxes to Stanislavski, Brecht and Copeau respectively, who, on the one hand, were significant figures of inspiration, teachers and models for Strehler, yet, on the other hand, posed the danger of one-dimensionality. Strehler talked about his teachers as 'cities'.[38] In a production such as *The Good Person of Szechwan* it is clear that the third (aesthetic) box, discreet and distinct at the same time, was not sufficient. All three boxes were in play in the staging, acting and the allusions.

Magic realism: The stage between dream and life

Strehler's thematic priorities varied between political and existential emphases. However, research into the text's historical and cultural premises was obligatory as a point of departure for the transformation of the text to a contemporary context. Throughout Strehler's entire oeuvre runs an exploration of the borderland between reality and illusion, dream, magic, the human being as actor, theatre as an existential metaphor, illusion as reality, and reality as illusion. This can be traced back to his early staging of Calderón's *Il mago dei prodigi* (*The Marvellous Magician*) in 1947 and to his productions of Pirandello's *Mountain Giants* (Piccolo Teatro, 1947; Zürich, 1949; Düsseldorf, 1958; Piccolo Teatro/Lirico, 1966 and 1994), as well as to his general interest in Pirandello. But what particularly marks the director's fascination with magic realism – the addition of an enigmatic dimension to the realist narrative – is his trilogy on illusion from the 1970s and 1980s, each play containing a 'wizard' in the leading role: *La tempesta* (*The Tempest*) by Shakespeare (Piccolo Teatro, 1978, following his earlier production of the play on an island in Giardino di Boboli, Florence, 1948), Corneille's *L'Illusion comique* (Odéon Paris, 1984) and Eduardo De Filippo's *La grande magia* (*Great Magic*. Piccolo Teatro, 1985). These productions demonstrate how Strehler placed increasing emphasis on the third of the Chinese boxes, while also further challenging the view of Strehler as a realist and 'text interpreter'.

The Tempest, Shakespeare's drama about power, magic, betrayal and reconciliation, was transformed by Strehler into an almost hallucinating cosmic liturgy, thanks to Fiorenzo Carpi's choral music and Luciano Damiani's scenography of an enchanted island that comprised a floor with a magic circle, covered with sand (see Figure 3.6). The white spirit Ariel weightlessly hovered, by means of wires, while the black Caliban – with tragic colonial connotations – came from a trapdoor in the floor. The comical characters wore masks taken from the *commedia dell'arte*. But, first and foremost, the island became a metaphor for the relation between life and the stage in the late 1970s, the so-called 'years of lead' in Italy, dominated by the horror of political terrorism. When the 'stage director' Prospero eventually discards his magic book, in Strehler's production the book had the shape of a theatre script, and in the epilogue the stage literally dissolved: the set simply collapsed. Up to this point, the performance had emphasized the need, expressed in Shakespeare's text, to face gloomy realities and to awake from a dream. This was pertinent in the Italian contemporary reality where utopian ideas of collectivism in the aftermath of 1968 had been replaced by the horror of terrorism. Strehler shifted the focus from reconciliation to the fragile island, equating it with the theatre, surrounded by merciless reality; even though philosophical themes were highlighted, he related it to political realities too, thereby making use of all three of the Chinese boxes.

In Corneille's *L'Illusion comique*, a father's desperate vision of his missing son's cruel fate appears to him in a magic cave until it is revealed that he has become an actor and his 'drama' is theatre. This became for Strehler a 'metaphor of life where theatre is employed as a poetic and disturbing demonstration of the relativity of the relationships of the characters who

FIGURE 3.6 *Luciano Damiani's set for Giorgio Strehler's 1978 production of Shakespeare's* The Tempest *(Photo: Luigi Ciminaghi/Courtesy of Archivio Piccolo Teatro di Milano – Teatro d'Europa).*

play out this human adventure on a world stage'[39] – a relativity that caused the boundaries between hallucination and reality, role-playing and life, to blur. This was achieved by Strehler via his choice to cast the same actor to play both the wizard Alcandre outside and captain Matamore within the play of illusion. This would challenge the author's logic almost to breaking point, but the complex mirror effect was contained within an illuminated scenographic clarity. The illusions – the scenes of the son's life – were evoked in a dark cave, connoting Plato's mythical site of illusions; and they reached a mystical visual culmination when the prompter's box burst into flames. Details – which were actually based on liberally interpreted historical research – appeared to be realistic, which paradoxically reinforced the impression of hallucination.

De Filippo's bitter 'Pirandellian' comedy meanwhile tells the story of a husband whose wife is 'conjured away' by a magician during a magic show, while in reality she has disappeared with her lover. The magician gives the man a 'magic' shrine that contains his wife. He is told that if he doubts that she is in the shrine, he will lose her forever. But when she actually returns, the husband prefers the illusion to the reality. Strehler's *mise en scène* referred to the fact that De Filippo had used the term 'a fairytale' on the title page of the playtext. He moved the staging from the author's Neapolitan environment to the Rimini coast, which enabled a richer orchestration in a variety of mixed dialects – literally a polyphony. The performance developed its own convincing reality, combining authenticity in material details alluding to the Italian coast with abstract and poetic stage images, to create a borderland between illusion and reality. In terms of the Chinese boxes, one could say that Strehler placed the accent towards the mythical-poetical box in this trilogy.[40] It was a question of selection, focus and montage. The details remained 'authentic' and referred to both psychology and history, but the emphasis was increasingly, at this stage of Strehler's career, on more universal and mythical dimensions. It is precisely this aspect that links Strehler, in a perhaps surprising way, to Robert Wilson (b. 1941). This, I suggest, offers an even more illuminating perspective on the often misunderstood core characteristics of Strehler's aesthetics.

Spaces around words and sounds: The different similarities between Strehler and Wilson

Shortly before his death in 1997, Strehler gave an interview for a book publication in which he describes his relationship with Wilson:

> When we meet, he always takes my hand and says: 'You are my father, my father.' There is a tremendous affection and respect between us. Where does it come from? God knows. [...] Recently, he told me about the start of his career: as a young man he had been taken to Europe. He was not really planning to make theatre. They took him to a performance. Which? The premiere of my production of *The Marriage of Figaro* in Versailles. He was totally excited when he saw the show: 'It cannot be true: how is he making that night, with the moon, is it there or is it not there, that sunrise in the room? Where did that light come from? How wonderful it is!' [...] From that day on he began to feel the pleasure of making theatre, and to recreate not what he had seen, but the feeling he had experienced, and to transfer it to his world which is very different from mine, but that has strange correspondences – points of contact that are hard to define and that I and he understand are borrowed from my practice, even if they are applied to other things: the use of light, certain forms of effects, the precision, the atmosphere. A testimony of the mystique of the handover of the baton from one artist to another.[41]

The passing of time (Strehler's *Figaro* premiered in March 1973) has slightly blurred the chronology relative to the career of Robert Wilson who at the time was already an emerging director with international acclaim. But there is a deeper truth in this anecdotal account, which is further unpacked in the introduction to that 1997 book, written by none other than Robert Wilson himself.[42] He takes his cue from a Strehler quotation: 'I am convinced that there is a mystical connection between Stanislavski, Meyerhold, Copeau,

Brecht and Chaplin.' Wilson defines this connection as the architecture of space and light – as the absolute point of departure for Strehler's work. He continues to recall his experience of *The Marriage of Figaro* in Versailles as an outstanding artistic experience, especially the light. 'Light is like an actor,' he states, describing visual architecture as a means of communication:

> Without light, no space. Without space, no time. Space and time coexist. For me, time is a vertical line that rises towards the sky and moves down into the earth. Space is a horizontal line. It is this intersection between time and space that makes up the architecture of all things: this is how you stand on the stage, play Mozart on the piano, sing, talk.[43]

Referring to John Cage (1912–92), he continues, talking about musicality as the guiding principle in the theatre. The greater the space that surrounds a tone – or text – the greater the weight it receives. We are in a continuum, according to Cage: there is constant music. Speech is a continuation of a line that was already there before the speech; when the speech ceases, the line continues. Everything is music. In a similar way, dancer Martha Graham (1894–1991) states that movement is there all the time. Immobility potentiates the experience of movement. When the gesture ceases, the movement continues. Wilson now transfers these considerations to Strehler and to his own work. He outlines two spaces: one filled with lines, the other with a single small line:

> The line in space two will always be bigger than in space one: there is more space around it. We often think when we are working in an opera house or in a theatre that we have to do big things. But paradoxically, one small thing can be bigger [...] the same thing goes for texts and music and gesture or whatever, as already said, it is the space around that makes it important, that highlights it [...] we are speaking here of real space, but also of mental and virtual space.[44]

Mental and virtual space is created by the actor who lets the audience come to her or him, leaving audience members space to participate in the stage work:

> Strehler knows this when he does theatre. I saw his *Don Giovanni* at La Scala [1987/8], and I found it such a thing of beauty, precisely because of this freedom that was afforded me, the spectator, to enter this mental space of my own accord; there was no bullying, no insistence to extort my attention. I admired Strehler for this, and I was able to feel an active participant in the process, but on my terms.[45]

Wilson develops this reflection by remarking that the urge to make theatre is related to a need to ask questions in dialogue with the audience: 'What is it? What do I say? What do I do? What does it mean?'[46] The space around the word and the sound, the movement's continuation in immobility, make up, he suggests, the interface between him and Strehler. What counts is the thread that runs through the director's work:

> a thread that keeps it all together: one idea, one visual way – theatre may wish to say a million things, but it must first and foremost intend to say one thing. If it does not intend to say one single thing, sooner or later it will fall apart and crumble to pieces – this continued thread that does not have beginning or end, but it always is there.[47]

It is interesting to see Wilson, the icon of visual theatre, celebrating Strehler, the stage director who called Stanislavski, Brecht and Copeau his teachers. This is also an indication that the cliché of both of them – as conceptualist vs. interpreter-directors – does not hold completely. Wilson is not just inaccessible; Strehler was not just straightforward. Wilson's highly controlled *mises en scène*, with his use of a shining backdrop and combinations of intensity and coolness, point to some significant similarities, not least in terms of their references to the aesthetics of the 1920s avant-garde, including Brecht. Unlike Wilson, Strehler, however, did not primarily pursue the era's stylized Expressionism, although it does occur in his work. Elsewhere in the 1997 publication, the director Stefano de Luca put it like this: 'Wilson and Strehler use the complete opposite techniques to achieve the same result, *a state of presence*.'[48] It is true and, at the same time, not quite true. It goes back to the number of Chinese boxes involved. The difference is about degrees of narrative complexity. Strehler thought out of three boxes, whereas Wilson tends to focus more on one. In his *Threepenny Opera* (Berliner Ensemble, 2007) for instance, Wilson quotes Strehler's illuminated wheels in a purely abstract context. Even his characters may recall Strehler's, albeit in an extremely stylized version.

Strehler had perfect pitch. He must have had a perfect eye, too, so his special talents went beyond mere musicality. The tension between semantics and aesthetics, the narrator and the conductor, the story and the music, created a constant urge in Strehler. De Luca offered further reflections concerning Strehler's

> very concrete intuition for what many oriental philosophies talk about [...] that *life* is rhythm, switching between light and shadow, the colour scale from cold to warm, light to dark. That *breath* is rhythm, that speech, the *word*, consists of rhythms. In this Strehler, who is a split man, is in harmony with the laws that regulate the life of things. In harmony in a mystical way. [...] Strehler is perhaps afraid of this, his ego is too strong, so he fights *against* it; his ideology prevents him from looking positively at this area. A man such as Peter Brook, for example, has managed to lead a more conscious 'spiritual' exploration into his theatre work. Strehler has

> not been able, or wanted to, permit himself that type of investigation: there is a void to be filled. *All* artists feel an urge to search for something they did not know, and beneath that operation there is always a deficiency, a void. The vacuum of a propulsion that forces them to seek what fills it.[49]

That Strehler denied the mystical aspects to his work does not mean they were not there, for instance in the third Chinese box. However, Strehler's main concern was to narrate, to communicate, to address time – the period in which the drama text was written and his own:

> My destiny is to narrate. To tell stories. I tell them from a wooden stage using people, objects and light. If there were no stage, I would tell them on the ground, in a square, in the street, at a corner, on a balcony, behind a window. If there were no people with me I would tell them with pieces of wood, rags, shreds of paper, tin, anything in the world. If there were nothing, I would tell them in a loud voice, and had I no voice, then with my hands, with my fingers. Had I no hands and fingers, then with the rest of my body. I would tell them silent, motionless [...] Do you not understand that the details do not matter? That the expression is only a transition, a thing, an excuse to talk to others about what is inside you? You talk about theatre, film and so on. To sit on a chair suspended on a cord twenty meters above a square, is also a way of telling what you can, alone, up there in your chair. Tell everyone that you exist, that you will not fall, that you can fall and do not fall, that you are afraid, but do not show it, and a thousand other things. Do you not understand it? You have never understood anything. The point is that it is not about being understood anymore. It is enough to be heard.[50]

Fifteen years later, Strehler elaborated his last comment in this long quotation: 'the problem is to tell our stories without telling too much'.[51] This last phrase contains a key to his artistic strategy: leaving out certain components which it is left to the audience to fill in, using an open and complex parabolic form, rather than counting on a clash between the text and staging. This makes his stagings appear organic and as interpretations of the text. But, as a matter of fact, this is an illusion. They were greatly conceptualized. But focus was not on the concept as such. So he was not a conceptualist; but neither was he an interpreter. The Chinese boxes implied a way of reading the text and a formula for the actors' complex communication with the audience. Regardless of the different phases and focuses in Strehler's career, this meticulous strategy – inspired by Brecht's weighting of contextualization in the dramaturgical preparations, expanded by Strehler to incorporate a psychological and a metaphorical level – dominated his production processes.[52] His fundamental urge, however, lay in the basic necessity to narrate. In the end, that is what made Strehler's theatre epic, in all senses of the word.

4

A Theatre of/for Europe: Giorgio Strehler and the Dream of a United Continent

Margherita Laera

> It is my firm belief that until a possible European unification places cultural events, art and cultural heritage at the top of the agenda for its construction, it will be destined to fail, even though it may succeed in constituting itself in some other form.[1]

To be writing about the dream of a united Europe today – particularly of the Europe that Giorgio Strehler had hoped would become united in the name of socialism, humanism and a common cultural heritage – is an ironic and somewhat uncomfortable task. From the current historical perspective in the mid-2010s, when the refugee crisis has unleashed the most unhuman and anti-communitarian side of the European Union (EU), when disaffection with the transnational political machine has become endemic in every corner of the Old Continent and when a neo-liberal agenda seems to have irrevocably prevailed in Brussels and Strasbourg, all hope of the outcome imagined by the Italian theatre director for the European project seems lost. Nonetheless, a reassessment of Strehler's thinking and legacy appears remarkably timely and necessary. On 23 June 2016, the British people voted to leave the European Union, in what was largely seen as a protest vote against immigration and the EU's policy on free movement of people and labour. It was a vote that, as studies have found, highlighted deep-rooted social divisions in British society and pushed the majority of marginalized, low-income voters – traditionally Labour's main constituents – to be persuaded by the Leave campaign's divisive rhetoric and its nostalgia for the country's 'lost sovereignty'.[2] The voting breakdown also demonstrated a marked division between younger voters who wanted to remain and older ones who chose to leave.[3] In the weeks and months immediately after the vote, a sharp rise in xenophobia and hate crimes was reported by Scotland Yard. In other parts of Europe such as France, Italy, Greece and the Netherlands, far-right, anti-establishment and anti-EU forces are on the rise.

What can we learn about our current situation from Strehler's vision for the future of Europe? And what do Strehler's words mean to us today, as the European project seems to be on the verge of collapse? How can we judge his legacy and ethics from our current perspective without falling into historical anachronism? This chapter examines the work of Giorgio Strehler as a director, artistic director, ideologue and politician from his theatrical beginnings in the 1940s to his death in 1997, fifty years after he founded the Piccolo Teatro in Milan. The study will focus not so much on Strehler's stage aesthetics, which are the subject of the previous chapter in this collection, written by Bent Holm, and much celebratory scholarship in Italian, but on his ideas and political engagement through programming, organizing, writing, parliamentary activities and cultural leadership.[4] I investigate the historical and social context in which Strehler operated, assessing his conception of theatre as a political battleground and nourishment for the (European) soul, and his efforts to put into practice his utopian dream of a unified Europe based not simply on free markets and consumerism, but on a rich cultural heritage and the values of 'poetry' and 'beauty'. Strehler's project for a 'humanist' Europe characterized by transnational 'fraternity' – and theatre's role in co-constructing it – will be dissected here in all its problematic yet still remarkably relevant purport. This chapter also offers a critique of Strehler's legacy: I ask what remains of Strehler's dreams in a European context hit by the most profound crisis since the Second World War, and where Strehler's own pioneering efforts to manufacture what I call a 'theatre of/for Europe' through dialogue and cultural exchange have ended up, in some cases, feeding the market-oriented machine of the European festival circuit as a new transnational establishment. Is it fair to argue that his project for furthering transnational cooperation has been co-opted by a neo-liberal logic? If so, what can be done to reclaim its focus on community and fraternity?

The chapter is divided into two main sections: in the first part, I provide a brief summary, periodization and contextualization of Strehler's work, mainly in Italy and France, concerning his ideas around theatre in Europe. In the second part, I examine some of Strehler's writings and speeches from the 1940s to the 1990s concerning theatre and Europe, positioning his thoughts within a constellation of philosophical discourses. I then investigate what is left of his teachings and ideas today: in particular, I reflect on the role that the practice of international co-productions has today in relation to cultural integration in Europe.

A battle on multiple fronts: Strehler's European work

Giorgio Strehler's work began as a vocation to 'Europeanize' Italian theatre, mainly by promoting the figure of the theatre director and the model of a state-sponsored, resident art theatre, both derived from European, particularly French and German, models. It evolved into a mission to 'transnationalize' theatres in Europe through his leadership of the Paris Odéon-Théâtre de l'Europe and the Union des Théâtres de l'Europe.[5] A faith in the European dream of togetherness despite differences characterizes his long and productive career, and almost every choice he made in the various roles he covered, from theatre programmer to director, from translator to writer, politician, organizer, magazine editor and campaigner can be seen to contribute to building that dream through theatre. Strehler's conception of theatre as the most 'human' and collaborative of art forms makes it in his view the optimal catalyst and paradigm for European integration and cooperation.[6] What emerges from assessing Strehler's multiple activities is a battle on multiple fronts to create not only a theatre *of* Europe – that is, a theatre that would display a European identity and explore a European heritage – but above all a theatre *for* Europe: a theatre that would actively build much-needed relations, cooperation and mutual understanding among European peoples. A theatre that would strive for, and begin to shape, European cultural integration.[7]

Strehler was born in 1921 in the culturally diverse town of Trieste into a distinctively multilingual and multicultural family (see also Bent Holm's preceding chapter for further biographical context).[8] Writing about how this multicultural family set-up impacted on his understanding of European politics, Strehler remarked, as he stood for the Socialist Party at the first European Elections in 1979:

> I really do not know [...] how much I can call my own personal culture Italian, Mediterranean, how much Middle-European, French, Slavonic, I do not even know, sometimes, how to distinguish the borders of these human and cultural lines that are intertwined in me.
>
> Of course, I belong to a 'naturally' European family, I was born at the crossroads of Europe, in Trieste, where Slavonic, Austro-German and Italian cultures blended and contrasted with one another in search of a new dimension and shared identity.[9]

It is important to situate Strehler in the specific historical context of Italian theatre at the time, so that his successful efforts to implement European experimentation in Italy can be seen to emerge out of an expedient social and political milieu, rather than appear as a single-handed feat springing out of a desert, which is what much celebratory scholarship around Strehler suggests. In his essay 'Il tramonto del grande attore' (The twilight of the star actor) (1929), D'Amico diagnosed that the reason why the Italian theatre scene had been lagging behind its European neighbours was that Italy lacked its own 'Antoine, Stanislavski Reinhardt or Copeau, a man capable of reforming our staging technique according to the needs of our time and country, like the abovementioned have done for their own [...] If that *maestro* does not appear, our theatre is doomed'.[10] Strehler may have been that 'maestro' so intensely longed for by D'Amico, but what is sure is that Strehler operated in a social, economic and political context that was ripe for change.

As Bent Holm has already outlined in the previous chapter, Strehler, graduating in 1940 from the Milanese Accademia dei Filodrammatici with a degree in acting, soon became disillusioned with the unrefined aesthetics of the distinctively national tradition of the star actor and the touring *compagnie*. In an interview with theatre critic Ugo Ronfani, Strehler depicted Italian theatre of the early 1940s in derogatory terms:

> I found myself living through the end of the glorious Italian tradition of making theatre (*teatro all'italiana*). It was quite a dishonourable end: what remained of that tradition had evolved either into 'sitting room comedy' (*commedia da salotto*) – which had more in common with French *boulevard* than with Pirandello – or into the theatre of the [fascist] regime.[11]

At the time of Mussolini's fascist regime (1922–45), traditional forms such as the masked comedy and dialect theatre had been suppressed as irreverent and contrary to the regime's strategies of homogenization and centralization. The repertoires of the touring companies had been forced to become inward-looking and provincial, focusing mainly on national writers, some of whom were active supporters of Mussolini – for example, Guido Cantini Teodosio Copalozza, Aldo De Benedetti, Gherardo Gherardi, Sergio Pugliese and Vincenzo Tieri – with a penchant for light entertainment, bourgeois family values or propagandist themes about war, patriotism and colonialism.[12] Before the fascist period, French authors had dominated Italian stages, but after 1922, importing foreign dramaturgy was actively discouraged by censorship, though classics such as Alexandre Dumas and Molière were of course present. During the 1930s, the fascist government began forcefully to regulate the theatre industry, not least by trying to influence artistic output and to promote large-scale open-air performances for the masses (*teatro di massa*).[13] The scarce funding distributed by the regime was channelled towards loyalists.[14]

Ever since the Futurists had proposed their theatrical manifestos in the 1910s, promoting a kind of fragmented, anti-intellectual and anti-realist entertainment, their enthusiasm had not been followed through with sustained stage innovation, and the avant-garde theatre scene in Italy had stalled. Moreover, the Italian stage had been cut off from the development of modern Western theatre. While during the first half of the twentieth century the figure of the theatre director had already become established in Central Europe – most notably through the work of André Antoine, Max Reinhardt, Vsevolod Meyerhold, Jacques Copeau and Erwin Piscator **[see Volumes 1–4]** – these new developments had not reached Italy. A healthy commercial scene focused mainly on the genres of comedy and drama in Italian, dialect theatre in regional languages, and opera; the latter generated by far the highest income. Until the early 1930s, stage arts relied entirely on private enterprise, touring companies and star performers whose declamatory delivery and textual semi-improvisation challenged the role of the playwright and excluded that of the director. Calls for modernization were frequent and loud, and the intellectual debate in specialized publications was lively,[15] but a combination of factors such as the rootedness of the old system, the scarcity of state funding, the economic precariousness in the 1920s and the growing competition from cinema meant that the Italian 'anomaly' dragged on until after the end of the Second World War. Ronfani argues that, 'in Italy at the time, the ineffective theatre policies of Giolitti [the long-serving liberal Prime Minister of the pre-fascist era] and Fascism, the average ideology of official culture and the authority of traditional actors made the relationship between our national scene and European theatre an anomaly'.[16]

Despite this inauspicious background, some innovators were active during the fascist period. Anton Giulio Bragaglia, a visual artist influenced by the Futurists, had founded the company Teatro Sperimentale degli Indipendenti (1922–36). Partly funded by the regime after the new state support system was inaugurated in the 1930s, Bragaglia introduced avant-garde authors such as Maurice Maeterlinck, August Strindberg, Eugene O'Neill, Frank Wedekind and even Bertolt Brecht to Italian audiences, directing productions himself and theorizing the role of the *regista*, the theatre director.[17] Simultaneously, Pirandello's experiments, especially with his company Teatro d'Arte in Rome (1924–8), saw the role of the *capocomico* timidly mutate into that of a de facto director.[18] Pirandello devised bold spatial and staging choices to match his meta-theatrical plays – for example, *Sei personaggi in cerca d'autore* (*Six Characters in Search of an Author*, 1921) – though he never actively theorized the shift to director's theatre, concentrating his campaigning instead on the need to establish quality art theatre repertoires in Italian stage venues and to offer stable, decent standards of living for performers. The most influential reformer of all was theatre scholar and pedagogue Silvio D'Amico, a close collaborator of the Ministry for Public Education – which at the time had jurisdiction over theatre – despite not being a fascist himself. In 1936, D'Amico left his office as government advisor to take up the position of Head of the Regia Scuola di recitazione in Rome (Royal Drama Academy), later to be named after him. In this role, D'Amico set out to shape the next generation of performers, who would be attuned to the sort of acting work undertaken under the guidance of a theatre director.

During the 1930s, the fascist regime opted for a more sustained involvement in the theatrical sector: first, in 1930, the Corporazione dello spettacolo, an organization that was partly a union and partly a government-run regulatory body, was created; in 1931, a tight system of censorship was introduced; then in 1935, the Ispettorato generale del teatro was established with the task of regulating repertoires and issuing funding, falling short of creating fully state-run venues.[19] This inaugurated an age of state intervention in the theatre industry, with considerable impact on the system that had thus far been left in the hands of private initiative. This paved the way for more intervention by the state after the fall of the regime. When Italy was liberated from fascism in 1945 and the war ended, the political and ideological climate shifted completely. A republic from 1946, Italy was on its knees but optimism was on the rise as the ensuing 'economic miracle' saw a period of remarkably strong economic growth. Therefore, the post-war generation was left with plenty to investigate, update, invent or reinvent, not least their own roots. Years later, Strehler described them as a 'generazione senza maestri' (generation without teachers).[20] Elsewhere, Strehler described Italian theatre of the early 1940s:

> Italian theatre was historically and humanly backward by at least fifty years. There were dreadful gaps. Those gaps were the spaces we occupied, with the intention, of course, of changing the world. Because, at the age of twenty, one wants to change the world.[21]

While the pioneering aspect of Strehler's activities and the influence of his work on Italian theatre is undeniable, our consideration of the historical context suggests that, building on the work of innovators such as Pirandello, Bragaglia and D'Amico, Strehler perhaps rather filled a leadership vacuum in the post-war economic boom period. He was the right man in the right place at the right time.

In 1947, Strehler and Grassi opened their Piccolo Teatro with *L'albergo dei poveri*, after Gorki's *На дне* (*Lower Depths*), which Strehler translated, adapted and directed himself. Later in the season, the Piccolo presented productions of plays by Salacrou, Calderón de la Barca, Pirandello, Carlo Goldoni and Alexander Ostrovsky, all staged with a semi-permanent ensemble directed by Strehler. This was certainly a revolutionary concept for a country such as Italy, and the Piccolo must be credited for leading the transformation of the entire national theatre system towards a more 'European' kind of practice (one characterized by a directorial aesthetics and funded by the state), which also incidentally significantly improved performers' working conditions. The Piccolo's overtly social and democratic mission, its exclusive dedication to directorial theatre and to building a stable ensemble, and its outward-looking programming choices were groundbreaking for Italy in the 1940s and 1950s. No such large-scale, consistent project had been attempted before in the country, and it was soon emulated, between 1950 and 1965, by other state-funded resident theatres in other major cities, such as Genoa, Turin, Trieste, Rome, and Palermo.

The manifesto for the new Piccolo wished to offer a programme of high-quality productions at reduced prices, rejecting both light entertainment and elitist experimentalism, construing theatre as a place where the community comes together to know itself and to accept or reject the behaviours it sees on stage.[22] Grassi and Strehler were named joint artistic directors, and the board of governors included local politicians from across the political spectrum. This management structure meant that elected public officials with little experience or knowledge of theatre would be able to influence decision-making at the Piccolo, something which Strehler found particularly detrimental to his artistic practice and freedom, especially in later decades.

Strehler's directorial style, known as 'symbolic realism', was based on the supremacy of the text and understood the director not as an artist in his own right but as an interpreter of the play.[23] Sustained by close readings of the script and prolonged ensemble work, Strehler's theatre was a 'poor theatre', in that it was based largely on in-depth work with actors and a simple set. Strehler's signature style combined the teachings of Copeau and Louis Jouvet on rigorous actor-training, a bare stage and 'authenticity' of delivery (that is, more naturalistic, less mannered and declamatory), with Bertolt Brecht's emphasis on the political, ethical and social role of theatre [**see Volume 2**]. As Strehler elaborated in an essay entitled 'I miei maestri' (My teachers), he considered these three practitioners as crucial in his personal and artistic development. From Copeau, Strehler wrote, he learned to understand the theatre as a kind of 'religion' prompting 'absolute devotion', despite not being a believer in God.[24] From Jouvet's work, he came to understand theatre as a profession to be practised day in day out in order to get better and better at it, while the actor should become a transient servant of eternal 'poetry', that is, dramatic literature.[25] From Brecht, Strehler absorbed a conception of theatre as a 'human' art, an art that is never disjoined from its historical, political and social context and that should never be practised for its own sake but instead to 'help [spectators] to make the world a better place'.[26] Strehler's faith in theatre's ability to mobilize spectators and achieve concrete political objectives – such as European unification – can be understood as the most significant aspect of Brecht's legacy on the Milanese director.

In the twenty theatre seasons that followed, Grassi and Strehler programmed a balanced selection of both 'classic' and contemporary texts by national, European and American writers who were often previously untranslated into Italian, such as Albert Camus, Ferdinand Bruckner, Jean-

FIGURE 4.1 *Giorgio Strehler in 1956, rehearsing Brecht's* The Threepenny Opera *with his Piccolo Teatro ensemble (Courtesy of Archivio Piccolo Teatro di Milano – Teatro d'Europa).*

Paul Sartre, Brecht, Friedrich Dürrenmatt, Anton Chekhov and Federico García Lorca. The Piccolo's 1947 manifesto was clear about the need to internationalize the repertoire:

> There is no need to claim a nationalist character for this theatre [...] Even if we are going to resort to words first spoken elsewhere to other peoples, we will realize the universally human traits that are revealed in them, while finding ourselves in the condition and situation of being Italian. We will not renounce the universal richness of men's words: we

> will only translate it for ourselves and communicate it among us. For this reason we will ask the translator to be an interpreter, almost a second author, poet added upon poet.[27]

Strehler's open and ongoing interest in translated plays was not only the result of what he perceived as a lack of high-quality contemporary Italian playwriting but it formed part of his internationalization plan, rooted in ideas of 'universality'. Between 1948 and 1968, creative fervour and enthusiasm meant that an average of ten plays were mounted each year at the Piccolo. The output was matched by a steady audience attendance, so much so that expansion plans were beginning to take form (though the funding for two new venues only materialized much later). National, European and intercontinental tours of the Piccolo ensemble already began the year after it was founded. By 1967, more than 4,300 performances of Strehler productions had been seen in 142 Italian venues and 116 foreign cities.[28]

While Strehler had first imagined that the Piccolo's relationship with its audiences would be open, dialogic and fresh, over the years it became far more institutionalized. Despite the theatre setting out to found a truly democratic art theatre for all, and practising a policy of subsidized theatre tickets, its audiences were mainly made up of the Milanese bourgeoisie who could afford a sustained engagement with the venue. Gradually, Strehler began to perceive the institutional dimension of the Piccolo and political interference as a weight on his artistic choices, which forced him to produce too many shows without allowing time for research and failure. Strehler's relationship with Grassi – who also pushed for a higher number of shows than Strehler would have wanted – began to deteriorate. Meanwhile, the political climate of the late 1960s saw a renewed hostility towards the role of the director, who was accused by anti-bourgeois ideologues of being the tyrant of the stage and colluding with the upper classes by furthering a hierarchical power structure.[29] In 1968, Strehler therefore handed in his resignation following a small student protest outside the Piccolo which accused him of authoritarianism and elitism. Strehler did not quit because of this demonstration, as has often been claimed,[30] but because he did not want his aesthetic choices to continue to be subjected to the will of Grassi and the board. Following his resignation, he founded the collective Teatro e Azione, supposedly bringing politically engaged theatre to factories and theatres around the country but actually performing mostly in conventional theatre venues. This experience drew to a close four years later when Grassi left the Piccolo to head Milan's opera house, La Scala. Strehler was then asked to return as sole director, which he did with a renewed sense of resolve and European impulse, implementing a plan to allow more experimentation, and to train new generations of theatre-makers. Shortly after his appointment, he set out the new strategy as follows:

> I thought of something more than a theatre that puts on shows night after night. I thought – with that element of dream and utopia that concretely underpins everyday action – of a *Theatre City* in the heart of Milan. And I thought of it for Milan but also for Europe: that Europe that is having so much trouble being born, but of which we detect the signs, and which in the fields of art and culture is a truer and more operative reality than in the field of politics. [...] In these coming years [...] a great *Theatre City* will begin its activities, a City that wants to be the heart of a *Theatre of Europe* in the heart of Milan.
>
> It will be a manifold organism, articulated over two theatres. The first is the Teatro Fossati, rebuilt within its perimeters, its volumes, its spirit, and dedicated to research; therefore, if you understand what I mean, we will be allowed to 'error'. Inside it – as I have said before – there will be a national and European drama school for actors, which will not of course solve all the problems for new generations, but will be a point of reference and development for 'modern' actors and actresses [...]
>
> Alongside this place – which I call a 'carte blanche' for theatrical research and the school – another theatre is being built [...] I think of it as a great European theatre, where different texts belonging to different ages and countries would be staged, where European directors could find an organized, human, protected space that would be devoted to realizing theatrical events under the guiding lights of invention and poetry.[31]

In the late 1970s and 1980s, as the European unification project gathered pace, Strehler's European work intensified with new commitments at the European Parliament in Strasbourg and at the Odéon theatre in Paris, and with his new productions in France, Germany and Austria.

As the task of 'Europeanizing' Italian theatre practice could be seen to have been accomplished by the late 1970s, Strehler therefore moved to a different objective: that of 'transnationalizing' European theatre. He stood for the Socialist Party in the European Parliamentary elections in 1979, but was only elected in 1982 and served for just over a year until the end of the first legislature. During his election campaign, Strehler declared that, 'In a possible future Europe, where little, too little, if anything, has been so far discussed about culture, my candidacy wants to represent [...] the idea of a community of culture over that of economy, rooted in shared ideas, brains, common cultural operations.'[32] His speeches in Strasbourg argued for a union based on a shared European cultural heritage. Strehler fought to give a voice to the arts sector in the new political project at a time when European institutions did not have a legal mandate for cultural affairs. His proposed plans for the arts in Europe, such as funding for transnational cooperation in cultural activities, were visionary for his time and were implemented in later years, after the Maastricht Agreement was signed in 1992.[33]

His vision for European collaboration in the theatre sector became more concrete in 1983, when France's Socialist Culture Secretary Jack Lang – who had met and worked with Strehler at the European Parliament – named him artistic director of the Odéon-Théâtre de l'Europe in Paris, a position that Strehler held for six years. The Théâtre de l'Europe, which shared the building with the Théâtre National de l'Odéon, was so baptized in order to sanction its mission to become the first truly European theatre – not just a hosting venue for ready-made productions from the Continent but a factory for theatrical creativity that was actively to promote 'collaboration among European theatre directors, actors, writers and other theatre-makers, with a view to creating new works and to enlivening Europe's dramatic heritage'.[34] For the Odéon's first season, Strehler proposed a selection of European classics in a variety of languages: Shakespeare's *La Tampesta* (*The Tempest*) in Italian, co-produced by the Odéon and the Piccolo and directed by the 'maestro' himself; Ramón del Valle Inclán's *Luces de Bohemia* (*Lights of Bohemia*) in Spanish, co-produced by the Odéon and Madrid's Centro Dramático Nacional, directed by the Catalan Lluís Pasqual; Corneille's *L'Illusion Comique* (renamed *L'Illusion*), produced by the Odéon and directed by Strehler in French; and Heinrich von Kleist's *Hermannsschlacht* (*Herman's Battle*) in German, produced by the Schauspielhaus Bochum and directed by Claus Peymann. In the programme notes introducing the 1983/84 season, Strehler hailed the new theatre as 'a step towards human knowledge [*connaissance des hommes*]' and characterized European identity as 'multiple, complex, contradictory [...] but recognizable as a red thread that weaves our history'.[35] He explained that the Odéon's mission would develop into several strands of activities:

> production of works that constitute European cultural heritage, coproduction of theatrical events with European organizations and institutions, performances in different languages (played by actors and directed by directors of international merit), research of links between different cultures and different theatre experiences, presentation *in* Europe of works produced by the Théâtre de l'Europe and creation of the 'company of the Théâtre de l'Europe'.[36]

The following seasons at the Odéon continued on the same track, with a blend of visiting productions and new commissions: in 1984, Strindberg's *Temporale* (*The Storm*) visited from the Piccolo in Milan; Dostoevsky's *The Possessed*, directed by the Russian Yuri Lyubimov in English, was co-produced by the Odéon, London's Almeida and the Piccolo; and Shakespeare's *Kung Lear* (*King Lear*), directed by Ingmar Bergman in Swedish, toured to Paris from Stockholm's Dramatiska Teatern. Under Strehler's directorship, the Odéon hosted visiting productions from Munich, London, Catania in Sicily, Milan, Moscow, Budapest, Madrid, Berlin and Lisbon in the respective languages. Plays presented in the Odéon's small venue comprised French translations of texts by Nâzim Hikmet (from Turkish), Lars Norén (Swedish), Alfred Döblin (German), Edvard Radzinski (Russian), and Krzysztof Zanussi and Edward Zebrowski (Polish). Notable international co-productions were Brecht's *L'Opéra de quat'sous* (*Die Drei Groschen-Oper/Threepenny Opera*), directed in French by Strehler with an international cast from France, Italy, Germany and Austria (with the Châtelet Theatre in Paris), and Pirandello's *Come tu mi vuoi* (*As You Desire Me*) in Italian (with the Piccolo and Madrid's Centro Dramático Nacional), again directed by Strehler with actors from Italy, France, Spain, Germany and the UK. Strehler described his work with international actors as 'at the same time human, symbolic and political [...] Not a point of arrival, but of departure.'[37] Working with international casts was a key aspect of Strehler's brand of a theatre *for* Europe, symbolically embodying the ideal of solidarity and cooperation among Europeans.

When considering Strehler's programming choices for the Parisian venue, it is important to mention that, in the 1980s, mechanisms of international collaboration and co-production were well established in the film industry but were not so frequent in the theatre sector,[38] despite having emerged as a practice in the 1960s.[39] Thirty years later, co-productions have become the norm and are part of the sector's survival strategy against a lack of funding and competition from other art forms. As Steve Wilmer has argued in his study of Western European national theatres, venues 'have become more transnational in their approaches in the late twentieth and early twenty-first centuries',[40] and international networks of European theatres have favoured co-productions from this period onwards. Back in 1984, when the practice of co-productions was still infrequent, Strehler remarked that, 'with our work we try to create a true circuit of European theatre arts which will have to grow and confirm itself in the future if the powers, the will and the means are up to the task'.[41] This is what happened when funding for international cultural collaborations within Europe was established a decade later. It could, therefore, be argued that the model of international co-productions proposed by Strehler at the Odéon provided a paradigm for what was later to become European cultural policy through its various programmes, such as Kaleidoscope 2000 (1995), Culture 2000 (1999) and more recently Creative Europe (2014). They promote 'bottom-up' cooperation for cultural events organized by partners in at least three member states. Strehler also envisioned what was later to become one of the pillars of European cultural funding, that of support for literary translation from and into European languages, listing it as one of the top priorities for a European cultural policy:

> I believe that one of the most fertile endeavours that could be undertaken under the banner of a communitarian cultural organism would be that of stimulating editions of works by authors from different nations in different languages on the basis of a complex programme that would take into account the gaps, the lacunae, of reciprocal differences. It is about

> planning a corpus of performable dramatic works, accurately translated into European languages, and presenting them to those responsible for different European theatres so that they might become part of their repertories.[42]

In the 1980s, Strehler was acutely aware that what he was doing at a cultural level was in many ways pioneering. In the programme note for the 1984/5 Odéon season, Strehler acknowledged that many Europeans were not 'ready' for what he was doing, but that it was still his duty to 'further the feeling of fraternity and unity' and help define the future of Europe through theatre:

> The Europe of politics still needs to be built. The Europe of culture, which is already a reality in its own right [...] demands new efforts and methods, for which many people are not yet ready, in order to blossom with the force of beauty and poetry. But this is precisely our duty ... the duty of those of us who 'make theatre', who witness the miracle of an art performed by human beings who are different, speak different languages, but who are tied by the same feeling of fraternity and unity in a world still too divided and solitary.
>
> To our audience, we ask nothing more than what it has already given us: presence, love, curiosity and perseverance in its will to be the protagonist of a fascinating adventure that is about to trace the profile of our continent's future.[43]

What is striking in this passage is Strehler's vision of theatre as the driving force for social and political change. Here, he communicates his belief that theatre is not simply commenting on the status quo but that it is doing 'social work' and influencing the political future of an entire continent. From 1987, when Jack Lang and Strehler created the Union des Théâtres de l'Europe (UTE) and Strehler became its first director, the 'maestro's' vision for the transnationalization of the theatre system in Europe entered a new and more effective phase.[44] The UTE, which is still an active organization today, was established to promote a network of producing theatre venues characterized by strong local traditions and international aspirations. The three founding members – the Odéon, the Piccolo and Madrid's Centro Dramático – were joined by twelve other members by 1995, including the Maly Teatr in St Petersburg, the Berliner Ensemble, the Royal Shakespeare Company and London's Royal National Theatre.[45] The primary aims of this new organism were to promote 'an Art Theatre that would oppose any commercialization of the theatrical event, seen as an instrument of both poetry and fraternity among peoples' and to devise a common policy that would encourage 'regular exchanges of European authors, actors, set designers and directors, overcoming any language barriers and concretely sharing different experiences and methodologies' through 'productions and co-productions'.[46] An annual festival hosted by one of the partners and a quarterly magazine called *Théâtre en Europe* (Theatre in Europe), initially edited by Strehler in French and Italian, were further initiatives conceived to strengthen the ties and opportunities for dialogue between the different institutions and their audiences. When Strehler died suddenly in 1997, having been at the helm of the UTE for ten years and at the Piccolo for fifty years, he left behind a remarkable legacy in both Italian and European theatre and culture.

For a 'common humanity': Strehler's European ideology and legacy

Strehler's career shows how his vision of theatre as an agent of social and political change developed into what we might see as his distinctive cultural strategy for European unification and integration. But what conceptions of identity, aesthetics and politics underpinned his European ideology? In assessing Strehler's legacy, one might rightfully ask whether his art, and particularly his transnational 'theatre of/for Europe', was more revolutionary or else more reactionary in nature. Did it serve the powers that be or did it struggle against them? At the beginning of his career, Strehler's efforts to break fascism's narrow-minded nationalism and bring Italy's theatre practices up to speed with European developments appeared groundbreaking and truly progressive. But later on, from the 1970s onwards, Strehler struggled to update his rhetoric, aesthetics and cultural references, remaining stuck in an essentialist Modernism, so to speak, which may provoke ambivalent feelings today. In this section, through a series of close readings, I shall assess more specifically what Strehler understood 'Europe' to be – a subject that previous scholarship on the 'maestro', most of which is in Italian, has so far omitted.[47]

In the following key passage, taken from an article first published in 1979, Strehler places what he terms a 'humanist ideal' (*ideale umanistico*) at the core of 'European identity':

> the idea of 'Europe' is for me an idea of Man [*sic*] before the creation of a system of government and of a more or less pacific association of interests: [...] this idea of the European man is born out of common heritage, of great shared themes that tie us together even beyond what is conscious and most definitely beyond our differences in language and customs.
>
> There is a humanist ideal that is tenaciously rooted in the heart of all of Europe, there is a theme that unites the different cultures of Europe in the name of those that made men modern, and this 'figured bass' [*basso continuo*] is at the same time national and European. Perhaps more European than national, such is the number of reciprocal exchanges, that

> it seems to me that we cannot exist within the circle of our own specific cultures without one another.
>
> Along the course of a history of 'European homicides' we have not only exchanged blood but also ideas, thoughts and art, words and images, in other words life and culture. We have made each other what we are today.[48]

Here, Strehler argues that all Europeans have common roots and that, culturally speaking, they belong to the same extended family – so much so that, using a musical metaphor, he likens European cultures to orchestra instruments that play a 'basso continuo', that is, a bass line providing the harmonic structure for a piece of music. In other words, European cultures are like different instruments that play to the same musical score. It is crucial to our investigation to begin to untangle what Strehler actually referred to by such nebulous phrases as an 'idea of Man', a 'common heritage' and 'humanist ideal' in his attempt to define European identity.

In philosophical terms, Strehler seems to posit here an 'essence' of 'European man', and to equate that 'essence' with a 'humanist ideal'. However, 'humanism' is an ambiguous philosophical term that is difficult to define. John C. Luik has argued that humanism's successive incarnations and definitions in history mean that it can now be thought of as a series of concentric circles, with the early modern notion of *studia humanitatis* – an educational programme that includes Greek and Latin 'classics' – at its heart, and Enlightenment humanism as the second circle.[49] Enlightenment humanism, in its most basic shape, makes ontological, ethical, educational, epistemological and political claims all centring on the core belief that human reason is the essence of 'man' – more precisely, an emancipatory essence – positing history as a progressive course towards realizing human reason's full potential. According to Luik, at the basis of humanism is a 'commitment to the perspective, interests and centrality of human persons', but 'to be helpful, a definition of humanism must be as much alive to what it excludes as to what it includes'.[50] In this sense, it may be useful to define Strehler's brand of humanism by considering how 1970s philosophers who called themselves 'anti-humanists' defined humanism itself. Louis Althusser, who was the first to coin the term 'anti-humanism', saw Marx's philosophy as progressively breaking away from humanism (the belief that history was tantamount to 'the unfolding of human essence') and Hegel's essentialism to anti-humanism, i.e. the view that 'history [is] a process without a subject'.[51] Later, the term 'anti-humanism' was appropriated by post-structuralists such as Michel Foucault, Jacques Derrida and Gilles Deleuze. Specifically, these thinkers attacked Enlightenment-derived humanism for its belief in the 'subject as a unified and sovereign entity',[52] and rejected the very notion of 'essence' as relative and historically, socially and culturally determined.

My assumption is that Strehler subscribed to the modernist current of thinking that was later to be rejected by post-structuralists and postmodernists such as Foucault, Derrida, Deleuze, Hélène Cixous and Judith Butler. In analysing his speeches, what seems evident is that the lineage of Strehler's beliefs with regard to 'Europeanness' can be traced back to Enlightenment humanism, and to Hegelian and Husserlian reinterpretations of it. Both Hegel, in his *Lectures on the History of Philosophy* (1819), and Edmund Husserl, in his 'Vienna Lecture' from 1935, discussed the 'essence' of the European 'man' as deriving from ancient Greek philosophy and went so far as to make claims about the superiority of Europeans over non-Europeans. While Strehler never made similar remarks, an element of essentialism undeniably permeates his thinking on Europe, and his vision of European unification as progress points to a sense of historical teleology. While he rejects essentialism at national level, he reinstates it at transnational level, unwittingly excluding 'non-Europeans' in his attempt to be more 'inclusive' and 'open'. Strehler understood 'Europeanness' as an autonomous entity and one absolutely distinct from, say, 'Asianness' or 'Africanness'. In Strehler's idea of European identity, there is little, if any, acknowledgement of the histories of colonialism, diasporas, migration and the porosity of European cultural borders in what was, by the late 1970s, already a multicultural continent with a shared past and inextricable cultural, economic and political ties with the rest of the world. Strehler's theatrical investigations and programming, albeit progressive and pioneering, focused on a kind of European culture and repertoire that, from a contemporary perspective, appears insular and autocratic – an accusation that Strehler himself had levelled at the fascist-approved repertoire in 1930s Italy.

A European 'common heritage', then, includes precisely the kind of texts Strehler staged over the course of his career – a mix of canonical and contemporary plays by European authors, including Russian writers, who were among Strehler's favourites, and some (white) North-Americans such as Wilder and O'Neill. By 'common heritage', then, Strehler refers to 'classics' that notoriously exclude women and 'foreign' authors, and forms of writing that rejected the traditional understanding of character and plot. By the 1960s, and particularly after Strehler returned to the Piccolo from his four-year break in the 1970s, the cultural climate had changed significantly. Challenges to the Western literary canon had become more widespread through the development of feminist, Marxist, post-structuralist and postcolonial literary critique (a group later dubbed 'the School of Resentment' by Harold Bloom in his 1994 book *The Western Canon*), and a growing number of theatre-makers realized the importance of acknowledging, legitimizing and engaging with non-Western cultures, notably Peter Brook and Ariane Mnouchkine [see **Volumes 5 and 7**].[53] Meanwhile, the 'idea of Man' postulated in Strehler's speeches and in the plays staged in his theatres continued generally to be that of a Western, white, male, straight and middle-class human being. While we must credit Strehler with being an innovator, the 'revolutionary' purport of his work does not lie in pushing the boundaries of Western thinking about subjectivity and identity – in fact, in this regard, Strehler's work can arguably be seen as fairly conservative.[54]

Creativity's role is, for Strehler, to unite 'our divided continent' by means of its ability to articulate Europe's distinctive and unified identity:

> That which united, that which will truly unite Europe will be above all love, understanding, the ability not to reassemble the fragments of an exploded culture, but to highlight more clearly and more courageously a culture that despite it all managed not to explode into pieces and to determine the distinctive character of our divided continent: this ability is that of creativity [...]
>
> Having said this, I want to say that if I think about a basic European culture, a culture that is everyday, real, sometimes hidden and sometimes evident, I think that there is a European culture that everyone dreams of (every intellectual, every worker and every man [*sic*] of good will), but that at the same time is almost denied and sometimes furiously prohibited by institutions. At best, culture is ignored.[55]

Strehler's faith in culture's power to generate social consensus, and his belief that culture's mission was precisely that of manufacturing agreement among what was already an essentially like-minded set of people, appears today as one of the most problematic aspects of his thinking. Inspired by Gramsci, Strehler imagined a European culture not for the few but for 'everyone', affordable and relevant to all – and yet we have seen how that 'everyone' was fairly restrictive and based on a normative understanding of subjectivity and an essentialist vision of identity. Strehler's outspoken desire for his work, and culture in general, to speak to 'everyone' also appears problematic because it suggests an understanding of democracy as the space of consensus rather than disagreement and contestation. Despite its self-declared openness and progressive objectives, Strehler's project identified the artist's task as that of enabling harmony, rather than celebrating difference, or problematizing 'common sense'. As a universalizing, harmonizing apparatus, culture and the arts – and theatre as a consequence – are tasked with 'catalogu[ing] all that exists and interpret[ing] it through the light of Tomorrow', as Strehler has it:

> I dream as a man of culture and a man of theatre (this simple and complex art that more than any other is made with others for others) of a Europe where culture and theatre would not be a privilege for the few but where authentically interdisciplinary cultural centres would be born, where propulsive cultural pivots would be able to catalogue all that exists [*l'Esistente*], but also able to interpret it through the light of Tomorrow. I dream – to give a few examples – of a Beaubourg that is not frigid, of a Biennale that is not disintegrating, and of a Kassel that is

> not autocratic. I think of a living European culture, a modern one that is affordable to all, and meets everyone's needs, in its most authentic Gramscian acceptation.[56]

Strehler's vision of culture as a unifying, universalizing device that produces 'happiness for all' can appear a deeply flawed attempt to normalize, standardize and exclude difference.

But as the world around the 'maestro' changed, he did not shift his beliefs to suit it. It is symptomatic that in 1968 student protesters chose to march to the Piccolo to point their finger against Strehler, singling him out as a symbol of authoritarianism and oppression, and his theatre as the bulwark of the bourgeoisie:

> The protest taught me a terrible lesson: one morning I found myself standing on the Right, perceived as retrograde by many, while the night before I thought I was on the Left and at the avant-garde. And I did not understand how such a transformation could have happened in twenty-four hours. And why.[57]

Finding himself thus on the 'wrong' side of history, his subsequent work to bring theatre to the factories with the collective Teatro e Azione almost appears as an act of apology and atonement. But as Renato Palazzi has argued, Strehler's four years away from the Piccolo never really marked a shift in his approach to theatre; his faith in the model of a state-funded public resident theatre and his less-than-collaborative creative processes remained largely unshaken – and as a result he fell back into his old habits.[58]

And yet, we dismiss his insistence on the need to use theatre politically to further kinship and solidarity among different cultures at our own peril. It is important to remember that the dream of European unity, that Strehler so passionately subscribed to, was the brainchild of a generation that had just resurfaced from the trauma of war and that had seen their lives wrecked by fascism, racism and unspeakable violence (see the Introduction to this volume). Despite Strehler's relative ethnocentrism and blindness vis-à-vis Europe's debt towards its former colonies and the rest of the world, his investment in a unified Europe as an instrument to further understanding among different peoples represents a crucial development in the history of the Continent, and it would be a mistake simply to dismiss it. While the notion of 'universality' has received thorough scrutiny and much-needed criticism in the past forty years, especially by post-structuralist and post-modern thinkers, the value of an ideal such as kinship among the peoples of Europe must return to the top of our agendas. As the European political climate has shifted again towards intolerance and hatred in the aftermath of the 2008 financial crisis, which unleashed nationalist, intolerant and xenophobic forces on the European political stage, might today be the moment to reassess our mistrust towards notions such as 'humanity' and 'universality'?

Strehler was drawn to exploring European 'humanity' through the lens of theatre-making. For instance, a reflection on the theme of 'illusion' or 'stagecraft' as metaphors for the human condition can be found in his celebrated productions of *The Tempest* (1948, 1978, 1983), in which the director identifies himself with the magician Prospero; in Pirandello's *I giganti della montagna* (*The Mountain Giants*, 1947, 1966, 1993), where the downfall of the actor troupe is a reflection on the condition of the artist in modern times; in Corneille's *L'Illusion* (1983), where the protagonist, the magician Alcandre, allows Strehler to explore the illusory nature of theatre and life; and in *Elvira, o la passione teatrale* (Elvira, or the Theatrical Passion) (1985, 1996), based on the writings of Louis Jouvet, a production which investigates the labour and backstage workings of performance-making and training as a metaphor of earthly existence. Strehler was more frequently attracted to plays that explored a psychological approach to character-building and human subjectivity, and only marginally drawn to his contemporary anti-realist, 'anti-humanist' and 'Absurdist' theatre, such as the work of Samuel Beckett and Jean Genet, by whom he only staged *Giorni felici* (*Happy Days*) in 1982, and *Il Balcone* (*The Balcony*) in 1976, respectively.[59] And yet the 'maestro' believed in the absolute value and power of 'poetry' – by which Strehler meant dramatic literature – whatever its focus, to further solidarity among different people and to heighten spectators' perception of themselves through sharing the live and collaborative experience of making or watching theatre.

In Strehler's writings and speeches, there is a clear yet under-theorized link between what audiences and theatre-makers do in the theatre and what they are then imagined to do and become in everyday life as a result of watching theatre. An almost Schillerian belief that a direct link between the experience of 'beauty' through 'poetry' in the theatre trickles down to other aspects of sociality outside the regime of art underpins all of Strehler's political campaigning and European engagement.[60] According to Strehler, an act of 'harmonization' between the performance and its audience is key to creating a 'collective fact' and turning spectators into a 'counter-chorus', that is, a collective entity that 'recognizes itself through theatre'.[61] If the theatre does not respond to the profound everyday concerns of ordinary people, then the power Strehler accorded to theatre – its ability effectively to shape more humane and intellectually open (European) citizens – will be less productive. Theatre, in Strehler's view, plays a crucial part in fostering a sense of community and shared humanity among people precisely because it is an essentially collaborative art 'that more than any other is made with others for others'.[62] A theatre director's mission is, therefore, that of turning silent spectators into a 'participating chorus' that gets to be 'one' with the performance, and in so doing 'transforming a simple numerical multiple into a collectivity'.[63]

In this sense, Strehler put his theatre at the service of European cultural and political unification on the basis of our common heritage despite differences. His support for the dream of a united continent was wholehearted, despite his dissatisfaction with what he saw as a disappointing beginning, dominated exclusively by discussions about markets, currencies and economic policy. He saw European unification as an unstoppable historical process and his own role in it as a kind of catalyst against conservative nationalist forces which were, in his view, rowing against history's flow. He considered it a duty of every person of culture to work for a (leftist) project for Europe that would prevail over capitalism and consumerism. Strehler's theatre, from the 1970s onwards, existed to make the project of a culturally united Europe possible – whether or not this coincided with the actual political machinery – by persuading theatre-going Europeans to subscribe to it. His insistence on the need to transnationalize European theatre must be read in this context as his attempt to 'change the world', demanding that the values of a pan-European project be adopted by every venue, artist, critic and theatre-goer. In the following passage, part of a speech delivered to an audience of theatre critics, he puts forward the image of the city-hopping theatre critic/ideal theatre spectator, whose job would be to communicate theatre being produced in every corner of Europe to his/her fellow national citizen:

> we need others to understand that theatre locked up in a single town or state is also finished. That the once-cherished concept of stability needs to be defended, but only *vis-à-vis* Europe, if not the world.
>
> Many times I have asked myself what made me, at a not so young age, what made me, tired theatre-maker that I am, tie certain knots with the world, found Theatres of Europe, travel here and there – me, the world's worst traveller?
>
> It was reality, history if you wish, that made me do it; it was the feeling of a reality in the making. And so for you there no longer is, there can no longer be the famous front row seat [...] But there can only be a jet, an aeroplane, a train. Mobility, that is. Today mobility is your front row seat [...] We need to tell others that we need to exchange our experiences more, attend more shows that deserve to be seen at least in the four corners of Europe.[64]

For Strehler, clearly Europe has become the limit. Cultural integration – which does not equate with standardization or the obliteration of local cultures, but with a celebration of their similarity within difference – should be pursued as the only possible basis for political and economic integration. In his parliamentary work as an MEP for the Socialist Party (1982–3) and, later, as an Italian Senator for the Independent Left party (1987–92), he never tired of lamenting how politics seemed to ignore culture, when in fact culture was the key to achieving the political goal of uniting the Continent.

If we really wanted to integrate Europe, the entire, still nationally-organized, European theatre system needed to reflect the paradigm shift to a transnational model, to what I have called a 'theatre of/for Europe': from funding to producing, from translation to criticism, from casting to touring, from programming to theatre-going practices and beyond.

Returning to the question I asked at the beginning of this section, we might wonder whether Strehler's theatre served the powers that be or strived for a revolutionary future. While Strehler had always distanced himself from the aesthetics of Italian anti-bourgeois, avant-garde theatre of the 1960s and 1970s, which he deemed too remote from everyday life and unable to connect with non-specialist audiences, he did construe his own theatre as 'revolutionary'. In 1967, as the Italian experimental scene – including Dario Fo, Leo de Berardinis and Carmelo Bene – met at a landmark conference in Ivrea, near Turin, and signed a manifesto entitled 'For a New Theatre', Strehler was the most noteworthy absentee, and for many he embodied the opposite of what 'New Theatre' stood for – a collaborative, proletarian, revolutionary practice that would bring about the fall of bourgeois society. From the height of his position of power as the artistic director of a state-sponsored theatre, who shared board meetings with elected local politicians, Strehler was not welcome in Ivrea, and certainly could not afford such subversive positions and class struggle rhetoric. Instead, Strehler always fought against what he perceived as the failures of the 'system' from within it, choosing dialogue and action over the antagonism and utopia of his less compromising colleagues in the 'experimental', anti-bourgeois camp. Writing in the 1990s, Strehler defended the 'revolutionary' significance of his theatre by placing it in direct opposition to the 'industrial scientific-technological system' (of capitalism), which in his view had led to a collective 'inability to access the notion of sublime':

> Caught between the messages of mass media, the isolation and disintegration of human beings, and the industrial scientific-technological system in which only the product is destined to become 'real', audiences look for oblivion, they seek to forget, not recognize themselves. Hypnosis is their everyday gesture. Now theatre, in its most truthful acceptation, is precisely the opposite of this. Theatre is a physical and psychic conflict-happening, and as such it demands our complete and active participation, which is therefore creative. It follows that theatre today is not in crisis or in decline [...] but that it is ever more an instrument of truth and opposition, a 'revolutionary' instrument in the sense that aesthetic and collective education through theatre seeks to recompose harmony and unity in the individual, who is pushed almost to dissolution and irresponsibility.[65]

In this Adornian reading of the culture and media industry, Strehler put forward his educational vision of theatre as a place for unlearning what the 'system' wishes us to learn, its commodity fetishism and alienation from our true selves.[66] Theatre's role, then, is that of reconnecting the fragmented twentieth-century individual to his/her humanity. With his engagement in Strasbourg and more generally with his cultural leadership, Strehler delivered a very simple message to the European Parliament: the European superstate must attend to the well-being of its citizens by sponsoring, organizing and intervening in the cultural sector, thus counteracting the alienating effect of our 'dehumanizing society'. Caring for people's 'happiness' was, for Strehler, a 'fundamental political gesture':

> Therefore a man [*sic*] of art, a normal thinking man, is entitled to intervene in this context, has the categorical duty to be there to struggle. To struggle because in a dehumanized and dehumanizing society like ours, discourses like these risk being understood as jest, an intellectual's jest. But I think that we need to tell *politics* that to think of man's happiness is a *fundamental political gesture*, that inventing places and modes to make people be together so that they can get to know and understand one another is a *fundamental* political gesture.
>
> I believe, for instance, that it is beautiful to be European, that it is right to feel proud of being a people not only of one country, but of a continent.[67]

Strehler's words here – as progressive as they may have been in the late 1970s – are easily subsumed by the cynical logic of 'happiness management' and the instrumentalization of culture by the powers that be. While Strehler fought for state and European sponsoring of culture in a world where such notion was not common practice, from our perspective in the twenty-first century, one can see how state or transnational cultural funding may become a means to manufacture social consensus, effectively neutralizing art's potential as a critical, subversive, non-aligned practice. From this perspective, Strehler's 'revolutionary' project could be seen to have been hijacked by the logic of capitalism.

Strehler's engagement in shaping European cultural policy permeated his very conception of the role of the director. His loud cries for more cultural funding at a transnational level were partially met by the establishment of European cultural funding programmes in the 1990s; however, the general trend at national level in many European countries from the 1980s onwards was precisely the opposite. Cuts to cultural budgets became the new neo-liberal common sense. Reflecting on the state of disarray in which Europe finds itself today, Strehler's words once again offer food for thought. Strehler wrote:

> It is my firm belief that until a possible European unification places cultural events, art and cultural heritage at the top of the agenda for its

construction, it will be destined to fail, even though it may succeed in constituting itself in some form.[68]

From the perspective of 2016, when this article is being written and European unification – political, cultural, economic, monetary and otherwise – appears an improbable feat, Strehler's vision resonates most strongly and prompts further reflection. Given the widespread and steady rise of anti-EU sentiments across European countries, we must ask: has European cultural policy failed for not securing a substantial enough budget and not being able to fill the gaps left by national governments, or is it the case that funding a continent's way to cultural integration through the arts is a flawed undertaking altogether? Scholars of cultural and European studies have highlighted how early European cultural policy and surrounding debates – polarized between those who favoured an approach promoting a pan-European culture and those who championed a regionalist agenda – were 'inadequate to the complexity of what Europe had actually become', blind as they were towards the impact of migration from other continents.[69] Strehler clearly stood in the pan-European camp: highlighting the 'great shared themes' and the 'humanist ideal', which he argued underpinned all European heritage, were among his priorities, but for him that never meant suppressing regional differences. Despite being a critic of many early decisions taken in Brussels and Strasbourg, Strehler never stopped considering his own 'Europeanness' as an imperative for supporting the cultural, political and economic unification project. But it is important that we are able to distinguish between 'feeling European' and subscribing to the European Union and its policies in their current shape.

Perhaps the lesson to be learnt from the current failures and shortcomings in European cultural policy, inasmuch as they partially reflect Strehler's thinking that funding culture transnationally would bring about a closer union, is that theatre's ability to offer critical paradigms for imagining subjective and social identity must never be confused with more 'ambitious' and problematic missions such as that of manufacturing political agreement and social consensus in a continent divided by competing national narratives, different histories and a rich multiplicity of attitudes towards being in the world. Perhaps that is asking too much of the theatre – or too little. Perhaps that is the wrong way of conceiving the political potential of theatre altogether. Theatre's political work is unpredictable because it depends on the spectators' 'unscriptable' response to an unforeseeable and unique performance event. As performance scholar Joe Kelleher has argued, theatre can be thought of as a faulty 'signalling machine' that is

prone sometimes to breakdown and irrelevance and miscommunication, not necessarily *doing* politics in any obvious way but bringing to the attention of us, its participants – actors and spectators all – the fact that some 'thing', some familiar stranger, is making an appearance here tonight and has a claim to make upon us.[70]

It may indeed be that the real political potential of theatre lies in that level of uncertainty, indeterminacy and unpredictability embedded in the live encounter of spectators and performers. The efficacy of any given piece of theatre's political message cannot be relied upon to lead the masses but it will act as an 'irritant' that gets 'under the skin' of audiences, if they are receptive to the ethical call before them.[71]

The most prominent aspect of Strehler's legacy is, however, the undeniably greater level of interconnectedness of the European theatre circuit since the 1980s through the practice of co-productions and exchange between venues and international festivals. Since the UTE was founded and the European Union started funding cultural activities in the 1990s, the number of inter-European partnerships has grown exponentially, now comprising collaborations such as the New European Theatre Action (NETA), the Prospero Network, Mitos21 and the International Young Makers in Action, to name but a few.[72] In an interview with Thomas Ostermeier on theatre, Europe and exchange between cultures carried out in 2007, the German director pointed to European networks of co-productions between theatres as a model for the future of the Schaubühne theatre in Berlin, mentioning Strehler and Lang as the first proponents of such a model.[73] Ostermeier's nod to Strehler's work in establishing closer networks among European theatres and theatre-makers is significant as it suggests how the 'maestro's' vision has influenced contemporary theatre-makers around Europe, beyond Italy and France. It would be misleading to suggest that Strehler was responsible for these developments that coincide with much larger factors such as the establishment of the single market and the rise of the neo-liberal economic paradigm, but he was certainly a catalyst in establishing the practice of co-producing theatre in Europe in order to ease internal distribution and tours.[74]

Greater collaboration between theatre institutions, such as venues and festivals, has in turn contributed to the creation of pan-European theatre 'products' and a certain international aesthetics that dominate the Continental theatre circuit, with a number of 'usual suspects' – currently artists such as Jan Fabre, Romeo Castellucci, Rimini Protokoll, Angélica Liddell and many others – travelling internally within Europe to perform at virtually all major venues and festivals, and intercontinentally as European export products. The relative ease with which some co-productions need to travel and 'translate' to culturally diverse audiences has in turn had an impact on the aesthetics and stage languages that some artists adopt in their 'ready-to-tour' creations, for instance introducing constraints such as limiting the number of performers or the kind of set that can be created, and limiting the use of text, which relies on sur-titling. According to the

French critic Jean-Pierre Han, theatre festivals have become like risk-averse 'supermarkets' that push a form of '"supranational" official art' based on an aesthetic that is 'accessible, conventional and identifiable'. This, according to Han, is currently a particularly established and recognizable brand which is positioned between the 'chic' and the 'shocking', and effectively erases cultural differences in favour of homogeneity and conformity to current market taste.[75] While not every European festival can be accused of contributing to the 'normalization of taste', and not every European theatre artist has been affected by this phenomenon equally, paradoxically, some of the mechanisms that Strehler adopted to establish European theatre circuits in order to further the values of 'poetry' and 'humanism', ended up feeding the process of marketization that has enveloped all aspects of public and private life with the neo-liberal turn. In other words, one could argue that Strehler's project for a 'humane' Europe driven by socialist ideals of solidarity and cooperation through shared cultural heritage has been in some cases appropriated and co-opted by a neo-liberal agenda. An urgent question, then, is how (and whether) theatre-makers and programmers may be able to disentangle the ideals of cooperation across national borders from neo-liberal market forces.

Roger Planchon

5

'Theatre's Beauty is its Death': Reflections on Working with Roger Planchon

Michel Bataillon

Translated by Clare Finburgh Delijani

> Theatre's beauty is its death. This is an idea that nobody is willing to accept, but that I hold very dear. You make something, and it disappears. I've always found that very elegant ...
>
> I dream of a theatre that would have no memory; I'd almost be inclined to say that we should burn everything ... leave nothing, even if this exasperates the professors of theatre history.[1]

Roger Planchon died in Paris on 12 May 2009, just after having finished a reading of his last play, *Sade, diptyque* (Sade, Diptych) that he left in draft form. Already, collective forgetting is conspiring to realize Planchon's dream of a theatre without memory. What remains of the hundred or so productions that he either conceived, wrote, staged or performed between 1949 and 2009 in his home city of Lyon, then in neighbouring Villeurbanne, and later on tour throughout the whole of France, through Europe and indeed the world, other than isolated moments, fixed in the memories of a couple of thousand ageing audience members by the phrase, 'I remember'?[2] 'I remember the fake paunch Jean Bouise wore when he played Falstaff in 19..'[3]

There are no recordings of Planchon's productions. Or almost none at least. Filming theatre is a fairly recent development that was formerly very costly, and that a production budget couldn't stretch to. Above all, Planchon refused to fix the flow of theatre, which he felt was intrinsically ephemeral, and which he wanted to maintain as ephemeral. He believed firmly that the playtext, the stage production and cinema were three distinct artistic languages. As I have already stated, he refused to allow his productions to be filmed. He never invested any money or time in the conservation of what, for him, was an ephemeral art. However, he was always open to the idea of adapting them for the screen but only managed to find the funds for this once, in 1988, in the case of Molière's *George Dandin*.

Photographs of his productions always disappointed Planchon. Paradoxically, however, for five decades the very best photographers were given access to his rehearsals and to productions of his shows: René Basset, Claude Bricage, Antoine Demilly, Brigitte and Marc Enguerand, Étienne Georges, Rajak Ohanian, Roger Pic, Jean-Marc Martin du Theil, Nicolas Treatt and others. Planchon admired their photographs and wrote cogently and touchingly on images taken, for example, by Demilly, Basset and Ohanian. I remember talking to Planchon about a couple of photographs of his two stagings of Molière's *Tartuffe* (1962 and 1972). He had chosen the images and recorded comments on them for educational use in schools. The combination of the images and recorded text that accompanied the slides was wonderful. He admired photography as an art in its own right without, however, trusting it to transmit the art of theatre. However, without the hundreds of images, prints and negatives preserved, notably at the Live Performance (Arts du spectacle) Department of the Bibliothèque Nationale de France (French National Library) and in private archives, it would be even harder to imagine and to understand why, for several decades during the second half of the twentieth century, Roger Planchon was the most important stage director in France.

Planchon found sound and video recordings even more pernicious than photos. He was quick to quote his own example, which referred to Gérard Philipe. How could a recording of Gérard Philipe's voice enable listeners to appreciate the charm of his presence in the courtyard of the Palais des Papes at the Avignon Theatre Festival in the role of Prinz Friedrich Arthur von Homburg in Kleist's *The Prince of Homburg* (1952) or Lorenzaccio in Musset's play of that name (1953)?[4] And yet Planchon himself got the Théâtre de la Cité de Villeurbanne to produce 12-inch vinyl recordings of extracts from his company's two major successes, his own adaptation of Alexandre Dumas's *Les Trois Mousquetaires* (*The Three Musketeers*, 1959) and Bertolt Brecht's *Schweyk dans la deuxième guerre mondiale* (Schweyk in the Second World War, 1961), where one can hear him actually haranguing audience members! This is a precious document that enables us to see what a superb ensemble director he already was as early as in 1960 (evident in the illustrations in the following essay).

Equally precious, or even more so, are two 'clandestine' recordings that were unearthed in the Falkoner Center sound archive fifty years after they had been forgotten about. Unbeknownst to the Théâtre de la Cité company, on 25, 26 and 27 April 1966 the sound technicians of this theatre in Copenhagen produced an excellent audio recording of the whole of *The Three Musketeers* and Molière's *Tartuffe* which were on an international tour in Scandinavia. Recently, the archival footage of these two productions was uploaded onto YouTube.[5] They are two key productions in terms of the Théâtre de la Cité de Villeurbanne's repertoire and Roger Planchon's own theatrical art. They differ radically from one another but both made him famous in France, in Europe and across the world, from New York to Tokyo. With them he invented a comic form that transcended class, cultural and linguistic barriers, and immediately reached out to audiences. And, by abandoning a fossilized academic approach to the dramatic text, Planchon brought to life the plays of classic authors such as Marivaux, Molière and Racine. Planchon read yesterday's and today's theatre for his contemporaries – audiences from the second half of the twentieth century – by enlisting his own intellectual arsenal inspired by the great thinkers of his era: Marx, Freud, Barthes, Lefebvre, Foucault and Brecht.

The Three Musketeers was the culmination of the ten years that the company spent developing a new dramatic genre, one that instantly brought them fame. In 1949 Planchon and his gang of amateur actor friends delighted their audiences with absurd gags inspired by the American burlesque tradition of the Marx Brothers and Buster Keaton, and by French comics such as the nineteenth-century humourist Alphonse Allais, the early twentieth-century poets André Frédérique and Jacques Prévert, the comic actor Jacques Tati and of course the Paris-based Romanian playwright Eugène Ionesco. They loved the Branquignols and the Frères Jacques, who dominated the cabaret scene.[6] The adventures of popular theatre heroes such as Cartouche, Rocambole and Casque d'Or formed the basis of their group improvisations.[7] In 1958 their theatrical form had matured. *The Three Musketeers* was the first masterpiece of their burlesque genre that the adjective 'wacky' (*loufoque*) can accurately be used to describe. They deployed an explosion of comedy to narrate Alexandre Dumas's serious affairs of state. Their most famous gag was the literal acting-out of the everyday phrase 'Go suck an egg!' (*Va te faire cuire un œuf!*). Ten years later, Planchon and his actors used the same dramatic format so that Pierre Corneille's *Le Cid* (1969) could be used to reflect on the May 1968 mass demonstrations and strikes.

During the 1950s Planchon explored other dramaturgical avenues which involved staging both playwrights from the past – Marlowe and Shakespeare, Lenz and Kleist – and above all, modern playwrights – Roger Vitrac, Arthur Adamov, Ionesco, Michel Vinaver and, notably, Brecht. When he was a teenager, the experience of reading Antonin Artaud's poetry had moved Planchon to the point where he deliberately turned away from it. But he never forgot how near to the abyss Artaud had stepped, nor the irrefutable poetry of that man's work. At twenty, the discovery of Brecht the playwright, but more so Brecht and his company the Berliner Ensemble as theatrical creators of stage poems [see **Volume 2**], nourished Planchon's reflections and decisions to such an extent that by 1960 he was considered France's first Brechtian director. Over the course of the 1950s times were changing, theatre was evolving, and Planchon was at the epicentre of these developments. He was fortunate enough to see the last embers of the Cartel.[8] Jacques Copeau and Charles Dullin died in the autumn of 1949, Louis Jouvet in 1951, Gaston Baty in 1952. When Jean Vilar created the Avignon Theatre Festival in 1947 and in 1951 took over the artistic directorship of the Théâtre National Populaire (TNP) at the Palais de Chaillot in Paris, he introduced a new model for theatrical institutions by demonstrating how theatre that was accessible to many people could be made both in Paris and outside the metropolitan centre (see the introduction to this volume). In addition, he enriched the repertoire of the arts theatre that had been founded by his predecessors; and he developed a stage art that was stripped back and at the same time generous and majestic, and, therefore, fit for the solemnity of the courtyard at the Palais des Papes at the Avignon Festival and also for the vast dimensions of the stage and auditorium at the Palais de Chaillot.

Quite naturally, Planchon and his company were inspired by Vilar's exemplary, innovative projects, that sought to create popular theatre for everyone, and that were also committed to decentralization. In the few photos that remain of Planchon's open-air production of *La Nuit des rois* (*Twelfth Night*, 1951) staged in the parc de la Tête d'Or in central Lyon, the style of the Avignon Festival is clear. In parallel, the permanent space that Planchon and his ensemble built with their own hands in the centre of Lyon, and that they named Théâtre de la Comédie, contained a stage and auditorium the size of a handkerchief. From 1953, with plays by Adamov, Ferenc Molnár and Kleist, they looked for a focused stage art that would turn its back on the attractive and decorative minimalist aesthetic that characterized their epoch. Despite their stage and auditorium being very cramped, they looked to attract an audience that was not acquainted with theatre or that was not interested in the touring productions from Paris. Thanks to the way in which the narrative was constructed, and how the mechanisms of the dramatic machine were overtly exposed, Planchon's production of Kleist's *La Cruche cassée* (The Broken Jug, 1954) appeared Brechtian before Planchon had even seen a Berliner Ensemble production with his own eyes, something he only did in 1955.

Among the directors who ensured Brecht's breakthrough on the French theatre scene in the 1950s – Jean-Marie Serreau, Jean Vilar and Jean Dasté – Roger Planchon, at only twenty-three years of age, was by far the youngest and the most ardent. He found in Brecht, in Brecht's plays, in his writings on the theatre and in the productions that Brecht presented at the Théâtre des Nations in Paris, answers to some of the questions that had been plaguing him for five years and also lines of enquiry that he would immediately take up in order to analyse texts, to work with actors, and to think about his relationship with his audiences and their social reality. However, since he was suspicious of the capacity of photographs to capture the spirit of a staging, he never followed the images and instructions set out in Brecht's *Modellbuch* to the letter. But the rigour and coherence with which Brecht conceived and realized his productions, suited Planchon. He rapidly became a brilliant dramaturg in the German sense of the term, in that he was careful to elucidate the narrative told by the dramaturg in the French sense of the term, namely the playwright. In other words, he took great pains to define for the audience the narrative he was presenting; and he took great pains to ensure that all of the arts that made up one of his stage productions converged and were placed under the service of the story being told.

In ways that appealed to Planchon, Brecht provided a solution to the apparent contradiction between literal realism in theatre and dramatic and stage poetry. He was fascinated by the manner in which Brecht took real human beings with their real acts and relationships, their real bodies, clothes and objects from their immediate and actual lives, and placed them in the theatrical frame. For a brief but decisive moment, the appeal that *Mother Courage, The Mother* and *The Caucasian Chalk Circle* had on Planchon, made him the most active of French Brechtians.

This was for a brief moment, simply because, very quickly, Brecht's dramatic works seemed to Planchon to be too complex, contradictory and, notably, to fly in the face of Brecht's own theoretical project. For example, Planchon felt that he would never solve the enigma of *The Good Person of Szechwan*, which eludes all logical reasoning. He was drawn more to the plays of Brecht's youth, where his ardour seems to be raw and not yet sublimated. The result of Planchon's attraction to Brecht's productions (rather than his plays) was that he developed a personal theatrical style in a highly productive collaboration with his friend, the painter René Allio, which began with Adamov's *Paolo Paoli* (1957) and ended with *Tartuffe*.

The only meeting and exchange of ideas between Brecht and Planchon took place in June 1955 in the dressing room of the Théâtre Sarah-Bernhardt in Paris. Planchon was showing Brecht photos of his production of *The Good Person of Szechwan* (1954; see Pia Kleber's chapter in this volume for an in-depth analysis), and Brecht was talking about Molière's *Dom Juan*. The nasty master character type was a subject of dramaturgical disagreement between the two because Brecht saw in Molière a critique of the aristocracy, whereas Planchon was interested in the progressive nature of the Libertine.[9] Brecht died too young to transcend the Marxist ideologies that dominated his thinking.

Later, Planchon combined his respect for Brecht's politics and aesthetics with the post-structuralist readings he conducted in the 1960s and his love of the surrealist poets, in order to avoid the dogmatism often associated with slavish Brechtianism. And so, in 1968 *George Dandin* was born. It contains everything that Planchon had learnt from Brecht's productions, and displays the special attention that Brecht paid to narrative thread and to gestures taken from everyday life. Indeed, Planchon talked of moments that he 'stole' from everyday life. In 1959, Planchon's production of Marivaux' *La Seconde Surprise de l'amour* (The Second Surprise of Love) broke with the tradition of *marivaudage*,[10] and even with the updated approach to Marivaux innovated by Jean-Louis Barrault and Madeleine Renaud [**see Volume 7**].[11] Planchon and his associate Allio read Molière and Marivaux through their *lecture* of Pierre Choderlos de Laclos and the Marquis de Sade. These two stages then led them to *Tartuffe*, their masterpiece of the 1960s. A clever architectural trick enabled audience members to feel as if they were infiltrating Orgon's house in the same way that Tartuffe does, and in the way that a worm eats into a piece of fruit. The stage space was at one and the same time intrinsically metaphorical and intrinsically literal. And within this space, the actors could play out the subtlest and strongest power dynamics that they had revealed in Molière's verses.

In 1963, just when *The Three Musketeers* and *Tartuffe* had become local, national and international hits, Jean Vilar gave up the artistic directorship of TNP and so gave up the stage of the Palais de Chaillot and all but stopped being a stage director in order to focus on managing the Avignon Theatre Festival. To this Festival, he invited Roger Planchon. Planchon was asked to direct *Richard III* for the festival (in 1966) and also to present his *George Dandin* and *Tartuffe* (in 1967) and *Bleus, Blancs, Rouges ou les Libertins* (Blues, Whites, Reds or the Libertines), his own play that spanned the period from the French Revolution in 1789 to its demise with the First Empire in 1800, which presented a couple of provincial heroes from that historical moment. The Théâtre de la Cité de Villeurbanne had thus become the most important producing house in France, and remained so until the 1970s, when it became the Théâtre National Populaire and was directed by Roger Planchon, who was joined by the rising star Patrice Chéreau.

6

Approaching Brecht – Documenting Planchon: Roger Planchon's Three Stagings of *The Good Person of Szechwan* (1954–8)

Pia Kleber

One of the defining challenges of Theatre and Performance Studies is bridging the gap between a work experienced in the present and its subsequent presence in scholarship. Necessarily, this challenge multiplies with time and can be further bolstered by an artist's stance on the nature of performance. Such is the case of Roger Planchon (1931–2009), who saw theatre productions as ephemeral and was 'opposed to theatre archives, to keeping photographs of performances'.[1] In this Planchon stands at cross-purposes with broader theatre and cultural discourse, since his work as a theatre director is significant both as a response to and a source of inspiration for other artists, and cannot but draw the interest of theatre scholars. This chapter aims to help those who are intrigued by his directorial work and, especially, by his engagement with Bertolt Brecht (1898–1956 [see **Volume 2**]), to reconstruct some elements of his three stagings of *Der gute Mensch von Sezuan* (*The Good Person of Szechwan*) and mark some paths of enquiry that remain open to future exploration.

I gathered much of the research presented here in the course of conversations and personal interviews that I had the privilege to hold with Planchon and his friends and colleagues during my own career as first a theatre costume designer, and now a theatre scholar.[2] I was guided by a general interest rather than the pursuit of a specific idea in my conversations with these artists, a reality that is reflected in the tone of this discussion. My aim here is to examine certain aspects of Planchon's evolving approach to Brecht, and in so doing to add to the scant documentation of his work. There is only one photograph and no surviving designs of Planchon's first *Szechwan* production, for instance, which makes these interviews (along with the photograph, one review article, and three press reviews) its only remaining evidence. And while there are more materials available for the subsequent productions, they too are hardly abundant. One reason for the sparse documentation is Planchon's already mentioned aversion to theatre documentation (see, too, Michel Bataillon's contribution to this volume), while another stems from the fact that Planchon's Théâtre de la Comédie was little known in France, even in Lyon, at the time. This deficiency of archives can partially explain the shortage of scholarly research into Planchon's early career. This is an issue worth addressing, however, for it is in those early stages that the seeds of his future as a director and playwright lie.

Of particular interest in the context of this discussion are Planchon's three stagings of Brecht's *Good Person of Szechwan*, which he directed for the first time in 1954 and, as was his practice, re-staged two more times, once more in 1954, and in 1958. An analysis of these three *mises en scène* will reveal the influences that Planchon was subject to during those years, including his deep roots in the French theatre tradition that he ostensibly rejected. Moreover, by tracing the changes in his presentation of *The Good Person of Szechwan* over the years, this analysis shows both the limits of his comprehension of Brecht's play at the time of the first production, and the ways in which Planchon's restagings allowed him to come ever closer to achieving a Brechtian *mise en scène*.

Planchon's beginnings

Roger Planchon was a voracious reader already as a teenager living in Lyon during the 1940s, as well as an enthusiast of both theatre and cinema, including American silent films. He was still able to see some of the theatre productions staged by the 'Cartel des Quatre', an association created in 1927 by four of the most prominent French directors of the 1930s and 1940s (Georges Pitoëff, Charles Dullin, Gaston Baty and Louis Jouvet). One common denominator of the French theatre style was the absolute authority of the written word, interpreted not by means of critical analysis but through feelings and intuitions, and guided by a desire to recreate the emotion and atmosphere intended by the author.[3] Opposed to naturalism, which aimed to create the perfect illusion of reality on stage, the Cartel's productions presented drama in a stylized manner. Although Planchon often rejected their aesthetics, he embraced their artistic courage and demanding repertoire: Shakespeare and the Elizabethans, Calderón and the Spanish golden age, and Molière. Meanwhile, and nearby, during the Festival d'Avignon, another prominent French theatre director and actor associated with the Théâtre National Populaire, Jean Vilar, excited a new generation of theatre goers (of which Planchon was a part) with his productions and performances of works by Georg Büchner, Pierre Corneille and Heinrich von Kleist (see also the introduction to this volume).

In 1950, the amateur theatre group that Planchon founded won a competition with a turn-of-the-century farce, turning professional overnight. Over the next three years, they moved from one improvised playing space to another, alternating their repertoire between Elizabethans, modern avant-garde and burlesque, while developing a style noted for the energy – if not precision – of the ensemble. Then, on 1 July 1954, at the same time as Brecht and the Berliner Ensemble (BE) gave their first guest performance of *Mutter Courage und ihre Kinder* (*Mother Courage and her Children*) in Paris, the Théâtre de la Comédie, as Planchon's group named itself, presented *The Good Person of Szechwan* for the first time at the casino Lyon-Charbonnières. Planchon was certainly aware of this guest performance, but the overlapping timetables made it impossible for him to see any of the Berliner productions. One year later, however, when the BE revisited Paris with Brecht's *Der kaukasische Kreidekreis* (*The Caucasian Chalk Circle*), Planchon interrupted his rehearsal of Calderón's *L'Alcade de Zalamea* (*The Mayor of Zalamea*) in order to see the performance and to meet Brecht himself:

> I introduced myself [...] with some photographs from our performance of *The Good Person of Szechwan* as my only recommendation. I spent five hours with him. He told me what he didn't like about our work and we talked about it. From this encounter, and from seeing the work of the Berliner Ensemble, I became convinced that the truth was *there*, and that one should not hesitate to copy it boldly.[4]

The photographs that Planchon showed Brecht were not of the first staging of *The Good Person* from July 1954, however. Aware that his first *mise en scène* was a complete failure, Planchon used the rest of that summer to study all the materials about Brecht available to him before starting again from the beginning. It was this completely new approach to the play, undertaken by the Théâtre de la Comédie in October 1954, that the photographs showed.

For all three of his productions, Planchon used Jeanne Stern's French translation of *The Good Person*, published in the literary journal *Botteghe Oscure* in 1950. Since the epilogue was missing in this translation, it was also absent in Planchon's first two productions; he did include it in his third staging, however, as is clear from its reviews. According to Planchon's own account, the only writings of Brecht that he had read before the summer of 1954 were an extract from *Das Badener Lehrstück vom Einverständnis* (*The Baden-Baden Lesson on Consent*) published in the journal *K* in 1949, three scenes from *Furcht und Elend des Dritten Reiches* (*Fear and Misery of the Third Reich*) published in 1939 by Pierre Abraham[5] and *The Good Person* in the literary journal *Botteghe Oscure*.

The first staging of *The Good Person of Szechwan*

In January 1954, Edouard Herriot, the then mayor of Lyon, invited Planchon to contribute to the drama programme of the Lyon-Charbonnières arts festival. Planchon's group decided to present two plays: Marlowe's *King Edward II* and Brecht's *Good Person*. They had to exchange their small Théâtre de la Comédie for a vast gambling casino, unequipped for theatrical productions. Short of money as usual, the company was forced to use everything available on site to construct the set. According to Planchon's own account, they erected a podium in the centre of the hall on table tops normally used in the restaurant and – using additional tables – built footbridges across the room, running through the audience, both to facilitate entrances and exits, and to establish 'a direct communication between the spectator and the performance'.[6] To maximize the close relationship with the spectator, Planchon and Pierre Doye, the designer of the show, built a set that enclosed the audience in another set of abstract, painted walls within the casino auditorium.

The only photograph from this production shows the first scene and gives a sense of the closeness of the audience to the stage (see Figure 6.1).[7] Shen Teh's tobacco shop is equipped with only the most important elements. The back wall is composed of two flats that differ in size and colour. A small shelf displays Shen Teh's tobacco goods. A wooden box that serves as a counter and the little stool on which Mrs. Shin sits, assign her to the background, creating room for the arrival of the elderly couple and their nephew. Interviews with members of the creative team reveal that each set was simply pushed aside for the mounting of the next scene. Isabelle Sadoyan, who made the costumes for this production, followed the tradition of the Cartel in using stylized, heightened and slightly exaggerated as opposed to strictly realistic designs. Even Planchon commented on this, noting: 'We staged the play using highly stylized costumes.'[8] Shen Teh (on the far left of the photograph) wore a kind of tunic over her trousers in order to facilitate her change into Shui Ta. The old couple's garments, in turn, belonged to a fairy-tale China or, as Sadoyan expressed it, 'a sort of China of the imagination, revisited by Bauhaus'.[9] Mrs. Shin's dress could have come from France in the 1950s. The nephew, seen from the back, wore a modern European overall. None of the actors wore masks since they were not trained to speak while wearing them.

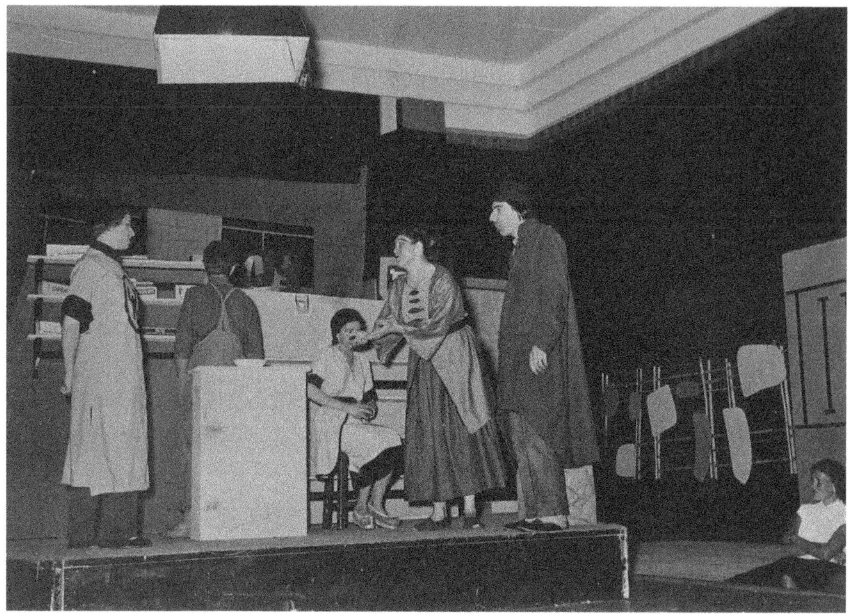

FIGURE 6.1 *The tobacco shop scene from Brecht's* The Good Person of Szechwan *in Roger Planchon's first production of 1954 (Photo: unknown/Personal collection Pia Kleber).*

Since there is so little available documentation of this staging, it is futile to comment now on either the acting or Planchon's blocking. At the time, all critics agreed on the professionalism of Catherine Sauvage's acting and singing (apparently without musical accompaniment), and the superiority of her portrayal of Shui Ta to her presentation of Shen Teh. Her voice evoked well the 'pathétique' (empathy), thus moving the audience and lending considerable 'warmth to the heartrending bitterness of the songs'.[10] These words of praise suggest a style of performance clearly not in harmony with Brecht's theory of acting. Since Catherine Sauvage was especially hired because she was a singer, Planchon assigned 'The Song of Green Cheese,' sung by Sun in Brecht's text, to Shen Teh. As a result, even this cynical song moved the spectators. This may well be one of the reasons why Max Schoendorff and Jacques Rosner thought that there was nothing worthwhile to be retained from this production.[11] This is counterintuitive, however, since this staging inaugurated Planchon's immense interest in Brecht. Moreover, this *mise en scène* tells us a lot about his closeness to the French tradition that he so often rejected.

As a young man of theatre, Planchon revolted against anything that adhered to tradition, the mediocrity of French theatre in general, and the aesthetics of the Cartel. None of the French theatrical groups addressed the major moral issues that arose in the aftermath of the Second World War, and from the seemingly endless wars that France waged with its colonies. It is not surprising that Planchon, with hardly any literary education, would be fascinated by the surrealist movement that originated in a counteraction to the cruelties of war. He was mesmerized by its search for a new form of life, one that was not rationally controlled by intellectual activity and which had nothing in common with the absurdity of life Planchon had experienced in the Second World War. He devoured the writings of the group whose central intention was to question radically not only reality but also all aesthetics. Planchon stated several times that the surrealist movement impacted him so deeply because he was exposed to their ideas at an early age: 'I soaked in the Surrealist texts when I was around 16 or 17. I read them like a mad man, very quickly.'[12] It was the surrealist movement that prepared Planchon well for the discovery of a man whose proclaimed goal was to overthrow all traditions and to change society: Bertolt Brecht. Despite their shared goals of breaking with tradition, changing society and renewing aesthetics, the fundamental intentions of the Surrealists and Brecht are, nevertheless, diametrically opposed. The Surrealists strove to destroy social fabric in order to discover a new set of values, those of the subconscious. They wanted to arrive at an intimation of a renewed consciousness, to develop a supplementary universe where the boundaries between reality and fantasy, conscious and unconscious, disappeared. Brecht, however, fought against the capitulation of rational behaviour.

In addition to the general ideas and goals of the surrealist movement, two specific Surrealists completed the foundation on which socially oriented theatre started to flourish: Antonin Artaud (1896–1948) and Arthur Adamov (1908–70). Young and lacking life experience when he first read Artaud, Planchon had no defence against the cruelty and violence he found in his writings:

> There came a point where I became afraid of that aspect, I feared I would lose my mind; I experienced a sort of vertigo in front of that [cruelty and violence]. I realized that it was a step towards an abyss, a step I did not feel capable of taking. So, like a coward, I closed these books and read something completely different. For the most part, I became interested in history, in anything that could be seen as a refusal of the abyss.[13]

Trying to escape from Artaud's spell, from this destroyer who came so close to shattering him, Planchon thus looked to the study of history for an antidote. In his study of Artaud and the Surrealists, Planchon was preoccupied with his own persona: conflicts concerning his present and future state of mind.[14] History, however, deals with specific events that occur at a specific time in a specific place. It deals with facts from the past that cannot be revoked and which offer fixed points of reference. Thus, history not only provided Planchon with a broader view of life than the merely individual but also supplied him with the kind of exciting tension that initially attracted him to Artaud. This conflict was now presented in an externalized and, therefore, less personal and destabilizing form, which gave him solid ground to stand on.

Planchon did not choose the historical events he wanted to study arbitrarily. Intoxicated by the concept of revolution, he started with an examination of its French and Russian incarnations: 'I was fascinated by history, still am, actually, and I tried to read in depth about the Russian Revolution, and I also read a great deal on the French Revolution.'[15] Both of these concrete historical developments provided practical examples of the fight for social revolution that he had already encountered through the Surrealists, with the October Revolution also familiarizing him with the historical passage from capitalism to socialism: a prerequisite for a fundamentally new way of thinking. At about this time, in 1952, Planchon met the playwright Arthur Adamov, who guided, taught, and thereby influenced him for many years to come. Adamov, a Surrealist despite not being included in the group, possessed an in-depth knowledge of German literature (he had lived in Germany from 1914 to 1924). He introduced Planchon to Kafka and the German writers of the eighteenth and nineteenth century, notably Kleist, Lenz and Büchner, whose literary works violated prevailing forms and conventions. In 1954, Adamov persuaded Planchon to stage Kleist's 1806 play *Der zerbrochene Krug* (*The Broken Jug*), which he had translated, together with his own *Professor Taranne*. This proved important to their professional relationship, as Adamov's account of his first meeting with Planchon reveals: 'One day, a young man came into my home. It was Roger Planchon. We quickly became friends. There was something grave about him that I immediately found endearing, but I didn't yet know what kind of work he was capable of. I found out when he staged *Professor Taranne*.'[16] The double billing reflected an interest in certain aspects of the surrealist movement that both men still had at this time, and particularly their continuing preoccupation with dreams.[17] Indeed, according to Adamov, *Professor Taranne* is a transcript of a dream. Moreover, the co-production signalled a growing awareness of social problems in Planchon's work.

Planchon consistently acknowledged his immense debt to Adamov, revealing the way in which he had inspired him:

> If I staged [...] *The Broken Jug*, it is thanks to [Adamov], because he made me read it very properly and thoroughly. Adamov read *The Broken Jug* through Kafka; he had been shaped by Kafka, who had perfectly understood what, under the guise of comedy, was important and grave about *The Broken Jug*. The idea of guilt that runs like a thread through the entire play, the judge's guilt, that was Adamov's idea. Professor Taranne's dream, that dream about guilt, that was Kleist's *The Broken Jug*.[18]

Planchon became extremely interested in the implications of the dream with its paired themes: the judge's desire and his feelings of guilt, and the judge's attempt to extricate himself from his desire and to prevent its disclosure. Both Adamov and Planchon saw *The Broken Jug* and *Professor Taranne* as accomplishing a reintegration of dream into reality – the union of dream and reality that is a fundamental intention of most Surrealists. Planchon's stress upon the admittedly tenuous connection between the dream world and *The Broken Jug* indicates just how strongly the surrealist bias gripped him at this stage. Planchon recognized that the idea of the judge's dream – the concept of profound culpability – is interwoven with political implications. Justice is only a relation of forces. He expanded on this thought by comparing Kleist's with Shakespeare's concept of justice: 'When Shakespeare writes, he speaks of justice *per se*; he doesn't ignore the fact that there are power struggles between men [*sic*], but outside of these struggles, there is the idea of justice *per se*.'[19] In 1960, the author and partner of Adamov, Jacqueline Autrusseau, interviewed five directors, including Planchon, about the validity of Brecht's theatrical principles for the French stage. During this enquiry Planchon described his three productions of *The Good Person*, his initial, inaccurate ideas about the play and the Brechtian *mise en scène*, and his discovery of the BE and admiration for its 'aesthetic success' and, above all, 'intellectual rigour':

> At the time, we had a lot of false ideas; a colleague told me: 'It is a play related to specific circumstances, filled with allusions to Brecht's stay in the United States. None of this has any general or "universal" meaning. One could even remove certain passages.' I saw things differently, but in a way that wasn't any more accurate.[20]

In addition to the Surrealists, other French theatrical conventions also influenced Planchon. One such convention, frequently found in French drama in the 1940s and 1950s, is the use of the closed-world image, a theme found, for example, in Ionesco's *La Leçon* (*The Lesson*, 1951) and *Les chaises* (*The Chairs*, 1952), as well as in Beckett's *En attendant Godot* (*Waiting for Godot*, 1952) and *Fin de partie* (*Endgame*, 1956). Likewise, in Sartre's *Huis clos* (*No Exit*, 1944), the whole action takes place in one single room. There is no way out of this imprisonment, no escape from the past. Planchon himself noted that he was under the spell of Sartre's existentialist viewpoint when he discovered Brecht: 'At the time, I was strongly influenced by the works of Sartre, who was confronting my generation with the very serious issue of commitment.'[21] One aspect of Sartre's work that caused Planchon to confront 'the serious issue of commitment' was freedom of choice. At this stage in Sartre's thinking (he was later to change remarkably in this regard), free choice was largely seen as an invitation to personal heroism. Collective actions were popularly seen as discredited by the chaos of French politics during and after the Second World War.

Sartre's influence on Planchon explains why he understood Brecht's postulate of social change as an individual moral problem, and thus concentrated on Shen Teh's personal dilemma and her choice to adopt the role of a cousin. Planchon admitted that he read a pessimistic message into *The Good Person*:

> I was really struck by the parable told by Wang, which ends thus: 'All (the trees) perish before their time, by the saw or the axe. That is the wage of the useful servant.' What mostly struck me was the pessimistic dimension (when Brecht says: 'find the solution', I understood: there is no solution) and the way in which the work comes across as an aesthetic fable.[22]

Planchon's conclusion that there is 'no solution' to the social dilemma has to be read in light of the fact that the translation of the play he was using did not have the epilogue in which Shen Teh invites the audience to look for their own solution, thus leaving the play open-ended. Planchon's misconception, nevertheless, provided an opportunity to realize one of Artaud's goals concerning the union between the auditorium and the stage, which for him had called for a shared space in which the spectator became part of the set, and thus of the performance. In order to recreate this world without escape, Planchon actualized Artaud's concept of surrounding the audience with walls: 'We staged the play with [...] painted decors enveloping the entire room, enclosing the audience.'[23] Yet Planchon did not go as far as abolishing the stage.

By the end of this rehearsal period, Planchon had distanced himself from the pessimistic French Existentialism and realized that the play did not deal with a closed world, but with a world in which solutions might be found: 'as we reached the final rehearsals, I understood that this was a false conception, that *The Good Person* was actually an "open" play'.[24] Even without the epilogue, a close study of Brecht's text reveals this authorial intention. To give some examples: in Scene 4, which takes place in the square in front of Shen Teh's shop, Shen Teh addresses the audience as she urges the protest against injustice: 'When an injustice takes place in a town there must be an uproar.'[25] In Scene 7, now in the yard behind Shen Teh's shop, she again tries to rouse the audience to help:

> Here, you! Someone begging for shelter.
> A chip of tomorrow begging you for a today.
> His friend, the conqueror, whom you know
> Can answer for him.[26]

By opening up the possibility of intervention, Brecht heightened the spectators' awareness that the audience can act to change this world in which good people cannot lead a decent life.

Georges Péju, a bookseller and source of Planchon's reading materials, confirmed the director's thirst for knowledge.[27] Once he became interested in an author, Planchon read his entire work and then studied the available secondary literature. In addition, he was surrounded by several men who spoke German fluently and shared his interest in Brecht: Max Schoendorff (1934–2012), a painter and production designer, and his father, a German scholar, who even knew Brecht personally and brought photographs, programmes and untranslated materials from Berlin; further, Arthur Adamov, who was deeply involved in the study of Brecht; and Jacques Rosner (b. 1936), an actor and collaborator of Planchon.

The second staging of *The Good Person of Szechwan*

In a 1972 interview for a British theatre journal, Planchon recalled the three stagings of *The Good Person,* classifying the first *mise en scène* as 'fairly unrealistic' and describing the second production as 'much more everyday'.[28] This account corresponds to the version he gave in 1960: 'The second staging, in the small theatre, was quite realistic. There was no aesthetic pursuit: we wanted to show simple misery, with a very rough style of acting.'[29] This is the most explicit, perhaps even the only statement on the concept of this production that Planchon ever made.

The working conditions at the Théâtre de la Comédie were better than at the Lyon-Charbonnières casino but still far from satisfactory. The move from the vast space of the casino into the small theatre with a proscenium arch theatre stage (size 6 × 7 metres) facilitated, and indeed forced, a complete reworking of the production in its concept, and also in its design. As it turned out, Planchon designed the set himself, also playing the role of Sun. The production pictures indicate that Planchon reminded his audience that they were at the theatre throughout the play. He suspended a title board above the stage and incorporated the stage frame into his design, working towards overcoming the major obstacle separating spectators from the performance (see Figure 6.2). The stage was flanked by a square pillar from which the plaster had crumbled away (stage right) and a partition of planks (stage left), with both designating the surrounding city. The side of the pillar facing the audience was covered with an imitation of Chinese writings and signs that were, in fact, meaningless. The sides of the stage remained unchanged throughout the performance. The shelves for Shen-Te's tobacco goods, on the right interior, were also seen in scenes played in front of the shop, in the park, and in the courtroom (see Figure 6.2). Each side provided two open spaces for the actors to enter and exit the stage. The published programme included one set sketch by Teo Otto (1904–68), designed for the staging in Frankfurt in November 1951.[30] Planchon adopted Otto's idea, transforming the fixed space into different locations with bamboo curtains and wooden blinds descending from the flies. The blinds, which constituted the back wall

FIGURE 6.2 *The first scene from Planchon's second production of Brecht's* The Good Person of Szechwan *in 1954 (Photo: Antoine Demielly/Personal collection Pia Kleber).*

of Shen Teh's tobacco shop, opened onto a view of the tree needed for the following scene in the park. This close-up picture reveals how primitively the blinds were constructed. The only furniture in the shop was a wooden counter and three stools. The set pieces were now more detailed and the counter appeared as if it had been in use for years. Figure 6.3 represents the square in front of the tobacco shop: the wooden blinds were raised and the park tree appeared in front of Shen Teh's shop.

In addition to ceiling lights that were part of the stage furnishing, Planchon employed recessed lighting hidden behind a row of unevenly cut pieces of wood, which suggested the roof of the tobacco shop in the outdoor scenes, as seen in Figure 6.3. A simple sign saying 'Shu Fu, Barber' was dropped from the flies to designate the barber's shop. The wooden blinds were closed to represent the back of the building, and hung far enough back to allow the two front exits to be used. A wheelbarrow with Shen Teh's laundry basket, a wooden box, and some sacks of tobacco, are the only objects on stage in this scene. The court scene brings us back to the setting of Scene 4, except that the bamboo curtain was slightly lowered to hide the wooden 'roof' (see Figure 6.4). Shen Teh's counter was moved from the right to the left to make room for the group arrangement of all the witnesses, and to serve as the judges' bench. The stage floor was covered with real sand in all of the scenes.

FIGURE 6.3 *The fourth scene (outdoors) from Planchon's second production of* The Good Person of Szechwan (*Photo: Antoine Demielly/Personal collection Pia Kleber*).

FIGURE 6.4 *The courtroom scene from Planchon's second production of* The Good Person of Szechwan (*Photo: Antoine Demielly/Personal collection Pia Kleber*).

Having seen photographs of the BE productions, Planchon was certainly aware that designers often surrounded the stage with a diorama, in white, grey or other neutral colours. Planchon did not employ a diorama, yet the back wall he used gave the impression of an endless horizon through the use of lighting techniques. The open position of the blinds in Shen Teh's tobacco shop prevented it from feeling like a totally closed environment. He did not create a milieu, rather a locale for the action on stage, by raising and lowering different sets of blinds from the flies. Each setting, each new scene, was defined by the action of the players. Following Brecht's postulate that props should be realistic signs, Planchon attempted to make the details of the set and props as realistic as possible and characteristic of the social class of those associated with them. Since he was still at the beginning of his career, he did not have a highly skilled workforce at his disposal, and had to build up and educate his staff from scratch. Nevertheless, the care he took in designing and building sets revealed Planchon's background: he came from a peasant environment where people developed the basic skills to make a living. He called his background 'outside of culture', and from the beginning desired to introduce everyday life onto the French stage: 'When I began to do plays, I always had this desire, and still have it deeply, to bring things away from literature and connect them with real life, the everyday life of the next-door neighbour, the butcher, the grocer on the corner.'[31]

The stage set from the second production clearly shows Planchon's distance from the French tradition that marked his earlier *mise en scène*. He now sought to establish a balance between open and closed spaces, using a few visual details to represent the specific milieu of the poor people of Szechwan, and the barber's shop emblem as a reminder for the audience that reality was here presented by artefacts. The tree growing in the courtroom, in turn, served as a clear source of a Brechtian *Verfremdungseffekt* (defamiliarization). Despite utilizing several ideas of Brecht's epic theatre, however, the appearance of the stage set as a whole missed the point of Brecht's stage conception. The clutter inside Shen Teh's tobacco shop, which we see in the photographs, hindered the audience from focusing on those few realistic elements that Brecht demanded, working against his directive of 'No atmosphere, everything clear, simple, visible!'[32] Brecht's text clearly describes living conditions under a capitalist system: the parasitic nature of human beings in a parasitic society. In contrast, Planchon's goal was to 'show basic misery'.[33] While falling short of fulfilling Brechtian theory, his second staging of *The Good Person* – the set, lighting, blocking and acting – suggest that Planchon had reached his own goal for the production.

He had left the creation of the costumes for the second staging completely in the hands of Isabelle Sadoyan (b. 1928), who also acted in all three productions.[34] She intuitively came close to Brecht's demands for costumes in her designs. She knew that she had to dress mostly poor people while also denoting variances in their social status. In giving the costumes an Asian character, she did not limit herself to copying traditional Chinese dresses but also drew upon certain 'Maoist' as well as Korean styles that were fashionable in France at the time. The costumes of the poor crowd evoked their misery through grey, dirty and faded colours, worn out materials and torn garments, prompting one critic to call the staging a 'concerto in grey'.[35] The garments of the gods were the only costumes consistently used for all three productions. They wore long Chinese tunics made from a shiny material, with wide sleeves and colourful embroideries, along with long Chinese fairy-tale moustaches, suggesting that neither the gods nor their costumes belonged to this world. The gods changed costumes for the court scene, however, appearing in black overcoats and bowler hats: clothes worn by the petite bourgeoisie or – as Claude Lochy (1929–91) expressed it – by 'minor civil servants'.[36] Thus, it is not difficult to decipher that Planchon parodied the god-like behaviours of French lawyers and civil servants, and their manipulations of legal arguments to serve their own aims. Sadoyan's costumes were, thus, never an end in themselves. While contributing to the play's social *Gestus*, meaning both the attitude visible in interaction between people and the social configuration of a milieu, they generally did not attract the spectators' special attention. As such, they did not succumb to what Roland Barthes calls the 'maladie du costume', but rather fulfilled the demand: 'The costume isn't designed to seduce the eye, but to convince.'[37] Still, experienced alongside the decor, they added to the busy effect of the whole stage.

The production photographs indicate that Planchon was by then familiar with Brecht's lighting techniques: the stage was mostly brightly lit, with the lighting sources exposed. As the images show, however, Planchon nevertheless incorporated invisible recessed lights into his design, which produced a certain, atmospheric effect. The combination of set, costumes and lighting conveyed a picture more reminiscent of Stanislavski's production of Gorki's sociopolitical drama *The Lower Depths* (1902), or of Antoine's naturalism [see **Volume 1**], than of Brechtian staging techniques.

From the beginning of his career, critics pointed to Planchon's superb sense and use of space, particularly the blocking of actors, as one of his talents. Planchon seemed to have sensed that people of the same social class are capable of both solidarity and mutual exploitation. Nearly all production photographs reveal the 'squeezing' together of people with shared problems or interests, as evident in the court scene. The theatre critic and scholar Bernard Dort (1929–94) postulates that an epic actor has to be highly trained and able to perform the same role on different levels. He expands on the Brechtian art of acting as follows:

> First, it is a matter of knowing how to observe – what Brecht calls 'the art of observation' – and, secondly, of knowing how to reconstruct on stage and communicate to the audience the product of this observation. In other words, to know how to capture behaviours and also how to recreate such behaviours, and highlight the contradictions between these

behaviours, whether they belong to different characters, or to the same character.[38]

Thus, the actor must not only be a good observer of people's behaviour and attitudes, but also be able to communicate the resulting knowledge to the public. The 'highlighting [of] the contradictions' – in other words, *Verfremdung* or *distanciation* – constitutes the most important technique for accomplishing this aim. When asked what *Verfremdung* meant to Planchon, or themselves, in 1954, all those interviewed gave vague answers, yet most began by talking about Planchon's sense of humour. Rosner emphasized, for instance, Planchon's 'very personal sense of the comic'.[39] This is significant since comedy is both an aspect of *Verfremdung*, and an evident element of *The Good Person*. Indeed, the central idea of the latter suggests comedy, since the double role of Shen Teh/Shui Ta rests on the discrepancy, or incongruity, between appearance and essence. The spectator is aware of the true identity of Shui Ta, a knowledge the other characters on stage do not possess, which makes their behaviour and language comical for the spectator, thereby creating a powerful *Verfremdungseffekt* and emphasizing the ambiguity of their actions and words.

Brecht operates with motives that traditionally express the social *Gestus* in *The Good Person*. Planchon, however, was not interested in the social *Gestus* in his second staging. Instead, he concentrated his humour on a combination of comical gestures and attitudes. The performance of Jean Bouise (1929–89), who played the double role of the barber Shu Fu and The Man, was noted for its comic effect: 'Jean Bouise continues to present characters that are surprising in their comedic power.'[40] The humour that Planchon evoked in the acting has strong ties to the American silent film tradition, while Brecht himself acknowledged his debt to the German comic cabaret sketch writer and performer Karl Valentin, silent films and Charlie Chaplin.[41]

Two critics characterized Planchon's second *mise en scène* as romantic, a trait that added a sentimental aspect to the comedy.[42] Since Planchon was not yet aware of the play's epilogue, his 'naturalistic' reading, combined with its comical effects, added up to a tragic, rather than a comic ending: there is no solution for Shen Teh's 'fate'. The audience is likely to have left the theatre crying tears that were mingled with laughter and reflective of a sentimental sadness arrived at in an amusing way, but without a new awareness of the possibility of their intervention in political processes, which was one of Brecht's main goals for the theatre. The acting style of Clotilde Robinovitch, who played Shen-Te/Shui Ta in Planchon's second production of *The Good Person*, was well suited to this tragic-comic mood: 'Clotilde Robinovitch creates, with the character of Shen-Te, a quite different image from the one previously rendered by Catherine Sauvage: in this new concerto in grey, she performs her solo in a more muted fashion, but with a more interiorized pathos and a most striking gravity.'[43] As it is here described, with its 'pathos' and 'gravity', Robinovitch's acting style was one that Brecht would have rejected. In fact, Planchon also declared his aversion to it in time. In 1971, he defined the acting style he was looking for as 'very [...] humorous', adding:

> My style is absolutely stripped bare of pathos. I think the Living Theatre and others like them are fatally tempted by pathos. Not me, absolutely not. I've no taste for it at all: excess repels me. When I see an actor plunging into pathos, I always feel he's lying. In this I'm very Brechtian [...] I don't have to ask myself questions about *feelings* – all kinds of other questions perhaps, but not those.[44]

In Brecht's text, music serves to comment on stage action by presenting a different viewpoint on the events, or by elevating them to a philosophical or universal dimension. This cannot be said for the music in Planchon's second production. The singing was no longer presented *a capella*: Paul Dessau's musical accompaniment was recorded on a tape; the same tape was later used for the third staging in 1958. One of two critics to comment on Dessau's music wrote that, 'Paul Dessau skilfully adapts these brief musical interludes and their heartrending tones to the spirit of the work, in which the cry uttered by Wang, the water carrier, resounds like a nostalgic song.'[45] Judging by the review, the songs did not as much comment on events as underline the misery and sentimentality of the *mise en scène*. None of the people interviewed recalled how the interludes, which Brecht also uses to present a different viewpoint to the audience, were handled. It seems there was no remarkable difference in their staging.

Due to this combination of factors, Planchon's second production appealed primarily to the spectators' emotions. The critic Robert Butheau compared Planchon's second *mise en scène* of *The Good Person* to Brecht's theatre as follows: 'The social reality of the play came through when it was presented in the small Théâtre de la Comédie, of course, but through a cloud of sentimentality that rendered neither the poetic weight of the Brechtian text, nor the scientific rigor of the German author's dramatic conception.'[46] Therefore, while Planchon reached his goal of showing the misery of Szechwan society, he did so without exposing the sources of its wretched condition. Moreover, despite his expressed disinterest in feelings, he was unable to contain their influence in his second staging.

The third staging of *The Good Person of Szechwan*

Four years elapsed between the second staging of *The Good Person* at the Théâtre de la Comédie and Planchon's third production of the play at the Théâtre de la Cité in Villeurbanne. Planchon devoted the interim period to deepening his knowledge of Brecht, and applying Brechtian methods not only to Brecht's own *Fear and Misery of the Third Reich* (1956) but to most of the *mises en scène* he produced during this period: *Les Coréens* (1956) by French writer and dramatist Michel Vinaver (b. 1927), as well as Adamov's *Paolo Paoli* (1957), Shakespeare's *Henry IV* and Molière's *George Dandin* (both in 1958). In an interview with Claude Sarraute in 1956, Planchon revealed that he wanted not only to direct each play several times but to stage its every scene in different versions before choosing the best just ahead of the opening: 'My dream, you see, would be to have the time and the means to rehearse the same scene twenty times, with different actors, to calibrate each scene in a number of ways, in order to choose, the day before dress rehearsal, the best version.'[47] In fact, Planchon's dream involved applying the methods of film editing to the theatre. Though he never had enough financial support to completely fulfil this dream, he re-staged several plays – quite often more than once – thus, reinterpreting his *mise en scène* or refining his production. Asked about the restaging of *The Good Person*, he answered that 'the substance of this play was so rich that, if one staged it a fourth and fifth time, one would always find something new'.[48] Given Planchon's attitude, it is only natural to look at the third production from the perspective of its difference from the previous versions. Available documentation of this production includes thirty reviews and several photographic prints. In addition, René Allio (1924–95) recalled the basic structure of the set in a sketch during his interview.[49]

Since his earlier productions, Planchon became aware that he had not fully grasped Brecht in 1954. After seeing performances of the BE, he came to understand that poetry and theatrical techniques were inseparable and dependent on a 'vision of the world'.[50] Therefore, he concluded that total commitment in politics and aesthetics is a prerequisite for staging Brecht:

> [The BE's productions] gave me the feeling that I had somehow missed Brecht's point, although not entirely. What impressed me about the Berliner's work was not so much its aesthetic achievements as its intellectual rigor. After seeing it, I felt that one is no longer permitted to do certain things. I had studied theatre in an incoherent manner, and then Brecht appeared. With him, it's no longer about 'the craft' – this 'craft' I was infuriated about lacking; rather, I realized that the craft was meaningful only when conditioned by a way of thinking. From then on, it was no longer possible to divorce poetry from technique; both are contained within a vision of the world. One cannot stage a Brecht play without total commitment, both aesthetically and politically.[51]

In effect, Planchon openly admits here that his third production of *The Good Person* was strongly influenced by the BE version. In one of his published notes on the production, he goes as far as to declare that he copied it: 'For us, Brecht's directorial work was equivalent to his work as a playwright. We, who are so respectful of the text of the author of *Mother Courage*, should respect his staging accomplishments to the point where, more than simply drawing inspiration from it, we should humbly copy it.'[52] It is crucial to emphasize though that Planchon had neither seen the BE's own version of *The Good Person* at this point, nor had a Modellbuch at his disposal. In addition to photographs of production, he read an article in the magazine *Théâtre Populaire* that gave a detailed description of Brecht's rehearsal of the second scene of the *Caucasian Chalk Circle*.[53]

By 1958, Planchon was more informed about Brecht's practice, and he had found a collaborator in designer René Allio, whose work was likewise strongly influenced by Brecht. Allio saw the BE's performance of *Mother Courage* in Paris in 1954 and felt it gave him a new definition of the designer's potential: 'This was the time when I was questioning my role in the theatre. And suddenly, Brecht's productions blew everything away! I persevered, because what I saw there was a way to continue in a new direction, one that reflected our concerns and provided a backbone to my research.'[54] These impulses proved fertile for this future collaboration with Planchon, which was founded on mutual confidence. They shared the same viewpoint on designing and staging plays, where the functions of directing and designing were no longer separate, but rather interrelated by mutual inspiration:[55]

> For *Henry IV*, we brought out the general meaning of the play, directed towards power. Then I created models; the guideline was: as many little objects as possible, 'create an abundance'. Rehearsals were structured around these maquettes. Sometimes we would make adjustments: in a street scene, for example, I removed a scaffold that would be put to better use elsewhere. One should avoid superimposing signs.[56]

Besides their fascination with Brecht, Planchon and Allio also shared a key interest in attracting new audiences to the theatre. They were looking for spectators, however, among people who preferred to go to movies and had never before set foot in a theatre.[57] While making them aware of social problems was one of their objectives, their most urgent issue was to convince newcomers that theatre is as much fun as a film, or a football game, thereby ensuring their return.

Recalling his working relationship with Planchon on *The Good Person*, Allio characterizes it as a 'complete collaboration'.[58] Still, Allio remembers the production for the extreme physical effort it demanded, owing to an untrained team and lack of time and money. Just as moving from the casino to the Théâtre de la Comédie prompted Planchon to rethink his concept of theatre in terms of open and closed spaces, the move to the Théâtre de la Cité in Villeurbanne had necessitated yet another revision. On a practical level, their new stage was much larger. Their solution was to create a smaller space within a bigger one, as Planchon explained: 'Our experience of the small stage at the rue des Marronniers taught me that the action should be concentrated in a limited space. And not because I had to move from a three by four meter stage to a nine by twelve meter stage.'[59] Planchon wanted to play on the contrast between, for example, the unrestricted space characteristic of the city and the limited space used in Shen Teh's tobacco shop scenes:

> [These two demands] are in fact contradictory, and this is the great challenge of the *mise en scène*. I believe that I have found a solution by playing upon this opposition: the overall scenography and work with the ensemble of actors aim to create the illusion of an unlimited scenic space, while the specific actions will be grouped in a very small section of the stage. Allio, the set designer, helped me in this task through the creation of his designs.[60]

The space restraint might have emerged from a conscious interpretation of Brecht's text, or from the public success of Planchon's earlier production. Moreover, Planchon had seen such a play of contrasts in Brecht's staging of *The Caucasian Chalk Circle*, and he was aware of the comical effect conveyed by the crowd jammed closely together in the wedding/deathbed scene. Planchon's approach and the large stage in Villeurbanne gave Allio an opportunity to create small islands of intimacy where some of the action occurred, and to surround these small islands with a neutral area suggestive of Szechwan's general urban environment. In an interview, Planchon explained that the set was meant to convey a realistic representation of China in the 1930s while emphasizing the mythical quality of the play: 'There again, we had to start with an opposition. Brecht's play takes place in China, probably [...] between the 1930s and the 1940s. So the set needed to underline the teeming, realist nature of the country in which the action took place, while highlighting how the play unfolds like a tale or a legend.'[61]

Allio solved the problem of uniting both demands within one setting by applying theories of Chinese visual arts and traditional pictorial representations to the decor. The set was a simple structure evocative of the complex reference system of Chinese culture. He developed the Chinese location by framing the large stage area with a huge backdrop of wash drawings, scroll banners painted with Chinese calligraphic designs and side partitions with some movable elements suggesting a poor area. The two scroll banners, located somewhat downstage, flanked the backdrop to create a dioramic perspective. While the big backdrop suggested an open space – a faraway horizon – the wash drawings evoked China in a very general way. The painted scroll banners mediating between the backdrop and side partitions referenced Chinese art far removed in time and space from the slums in which the poor of Szechwan lived during the 1930s. Along with the scrolls flanking the backdrop, others were lowered and raised during the performance. These scrolls denoted an art that has served the needs of the privileged classes, an art of extreme beauty showing the highest degree of technical skills. Why would the gods want to change this beautiful world where the visualization of cultural ideas provides a decorative vocabulary with which to ornament the surroundings of human existence? The slums of Szechwan do exist, certainly, but who wants to see them, given the choice of escaping into the world of painted scrolls?

Preserving this privileged world demanded a compromise: the good woman of Szechwan was allowed to have her cousin as long as she did not need him too often: 'once a month: that will be enough!', proclaimed the first god before the trio flew away into their 'nothingness'.[62] They had to leave quickly for the beautiful deceit cannot be maintained for long – Shui Ta might have destroyed the illusion: 'Shrewdly studied, closely fingered / Precious treasures melt away.'[63] The refined beauty of classical Chinese art, with its every detail painted with utmost care and creativity, contrasted strikingly with the neglected state of shelters that did not fulfil even their basic function. Allio's designs thus established a relationship between the two worlds that reinforced the atmosphere of total disjunction. The basic structure of Allio's design also corresponded to the textual structure of the play. As the first god notes, complaints about the world have a long history that, implicitly, resists mitigation by the beauty of ancient scrolls: 'For two thousand years we have been hearing the same complaint that the world cannot go on as it is. No one can stay on earth and remain good.'[64] The sister-in-law describes the shelters provided by Shu Fu (depicted on stage by the side partitions) as 'A damp rabbit-warren with half rotten floors!'[65]

As his sketch reveals, Allio also superimposed another level of reference onto his set by putting a wall covered with aggressive Western advertising posters in front of the backdrop. One reason why the designer mixed signs of Western publicity with Chinese elements was most certainly to mark the impact of Western capitalism on Asia. To a great extent, however, the play is not about China but about the task of living a decent life in any society that puts moneymaking ahead of other values. The crucial contrast, therefore, is between urban commercialism and the serenity – represented by the stylized art – that was valued and accessible only to the upper classes, and thus *never* applied to the Chinese people as a whole. Both art and religion are escapist and essentially anti-realist, which is why the gods are so strongly associated with the art world. This is not a matter of choosing between societies that produce either delicate traditional art or loud 'American' posters (the art of posters, in its agitprop form, is a legitimate art form that reached some of its greatest heights in the service of socialist and revolutionary causes). At stake here is the creation of a world in which one does *not* have to choose between two self-serving, exploitative worldviews.

Several critics were aware of the *Verfremdung* that Allio achieved through the contrasts outlined above. By its means, the designer created a relationship between the sombre, bleak reality of Szechwan and the reality of the fable that corresponded with Brecht's intermingling of everyday language with poetic passages:

> A detachment is also created by the costumes and René Allio's beautiful set design, which accurately replicates a picturesque and sordid image of China, one that has been soiled by modernity's motley assortment of posters, among which float traditional banners, with their calligraphy and decorations. The relationship between the latticed huts teeming with life and the delicately painted rolled curtains, between the dark realism and the fable, offers a kind of provocation that is suited to Brecht's poetry.[66]

Allio bestowed the same care in creating interior spaces (see Figure 6.5). Unfortunately, no photograph remains showing Shen Teh's tobacco shop. Jean Beaumont's review informs us that Allio limited the set of the Chinese shops to screens that folded and unfolded. These screens, signifying either the exterior or the interior of the shop, were lowered from the flies and placed in the middle of the stage.[67]

In Scene 8, set in the factory, a wooden pole was lowered from the flies as a railing to control the workers' passageway, creating a kind of maze for them to walk through, in which it was nearly impossible to find the exit, as Allio notes.[68] Robert Butheau analysed Allio's decor for this scene and concluded that the set supported the action, while provoking a reaction in the audience against not only assembly line work but also the way enchained factory labourers became part of the machine.[69] His review strikes a clearly Brechtian note, suggestive of Allio's understanding of the authorial intentions in this scene. Planchon informs us that Allio created 'quite realistic props' modelled on objects depicted in historical documents of China in the 1930s

FIGURE 6.5 *The wedding scene from Planchon's 1958 production of* The Good Person of Szechwan (*Photo: Rajak Ohanian/Personal collection Pia Kleber*).

and 1940s, as exemplified by the lamp and set pieces in the wedding scene (Figure 6.5).[70] Remarks on the production published on 15 January 1959 in *Les Lettres Françaises* must derive from Planchon's own words, which appeared in the same newspaper on 25 December 1958: 'and the realistic details set the tone for this swarm of activity and facilitate the action by delimiting it to a specific location'.[71] Most of the props were in harmony with this statement. Two different photographs display the Chinese lanterns that wedding guests carried in their hands, which reinforced the gay mood of the wedding.[72] There is a shift in atmosphere between Shen Teh's arrival at the restaurant and later in the scene, when it becomes apparent that the ceremony will be cancelled.

One aspect in which Planchon's third production worked against Brechtian aesthetics is in its unusual combination of two *mise en scène* elements: props and lighting. According to Brecht, the stage should always remain brightly lit, whereas in Planchon's third staging, the props and set elements were lowered from the flies and changed in half-darkness. This fact was remarked on by a number of critics. In Jean Beaumont's opinion, Planchon's choice was objectionable:

> During the set changes which took place in full view of the audience, in half-darkness (which I would prefer to be slightly less dark), some of the actors plant small fences, while others, who are backlit, come and go at the front of the stage. It's quite beautiful, but these are not so much Chinese shadows as what one would find in Callot (the grotesques) or Piranesi (the cables).[73]

The reference to these two painters is helpful in recapturing the impression evoked by these scene changes. Beaumont's specifications – 'les grotesques' and 'les cordages' – direct our attention to Callot's print *The Temptation of Saint-Antoine* and Piranesi's series of 'Prisons' etchings, respectively. Because of the half-darkness, it is possible that the actors were reminiscent of the strange animals, grotesque figures and acrobats scattered throughout Callot's bizarre landscape. Alternatively, the actors may have been reminiscent of stock *commedia dell'arte* characters. Beaumont's shrewd observation is thus a useful guide to the nature of Planchon's 'theatricality' in this production.

As already indicated, the lighting design of the Villerbanne *Good Person* was more theatrical and dramatic than Brechtian. The shadows projected on the wall during the wedding scene imply the use of spotlights. Planchon probably intended to thus create a more sombre atmosphere, or to heighten the suspense caused by waiting for Shui Ta.[74] Based on accounts of the lighting design, it seems to have grown out of the world of film that prepared Planchon for his theatrical career. Nevertheless, despite its cinematic lighting, Jean Beaumont observed a difference in Planchon's use of the third *mise en scène*: 'On the whole, the production is less "cinematic" than is customary: Brecht never lets the realism overshadow the poetry. Planchon feels and expresses that.'[75]

Allio's theory that all objects on stage must be chosen with a view to conveying interrelated meanings applies also to the costumes (Figure 6.6). When questioned by Gérard Guillot about the costumes for *The Good Person*, Planchon explained that René Allio designed them after studying historical documents: 'The costumes were also designed by Allio, based on documents, although this proved difficult, given that the play is filled with beggars, paupers, wretches.'[76] More recently, Allio has slightly modified this statement: although he designed most of the costumes, a few were from previous productions.[77] The three gods, for example, did not appear in the court scene dressed as 'minor civil servants', as in the second production, but retained the beautiful, embroidered Chinese costumes made for the first staging. Allio's stated reason was that court coats were seen 'in all the Chinese prints'. It is not known whether the Western-looking costumes worn by the gods in the epilogue were created specifically for the third staging, or reused from previous productions. According to Allio, the rest of the costumes resembled ones 'that one may find in Hong Kong, a mixture of European and Chinese'. Asked if he distinguished the different social statuses of the characters through their clothing, he answered laughingly: 'We would not have committed the sin of not showing the social classes!', immediately adding that 'they were all in shades of grey'. Most of the critics abstained from long comments on costumes in the third staging. Unlike the two previous productions, this one presented Shen Teh in a half mask when

FIGURE 6.6 *Isabelle Sadoyan as Shen-Te in Planchon's 1958 production of* The Good Person of Szechwan (*Photo: Rajak Ohanian/Personal collection Pia Kleber*).

she was disguised as Shui Ta. No other characters were masked, however. In 1959, *Le Travail au Théâtre de la Cité* published an article entitled 'To the Actors of *Dandin* and *The Good Person*, etc.', which outlined Planchon's theory of acting and explained his choice not to use masks in the production: 'Would not our lack of experience acting behind masks have steered the play towards a simplistic imagery, one that was incapable of rendering its full content? Would we not have risked giving it the appearance of naive imagery? Would our interpretation not have been like a symphony for orchestra performed on a harmonica?'[78]

Planchon believed that characters were primarily social beings, determined by their time and situation and distinguished by their behaviour. As always, he demonstrated his point by a practical example: 'In a street, no two paving stones are identical; there are only families of paving stones.'[79] Producing a play involved assembling a heterogeneous group of actors representative of all milieus: 'It would be like asking a well-defined category of paving stone to evoke all the possible ground covers: sand, tar, marble, gravel, soil, mud.'[80] According to Planchon, therefore, each role must be regarded as a composition, a structural entity, and each character must be both typical and unique. Planchon's goal was not to unify his ensemble with one common style of acting but to compose on stage a society with all different social levels and different social behaviours. He cautioned his actors against overplaying and internalizing a role: 'Some actors let their role escape them: it is the most skilled actors who always add legs to the snake. They do not always do this for a pitcher of wine or a round of applause. No, they think they are doing the right thing. They think that they are adding depth to their role.'[81] He also told them the story of 'Suspicion': a tale of a farmer who loses his axe and believes his neighbour's son has stolen it. He becomes suspicious that the young man is a thief when he observes him and finds his way of walking, voice and facial expression strange. When the farmer discovers the axe where he himself had placed it, however, the young neighbour's behaviour suddenly appears absolutely natural to him. This story was meant as a warning to his actors not to rely on a psychological analysis. Only facts count; a tone of voice, a facial expression or a certain walk might be deceitful. Planchon urged his actors to observe human beings in real life and to show with precise gestures the specific attitude of a person in a particular situation. He proposed two main guidelines: that actors must subordinate their acting to the events of the play and that everything which reinforced the story was justified.[82]

So how did Planchon's work with his actors to accomplish this task in 1958? Contrary to his later working methods, when he insisted on detailed studies of the text with the whole ensemble, there was no theoretical discussion between him and the actors. Jacques Rosner confirms this, adding that Planchon always had one 'interlocutor' with whom he was in constant dialogue – whether Claude Lochy, Allio or Rosner himself – but that this exchange of ideas did not extend to other members of the group.[83]

While Planchon may not have communicated his thoughts to the actors verbally, nonetheless, he worked very closely with them, showing them different ways of playing specific scenes during rehearsals. Since he was an actor himself, these demonstrations were also tools for expressing his ideas. Clarity of thought was of utmost importance to him at that time. He prepared himself thoroughly for rehearsals without imposing preconceived ideas about staging upon the actors. They had to find their own personal way of translating certain behaviours. Thus, Planchon challenged them continuously while simultaneously breathing into them his own energy and dynamism. According to his own account, he gave his actors some freedom of thought and expression, but also provided them with a definite framework to work within. When asked, in 1981, if he allowed the actors to improvise and contribute their own thoughts, he replied:

> Let's say yes and no. This is a bit complicated. I am a director who is fairly dictatorial on stage. I tell the actors what they have to do on stage and which liberties they can take. But since I am an actor myself, I usually seek solutions which favour the actor's creative collaboration. Therefore, I often do it in the following way: I tell the actor 'you can do it in this way', and show it to him [*sic*], or 'you can also do it in this way', and show it to him as well, and then leave the actor the choice. Naturally I know beforehand what he will decide, but first I let him choose from among these three possibilities.[84]

Conclusion

Despite some similarities in the concept of set design (for instance, the relationship between small and large spaces), Planchon's third *mise en scène* cannot be called a synthesis of the two preceding ones. The first production had a picturesque, fairy-tale character, while the second leaned towards naturalism *à la* Antoine and concentrated on showing the misery of the people in a sentimental way. The third staging, in turn, was directed towards two goals: firstly, the search for a popular audience new to the theatre and brought up on film, and, secondly, the achievement of a Brechtian *mise en scène*. As a result, the theatre Planchon strove for was neither a theatre 'of culture' nor one 'of pure entertainment'.[85] Although Planchon's definition of theatre and his theoretical pronouncements corresponded to Brecht's understanding of theatre, his desire to attract new spectators, his debt to film and belief in the validity of applying cinematic techniques to the theatre, prevented him from applying Brecht's methods to his Villeurbanne stage in an orthodox way, despite his declared intention to copy Brecht. Instead, Planchon attempted to raise the spectators' consciousness of their social responsibilities in his own 'Planchonian' manner: by creating (along with Allio) a narrative space where various superimposed signs commented on the play. The set, props and costumes, as well as stage action, further defined the environment and exterior *habitus* of the portrayed characters. These pictorial means narrated the action as elaborately as the text and can legitimately be called epic. Planchon inserted theatrical inventions such as the shadow plays and the wedding scene with Chinese lanterns to entertain the spectators, using an atmospheric lighting design familiar from film to create a sense of suspense for audiences.

While deviating from Brechtian principles of epic theatre, Planchon nonetheless succeeded in shaking up the audience and making spectators aware of their responsibilities. He analysed the play from a sociological rather than psychological point of view, paying particular attention to any arising contradictions. While his *mise en scène* was strongly marked by his own personality, it nevertheless fell within the boundaries of Brecht's realm. After all, it was Brecht himself who had warned against too narrow an understanding of epic theatre. For his part, Planchon had modestly declared in 1958 that 'Showing life isn't so easy. For now, we are still at the learning stage.'[86]

NOTES

Introduction to the Series

1 Simon Shepherd, *Direction* (Basingstoke: Palgrave Macmillan, 2012).

2 P.P. Howe, *The Repertory Theatre: A Record & a Criticism* (London: Martin Secker, 1910).

3 Alexander Dean, *Little Theatre Organization and Management: For Community, University and School* (New York: Appleton, 1926), 297–8.

4 Constance D'Arcy Mackay, *The Little Theatre in the United States* (New York: H. Holt, 1917).

5 William Lyon Phelps, *The Twentieth Century Theatre: Observations on the Contemporary English and American Stage* (New York: Macmillan, 1920); Hiram Kelly Moderwell, *Theatre of Today* (New York: Dodd, Mead & Co., 1914, 1923); Dean, *Little Theatre Organization and Management.*

Introduction to Volume 6

1 Fellow director Patrice Chéreau (1944–2013) links the latter two: emerging from the popular performance practice stimulated by Jean Vilar's TNP traditions in the Paris *banlieus*, which this chapter will introduce presently, he initially worked with Strehler at the Piccolo Teatro from 1968 before joining forces with Planchon, as co-director of the new TNP Villeurbanne from 1972 to 1982.

2 Littlewood in 1945, cited in Nadine Holdsworth, *Joan Littlewood's Theatre* (Cambridge: Cambridge University Press, 2011), 10.

3 Jürgen Habermas, *The Structural Transformation of the Public Sphere*, trans. Thomas McCarthy (Cambridge: Polity, 1992 [1962]).

4 In Europe, the 'axis' also consisted of Austria, Hungary, Romania, Bulgaria and Finland.

5 Our historical survey is particularly indebted to Tony Judt, *Postwar: A History of Europe since 1945* (New York: Penguin, 2005). For the death toll, see ibid., p. 17f.

6 Eric Hobsbawm, *Age of Extremes: The Short Twentieth Century 1914–91* (London: Abacus, 1995).

7 Max Horkheimer and Theodor W. Adorno, *Dialectic of Enlightenment: Philosophical Fragments*, trans. Edmund Jephcott (Stanford, CA: Stanford University Press, 2002 [1947]), chap. 4, 'The Culture Industry: Enlightenment as Mass Deception', 94–136.

8 Bertolt Brecht, *Brecht on Theatre*, ed. Marc Silberman, Steve Giles and Tom Kuhn (London: Bloomsbury Methuen, 2015), 69, 229.

9 Hannah Arendt, *The Origins of Totalitarianism,* new edn, with added prefaces (San Diego, CA: Harvest Harcourt Brace, 1973).

10 Hannah Arendt, *Eichmann in Jerusalem: A Report on the Banality of Evil* (London: Penguin, 2006 [1963]).

11 See Simona Forti, *New Demons: Rethinking Power and Evil Today*, trans. Zakiya Hanafi (Stanford, CA: Stanford University Press, 2015).

12 Albert Camus, *Le Mythe de Sisyphe* (Paris: Gallimard, 1942), 18, in Martin Esslin, *The Theatre of the Absurd* (London: Bloomsbury Methuen, 2013 [1961]), 5.

13 See Esslin, *The Theatre of the Absurd.*

14 Philippa Burt, 'Punishing the Outsiders: Theatre Workshop and the Arts Council', *Theatre, Dance and Performance Training* 5, no. 2 (2014): 127–9.

15 Marshall McLuhan, *The Gutenberg Galaxy: The Making of Typographic Man* (Toronto: University of Toronto Press, 1962).

16 Herbert Marcuse, *One-Dimensional Man: Studies in the Ideology of Advanced Industrial Society* (Abingdon and New York: Routledge, 2002 [1964]).

17 The Red Army Fraction (RAF), founded by the former investigative journalists Ulrike Meinhof and Andreas Bader, which emerged from this protest movement, then went on systematically to abduct and kill alleged former Nazi perpetrators who had never been called to justice for their crimes.

18 Giorgio Strehler, 'Ci siamo scambiati omicidi ma anche molta cultura', *La Stampa*, 8 June 1979, Piccolo Teatro Archive, quoted in Margherita Laera's chapter in this volume.

19 Jaime Torres-Bodet, UNESCO general secretary, quoted in Joseph Gregor, *Grosse Regisseure der modernen Bühne* (Vienna: UNESCO Commission, 1958), 3.

20 See Pierre Bourdieu, *Distinction: A Social Critique of the Judgment of Taste*, trans. Richard Nice (Abingdon and New York: Routledge, 2010 [1984]).

21 L'ANRAT, 'Sans amnésie', in Robert Abirached, *La Décentralisation théâtrale 1. Le Premier Âge* (Arles: Actes Sud, 1992), 7.

22 Romain Rolland, *Le Théâtre et le peuple* (Paris: Cahiers de la Quinzaine, 5.4, November 1903), quoted in Paul Blanchart, *Firmin Gémier* (Paris: L'Arche, 1954), 234.

23 Blanchart, *Firmin Gémier*, 229–58. For further details on Gémier see Catherine Faivre-Zellner, *Firmin Gémier. Théâtre Populaire Acte I* (Lausanne: L'Age d'Homme, 2006).

24 Jean Vilar, 'The T.N.P. – Public Service', in *Twentieth-Century Theatre: A Sourcebook*, ed. Richard Drain (London and New York: Routledge, 1995), 193. The quotations in this paragraph are from this source.

25 Quoted by Émile Copfermann, 'Enjeux politiques et sociaux du théâtre populaire', in *La Décentralisation théâtrale 1. Le Premier Âge*, ed. Robert Abirached (Arles: Actes Sud, 1992), 143–53, 144. The idea of bringing theatre of the highest quality to broad audiences was central to the ethos of the Cartel of Paris directors that dominated the interwar years: Charles Dullin, Louis Jouvet, Georges Pitoëff and Gaston Baty.

26 See Philippa Wehle, *Le Théâtre populaire selon Jean Vilar* (Arles: Actes Sud, 1991).

27 See Bernard Dort, 'La Revue *Théâtre Populaire*, le brechtisme et la décentralisation', in *La Décentralisation théâtrale 1. Le Premier Âge*, ed. Robert Abirached (Arles: Actes Sud, 1992), 125–41, 128. Without subscribing to the hard-line Stalinist or Maoist communist politics to which a number of French intellectuals and trade unionists in the 1950s adhered, *Théâtre Populaire* was a post-Marxist journal that believed firmly that, 'if the theatre tells things how they are, it can help people to understand the world and change it' (Editorial, *Théâtre Populaire*, February 1963, 49). (trans. CF)

28 See Jen Harvie, *Staging the UK* (Manchester: Manchester University Press, 2005), 16–22.

29 Nadine Holdsworth, '"They'd have pissed on my grave": The Arts Council and Theatre Workshop', *New Theatre Quarterly* 15, no. 1 (1999): 3. See also Holdsworth, *Joan Littlewood's Theatre*, 24–8; and Burt, 'Punishing the Outsiders'.

30 Brecht, *Brecht on Theatre,* 70.

31 Juliet Rufford, '"What Have We Got to Do with Fun?": Littlewood, Price, and the Policy Makers', *New Theatre Quarterly* 27, no. 4 (2011): 316, 326.

32 Giorgio Strehler, *Für ein menschlicheres Theater*, ed. Sinah Kessler (Frankfurt am Main: Suhrkamp, 1975), 32f. (trans. PMB).

33 Louis Althusser, 'The "Piccolo Teatro": Bertolazzi and Brecht – Notes on a Materialist Theatre', in *For Marx* (London and New York: Verso, 2005), 129–51.

34 Decentralization began in French theatre in 1947 with the creation, in Saint-Étienne, of the first state-subsidized theatre outside Paris.

35 As a Germanist, Bataillon has translated a number of works from French and is a specialist in German theatre, notably Brecht.

36 Planchon, cited in David Bradby, *Modern French Drama*, 2nd edn (Cambridge: Cambridge University Press, 1991), 107. Originally in Michel Bataillon, *Expoplanchon. Exhibition Catalogue* (Vénissieux: Centre Culturel, 1982).

37 Yvette Daoust, *Roger Planchon: Director and Playwright* (Cambridge: Cambridge University Press, 1981), 14.

38 David Bradby and Annie Sparks, *Mise en Scène: French Theatre Now* (London: Methuen Drama, 1997), 41.

39 Roger Planchon, 'Où en sommes-nous avec Brecht? Entretien avec Roger Planchon et René Allio', in *Ici et maintenant*, ed. Arthur Adamov (Paris: Gallimard, 1964), 214, emphasis in the original.

40 Planchon cited in Daoust, *Roger Planchon,* 15.

41 See David Bradby and David Williams, *Directors' Theatre* (London: Macmillan, 1988).

42 The Théâtre des Nations annual festival played a capital role in renewing theatre forms and ideas across Europe, since it invited some of the most innovative productions from around the world – Brecht, Littlewood, the Living Theatre and Grotowski to name but a few – to Paris, where they were viewed by large audiences and where exchange between theatre-makers guaranteed the international impact of shows.

43 The scholars who argue that Littlewood inaugurated Brechtian theatre in the UK include John L. Styan, *Modern Drama in Theory and Practice*, Volume 3: *Expressionism and Epic Theatre* (Cambridge: Cambridge University Press, 1981), 185; and Margaret Eddershaw, *Performing Brecht: Forty Years of British Performances* (London and New York: Routledge, 1996), 45.

44 Joachim Fiebach, *Von Craig bis Brecht: Studien zu Künstlertheorien des 20. Jahrhunderts*, 3rd rev. edn (Berlin: Henschel, 1991), 368. The following relies on the chapter 'Brecht und Darstellungskulturen im 20. Jahrhundert', in Fiebach, *Von Craig bis Brecht*, 365–90.

45 Fiebach, *Von Craig bis Brecht*, 368. For his analysis, Fiebach specifically points to the summary of the French reception of Brecht following his Paris visits in Richard Demarcey, *Éléments d'une sociologie du spectacle* (Paris: Union générale d'éditions, 1973), 242–317.

46 Strehler, *Für ein menschlicheres Theater,* 51, emphasis in the original (trans. PMB).

47 Brecht, *Brecht on Theatre,* 144.

48 Ibid., 230.

49 Ibid., 235f.

50 Marcuse, *One-Dimensional Man,* 64.

51 Ibid., 65.

52 Ibid. – Marcuse asserts and further develops this argument in his final publication 'The Permanence of Art: Against a certain Marxist aesthetics' from 1977, published in English as *The Aesthetic Dimension: Toward a critique of Marxist Aesthetics* (Boston, MA: Beacon, 1978).

53 Horkheimer and Adorno, *Dialectic of Enlightenment,* 94.

54 Günther Rühle, 'Die fortschrittliche Revision: Die Bühne als Schauplatz der Kritik', in *Anarchie der Regie? Theater in unserer Zeit, Vol. 2* (Frankfurt am Main: Suhrkamp, 1982), 51f. (trans. PMB).

55 Piscator, cited in ibid., 52.

56 Howard Goorney and Ewan MacColl, eds, *Agit-Prop to Theatre Workshop: Political Playscripts 1930–50* (Manchester: Manchester University Press, 1986), ix.

57 This was emphasized at the time by the groundbreaking work of East German Shakespeare expert Robert Weimann, see his *Shakespeare and Popular*

Tradition in the Theatre: Studies in the Social Dimension of the Dramatic Form and Function (Baltimore, MD: Johns Hopkins University Press, 1978 [1967]).

58 Joan Littlewood, quoted in Howard Goorney, *The Theatre Workshop Story* (London: Methuen, 1981), 154.

59 See Diana Taylor, *The Archive and the Repertoire: Performing Cultural Memory in the Americas* (Durham, NC, and London: Duke University Press, 2003).

60 Strehler in Herbert Mainusch, 'Kunst ist die wirklich aktive Seite des Menschen: Gespräch mit Giorgio Strehler', in *Regie und Interpretation: Gespärche mit Regisseuren* (Munich: Wilhelm Fink, 1985), 127 (trans. PMB).

61 Strehler, *Für ein menschlicheres Theater*, 33f. (trans. PMB).

62 Vilar, 'The T.N.P', 193.

63 This criticism was levelled at Vilar in the editorial to *Théâtre Populaire*, 16, November–December 1955, marking the schism between the journal and Vilar.

64 André Malraux, appointed head of France's first Ministry for Cultural Affairs in 1959, had declared that culture, like education, should be a basic human right.

65 Patrice Chéreau, *Partisans*, 1 May 1969, quoted in Émile Copfermann, 'L'Avant-Mai: une crise rampante', in *La Décentralisation théâtrale 3. 1968, le tournant*, ed. Robert Abirached (Arles: Actes Sud-Papiers, 1994), 13–37, 19.

66 Carl Lavery, 'Between Negativity and Resistance: Jean Genet and Committed Theatre', *Contemporary Theatre Review* 16, no. 2 (2006): 223.

67 'La Déclaration de Villeurbanne', in Robert Abirached, *La Décentralisation théâtrale 3. 1968, le tournant* (Arles: Actes Sud-Papiers, 1994), 195–200, 196.

68 David Bradby, and John McCormick, *People's Theatre* (London: Croom Helm, 1978), 138. See also Daoust, *Roger Planchon,* 10f.

69 'La Déclaration de Villeurbanne', in Abirached, *La Décentralisation théâtrale 3*, 195–200, 196.

70 Daoust, *Roger Planchon,* 11.

71 Jacques Duhumel, quoted in 'Editorial', *Travail théâtral*, July–September 1972, 8, 3–8, 4.

72 Strehler, *Für ein menschlicheres Theater,* 41 (trans. ML).

73 Gayatri Spivak, 'Can the Subaltern Speak?', in *Marxism and the Interpretation of Culture*, ed. Carey Nelson and Lawrence Grossberg (Urbana and Chicago: University of Illinois Press, 1988), 272.

74 *Le Monde*, 21 October 1971.

75 These points are debated by Anne-Marie Gourdon, 'Le Théâtre populaire. Point de vue du public du T.N.P.', *Travail théâtral*, July–September 1972, 8, 9–18, 14.

76 'La Déclaration de Villeurbanne', in Abirached, *La Décentralisation théâtrale 3*, 195–200, 195.

77 Brecht, *Brecht on Theatre,* 145.

Chapter 1

1 Littlewood quoted in Charles Marowitz, Tom Milne and Owen Hale, *The Encore Reader* (London: Methuen, 1965), 133.

2 Michael Arditti, 'Joan Littlewood is making a scene', *Independent Magazine*, 26 March 1994, http://www.michaelarditti.com/non-fiction/joan-littlewood-making-a-scene/ (accessed 30 November 2017).

3 Joan Littlewood, *Joan's Book* (London: Methuen, 1994), 74.

4 Douglas Geoffrey Bridson, *Prospero and Ariel: A Personal Recollection* (London: Golancz, 1971), 30.

5 Ibid., 69.

6 Ewan MacColl, *Journeyman: An Autobiography* (London: Sidgwick and Jackson, 1990), 266.

7 Howard Goorney, *The Theatre Workshop Story* (London: Methuen, 2008), 41–2.

8 Ballad opera is a popular eighteenth-century English satire of opera, with spoken dialogue.

9 Ewan MacColl, *Uranium 235* (Glasgow: William MacLellan, 1946).

10 See Goorney, *The Theatre Workshop Story*, 50.

11 On their influences, see also Leach's chapter below. On Stanislavski and Meyerhold, see also *The Great European Stage Directors*, vols 1 and 2.

12 Richard Runkel, Theatre Workshop: Its Philosophy, Plays, Process and Productions (PhD thesis, Texas University, 1987; British Library).

13 On Brecht and Piscator, see *The Great European Stage Directors,* vols 2 and 4.

14 Derek Paget, 'Theatre Workshop, Moussinac and the European Connection', *New Theatre Quarterly* 11, no. 43 (August 1995): 214.

15 Léon Moussinac, *The New Movement in the Theatre: A Survey in Developments in Europe and America*, trans. B. Bloom (London: Batsford, 1931).

16 See *The Great European Stage Directors*, vol. 3.

17 Marowitz, Milne and Hale, *The Encore Reader.*

18 Goorney, *The Theatre Workshop Story*, 41.

19 Personal correspondence between the author and Clive Barker, dated 7 April 2002.

20 Agitprop began in revolutionary Russia in the 1920s and quickly spread to Europe and the USA as a tool to educate and awaken political consciousness among the people. It took different forms: plays performed on bare stages with minimal props, or else pamphlets, posters and films.

21 These were theatrical propaganda productions that consisted in dramatizing current events and social and economic problems. Both traditions inspired Erwin Piscator and Bertolt Brecht's epic theatre practice during in the 1920s; see *The Great European Stage Directors,* vol. 2.

22 Clifford Odets, *Waiting for Lefty and Other Plays* (New York: Grove Press/Atlantic Monthly Press, 1994). MacColl's connections were mainly American.

The American Laboratory Theatre provided him with scripts, for example *Last Edition* (1940). MacColl's first plays drew directly in style from agitprop sketches and Living Newspapers. His post-war plays, *Johnny Noble, Uranium 235* and *The Other Animals*, explored a more elaborate style, related to Brecthian 'epic' theatre.

23 Robert Leach, *Theatre Workshop: Joan Littlewood and the Making of Modern British Theatre* (Exeter: University of Exeter Press, 2006), 25.

24 Littlewood, *Joan's Book*, 101. Littlewood's heavily annotated directors' script can be seen in a digitized version at the British Library at https://www.bl.uk/collection-items/manuscript-of-john-bullion-the-first-collaboration-between-joan-littlewood-and-jimmy-miller (accessed 30 November 2017).

25 MacColl's daughter with dancer Jean Newlove, Kirsty MacColl (1959–2000), also followed in his footsteps as a folksinger.

26 Murray Melvin, interview, BBC Radio 4, 9 February 2004, transcript.

27 This and the previous quotations are from an interview with Melvin by the author, that took place on 5 June 2000. It was first drawn on in Danielle Mérahi, *Joan Littlewood l'insoumise et le Theatre Workshop* (Paris: L'Entretemps, 2010). While these are the recollections of just one of Theatre Workshop's actors, they are nonetheless valuable for their insights into Littlewood's directorial practices.

28 Behan had originally written the play, which received its premiere in Dublin in 1957, in Gaelic and translated it into English during the rehearsals at Stratford.

29 Melvin, interview transcript.

30 Quoted by Claude Planson, *Il était une fois le Théâtre des Nations* (Paris: Maison des Cultures du Monde, 1984), 28. The preceding account draws on this source.

31 Françoise Kourilsky, 'Nouvelle Compagnie d'Avignon, l'exemple', *Travail Théâtral* 5 (1971): 3–25, 10.

32 Debauche was a vital voice in the *théâtre populaire* policy in France in the 1960s and 1970s, discussed in the introduction to this volume. Following Jean Vilar, he sought to 'decentralize' theatre by affording access to audiences of all social classes, notably those outside the capital city, Paris. He consequently founded the Théâtre des Amandiers in the Paris suburb of Nanterre.

33 Marowitz, Milne and Hale, *The Encore Reader*, 66.

34 MacColl made this remark in relation to the West End production of *Oh What a Lovely War*. See Derek Paget, '*Oh What a Lovely War*: The Texts and their Context', *New Theatre Quarterly* 6, no. 23 (August 1990): 258.

35 His 'Hammamet Festival' in the former French colony began in 1964, following the Hammamet workshops that had started in 1955, immediately after Tunisian independence. Between 1955 and 1963, Hammamet, Planson's utopian dream to bring together theatre companies from around the world, welcomed 165 companies from 51 countries in Western and Eastern Europe, Africa, Asia and the Americas. Hammamet included various performance forms such as theatre, choreography and to a lesser extent, music. See Planson, *Il était une fois*.

36 Littlewood, *Joan's Book*, 748.

37 Ibid.

38 *Homo Ludens*, following the famous idea developed by Dutch cultural historian Johan Huizinga in 1938, is the term used by Littlewood (*Joan's Book*, 704).

39 This and the following quotations are from Melvin, BBC Radio 4 interview.

40 Jean Newlove, *Laban for Actors and Dancers* (London: Nick Hern, 1993), 8.

41 Clive Barker, *Theatre Games: A New Approach to Drama Training* (London: Methuen, 1977)

42 See introduction to this volume.

43 Dennis Kennedy, 'Shakespeare and the Cold War', in *Four Hundred Years of Shakespeare in Europe*, eds Luis Pujante and Ton Hoenselaars (Newark: University of Delaware Press, 2003), 163.

44 Goorney, *The Theatre Workshop Story*, 167.

45 Ibid., 101.

46 Ibid.

47 Littlewood, *Joan's Book,* 132.

Chapter 2

1 Simon Callow, 'Character Building Stuff', *The Guardian Review*, 13 March 2013, 12.

2 The aim of the Drama Centre, founded in 1963, was to focus on character acting. Stanislavski was, therefore, a major influence on the actor-training methodology.

3 Marowitz, Milne and Hale, *The Encore Reader*, 133.

4 MacColl, *Journeyman*, 211.

5 See Raphael Samuel, Ewan MacColl and Stuart Cosgrave, *Theatres of the Left, 1880–1935* (London: Routledge and Kegan Paul, 1985), 13–16.

6 Ness Edwards, *The Workers Theatre* (Cardiff: Cymric Federation Press, 1930), 3, 67, 68.

7 Samuel, MacColl and Cosgrave, *Theatres of the Left*, 55, 58.

8 Émile Durkheim, *Selected Writings* (Cambridge: Cambridge University Press, 1972), 100.

9 Samuel, MacColl and Cosgrave, *Theatres of the Left*, 138–46.

10 Zygmunt Bauman, *Community: Seeking Safety in an Insecure World* (Cambridge: Polity, 2001), 1, 2.

11 Martin Buber, *Between Man and Man* (London: Fontana, 1961), 51 (emphasis in the original).

12 Victor W. Turner, *The Ritual Process* (Harmondsworth: Penguin, 1974), 83.

13 Ibid., 105.

14 Kevin Morgan, Gideon Cohen and Andrew Flinn, *Communism and British Society* (London: Rivers Oram Press, 2007), 3.

15 See Colin Chambers, *The Story of Unity Theatre* (London: Lawrence and Wishart, 1989).

16 Ibid.

17 Ibid.

18 Goorney, *The Theatre Workshop Story*, 25.

19 Allardyce Nicoll, *World Drama* (London: Harrap, 1976), 168, 170.

20 Ewan MacColl, quoted in Leach, *Theatre Workshop*, 37.

21 Littlewood, *Joan's Book*, 763–4.

22 Goorney, *The Theatre Workshop Story*, 20.

23 Littlewood's notes, quoted in Leach, *Theatre Workshop*, 81.

24 Goorney, *The Theatre Workshop Story*, 19.

25 Quoted in Leach, *Theatre Workshop*, 92.

26 Littlewood's notes, quoted in Jonathan Pitches, *Russians in Britain* (London: Routledge, 2012), 122 (emphasis in the original).

27 Konstantin Stanislavski, *An Actor Prepares* (London: Bles, 1937), 13 (emphasis in the original).

28 Littlewood's notes, quoted in Pitches, *Russians in Britain*, 123 (emphasis in the original).

29 Stanislavski, *An Actor Prepares*, 14.

30 See Volume 2 of *The Great European Stage Directors* series for a full account of Brecht's directorial practices.

31 David F. Kuhns, *German Expressionist Theatre: The Actor and the Stage* (Cambridge: Cambridge University Press, 1997), 107, 109.

32 Patrice Pavis, *Dictionary of the Theatre* (Toronto: University of Toronto Press, 1998), 171.

33 Bertolt Brecht, *Brecht on Theatre*, ed. and trans. John Willett (London: Eyre Methuen, 1964), 60, 58.

34 Ibid., 26.

35 Ibid., 28.

36 Stephen Parker, *Bertolt Brecht: A Literary Life* (London: Bloomsbury, 2014), 263.

37 Brecht, *Brecht on Theatre*, 58.

38 Ibid., 83.

39 Ibid., 42.

40 Ibid., 104.

41 Ibid., 55.

42 Ibid., 129.

43 Ibid., 138.

44 Ibid., 191.

45 Friedrich Nietzsche, *Basic Writings of Nietzsche*, trans. Walter Kaufmann (New York: Random House, 2000), 33.

46 Ibid., 35.

47 Ibid., 37.

48 Ibid., 48, 52.

49 Erwin Piscator, *The Political Theatre* (London: Eyre Methuen, 1980), 264.

50 Ibid., 269.

51 Brecht, *Brecht on Theatre*, 92–3.

52 See also Michael Schwaiger, *Bertolt Brecht und Erwin Piscator* (Vienna: Christian Brandstätter, 2004), 47–9.

53 Littlewood, *Joan's Book*, 106.

54 Ewan MacColl, *The Good Soldier Schweik*, typescript in Ruskin College Library, Oxford.

55 Goorney, *The Theatre Workshop Story*, 19.

56 Reviews from *The Daily Mail* and *Evening Standard*, quoted in Leach, *Theatre Workshop*, 130.

57 Goorney, *The Theatre Workshop Story*, 100.

58 Bertolt Brecht, 'Schweik in the Second World War', in *Collected Plays Vol. 7* (New York: Random House, 1975), 65.

59 Ibid., 132–3.

60 Ibid., 229.

61 Littlewood's notes, emphasis in the original, quoted in Leach, *Theatre Workshop*, 84.

62 Quoted in ibid., 89.

63 Goorney, *The Theatre Workshop Story*, 160.

64 Marowitz, Milne and Hale, *The Encore Reader*, 133.

65 Quoted in Leach, *Theatre Workshop*, 175.

66 Goorney, *The Theatre Workshop Story*, 126–7.

67 Ibid., 194 (emphasis in the original).

68 Quoted in Leach, *Theatre Workshop*, 178.

69 Ibid.

70 Nigel Hawthorne, *Straight Face* (London: BBC Audiobooks, 2004), 217.

71 MacColl, *Uranium 235*, 6.

72 Goorney, *The Theatre Workshop Story*, 168.

73 Robert Leach, *Stanislavsky and Meyerhold* (Oxford and New York: Peter Lang, 2003).

74 Quoted in Kenneth Tynan, *Tynan on Theatre* (Harmondsworth: Penguin, 1964), 90.

75 *Omnibus*, BBC Television, 19 April 1994.

76 Alison Hodge, *Actor Training*, 2nd edn (Abingdon and New York: Routledge, 2010), 139.

77 Aleksandr Gladkov, *Meyerhold Speaks, Meyerhold Rehearses* (Amsterdam: Harwood Academic, 1997), 108.

78 Paul Schmidt, *Meyerhold at Work* (Austin: University of Texas Press, 1980), 207.

79 Littlewood's notes, quoted in Leach, *Theatre Workshop*, 184 (emphasis in the original).

80 Goorney and MacColl, *Agit-Prop to Theatre Workshop*, 64.

81 Ewan MacColl, *Landscape with Chimneys*, typescript in Ruskin College Library, Oxford, 67–70.

82 Kenneth Tynan, *Tynan Right and Left* (London: Longmans, 1967), 317.

83 Henri Bergson, *Laughter, and an Essay on the Meaning of the Comic*, trans. Cloudesley Brereton and Fred Rothwell (London: Macmillan, 1935), 4, 5, emphasis in the original.

84 Ibid., 6, 8, 20 (emphasis in the original).

85 Ibid., 33.

86 Walter Benjamin, *Understanding Brecht*, trans. Anna Bostock (London: New Left Books, 1973), 3.

87 Ibid., 3.

88 Bergson, *Laughter,* 197.

89 Frank Norman, *Fings Ain't Wot They Used T'Be* (New York: Grove Press, 1962), 9.

90 Shelagh Delaney, *A Taste of Honey* (London: Methuen, 2000), 34, 84.

91 Ibid., 54.

92 Brendan Behan, *The Hostage*, in *The Complete Plays* (London: Eyre Methuen, 1978), 148–9.

93 Norman, *Fings*, 95.

94 Theatre Workshop, *Oh What a Lovely War*, rev. edn (London: Methuen, 2000), 75–7.

95 Pam Morris, ed., *The Bakhtin Reader* (London: Edward Arnold, 1994), 197, 199.

96 Ibid., 200, 209.

97 MacColl, *Landscape with Chimneys*, 3, 4, 28.

98 Behan, *The Hostage,* 169.

99 Ibid., 134–5, 231.

100 Theatre Workshop, *Oh What a Lovely War*, 9.

101 Ibid., 92.

102 Holdsworth, *Joan Littlewood's Theatre*, 193.

103 Bertolt Brecht, 'The Caucasian Chalk Circle', in *Collected Plays*, Vol. 7 (New York: Random House, 1975), 199.

104 Marowitz, Milne and Hale, *The Encore Reader*, 133.

105 John Arden, *Plays: One* (London: Eyre Methuen, 1977), 113.

Chapter 3

1 Quoted in Giancarlo Stampalia, *Strehler dirige: Le fasi di un allestimento e l'impulso musicale nel teatro* (Venice: Marsilio, 1997), 246. All translations from foreign language sources are by the author.

2 Ibid., 36. For further biographical context, see ibid., 244–7, and Alberto Bentoglio, *Invito al teatro di Strehler* (Milan: Mursia, 2002), 5–23.

3 Clarissa Egle Mambrini, *Il giovane Strehler: Da Novara al Piccolo Teatro di Milano* (Milan: Lampi di stampa, 2013), 287–314; Giorgio Strehler and Stella Casiraghi, *Lettere sul teatro* (Milan: Archinto, 2000), 61–71.

4 Famous Italian theatre personalities such as actor-playwright Eduardo De Filippo (1900–84) and Dario Fo's partner Franca Rame (1929–2013) originated from such theatre dynasties that dominated this traditional system. Eduardo's artistic heritage was handed over to his son Luca, after whose death in 2015 the De Filippo company moved on under the direction of Luca's widow.

5 Joseph Farrell and Paolo Puppa, eds, *A History of Italian Theatre* (Cambridge: Cambridge University Press, 2006), 271.

6 Quoted in Andrea Nanni, ed., *Giorgio Strehler o la passione teatrale* (Milan: Ubulibri, 1998), 100.

7 Giorgio Strehler and Sinah Kessler, *Per un teatro umano: pensieri scritti, parlati e attuati* (Milan: Feltrinelli, 1974), 23–4.

8 See Catherine Douël Dell'Agnola, *Gli spettacolo goldoniani di Giorgio Strehler 1947–1991* (Rome: Bulzoni, 1992), 25–82.

9 The school was run as an integral part of the theatre until 1967, when its formal status was changed; it was then re-opened as part of the theatre again in 1987.

10 Strehler and Kessler, *Per un teatro umano*, 165–8.

11 Bentoglio, *Invito al teatro*, 34–5; Farrell and Puppa, *A History of Italian Theatre,* 276.

12 Strehler and Kessler, *Per un teatro umano*, 58–60, 68 and 117–19; Stampalia, *Strehler dirige*, 151–2.

13 In the 1970s, Strehler was then offered the artistic directorship of the French national theatre, the Comédie-Française, but declined. In 1982, however, the French Minister of Culture Jack Lang appointed him as head of the new Théâtre de l'Europe at the Odéon théâtre de Paris, one of Strehler's favourite stages (see Laera's chapter in this volume).

14 Both Bragaglia and Pandolfi produced groundbreaking works in connection with the artistic and academic revival and exploration of the Italian masked comedy after the war, demonstrating their desire both to engage with modern European influences and to develop their own domestic heritage.

15 Franco Quadri, *Il teatro del regime* (Milan: Mazzotta, 1976), 37.

16 Ibid., 37–49. For further information on the Piccolo Teatro and the history of Brecht in Italy, including a focus on the role of Grassi in that connection, see

Alberto Benedetto, *Brecht e il Piccolo Teatro. Una questione di diritti* (Milan: Mimesis, 2016).

17 Strehler and Kessler, *Per un teatro umano*, 101ff.; Bunge in Siegfried Unseld, ed., *Bertolt Brechts Dreigroschenbuch: Texte Materialien Dokumente* (Frankfurt am Main: Suhrkamp, 1960), 130–4.

18 The same setting appears in Strehler's production of *El nost' Milan* (1955).

19 Strehler and Kessler, *Per un teatro umano*, 103ff.

20 Ibid., 106.

21 David Hirst, *Giorgio Strehler* (Cambridge: Cambridge University Press, 1993), 97.

22 Werner Hecht, *Bert Brecht. Sein Leben in Bildern und Texten* (Frankfurt am Main: Suhrkamp, 1978), 305.

23 Ibid.

24 Quoted in Hirst, *Giorgio Strehler*, 93.

25 Quadri, *Il teatro del regime*, 37–8. Massimo Bucciantini, *Un Galileo a Milano* (Torino: Einaudi, 2017), 134–82. For information on Fo's 'Brechtian' play about Columbus, *Isabella, tre caravelle e un cacciaballe*, performed in the same season in Milan, and for a comparison between this, and Strehler's show, see Bent Holm, 'Dario Fo's Bourgeois Period. Carnival and Criticism', in *Dario Fo: Stage, Text and Tradition*, ed. Joseph Farrell and Antonio Scuderi (Carbondale and Edwardsville: Southern Illinois University Press, 2000), 130–3.

26 Benedetto, *Brecht e il Piccolo Teatro*, 16, 37.

27 See Fn. 23 above.

28 Quoted in Hirst, *Giorgio Strehler*, 103.

29 This kind of minimalism or micro-realism is comparable to Samuel Beckett or the Polish avant-garde theatre artist Tadeusz Kantor, even though they focus on existential absurdities in contrast with Strehler's social commitment.

30 Catherine Douël Dell'Agnola, *Strehler e Brecht* (Rome: Bulzoni, 1994), 69–74.

31 According to Douël Dell'Agnola (*Strehler e Brecht*, 57), the remains of the plane, namely a wing, had been omitted by Strehler because of his reluctance to use symbols. However, according to a letter from Luciano Damiani to me (26 October 2001), Strehler had nothing against symbols. It was more a technical question. Finally, in 1996, at the Teatro Studio, Damiani got the chance to realize his original idea full-scale.

32 Quoted in Bentoglio, *Invito al teatro*, 131.

33 Hirst, *Giorgio Strehler*, 17. See also Nanni, *Giorgio Strehler o la passione*, 115.

34 See Bentoglio, *Invito al teatro*, 132–3.

35 Stampalia, *Strehler dirige*, 38.

36 In various abstract and theoretical optics, 'text' figures as a predominant component in theatre. To practitioners, however, it has been clear for centuries that theatre is a performative art form. The audience perceives in three dimensions and with five senses and has always done so. From a cognitive point of view the semantic aspect of a performance is minute compared to the

visual, auditory and mimic qualities. In practice the dichotomy of textuality and performativity is, therefore, problematic.

37 Strehler and Kessler, *Per un teatro umano*, 260–3.

38 For further information on the Chinese boxes, see Valentina Cortese, 'Le scatole cinesi', in *Piccolo Teatro di Milano*, ed. Maria Grazia Gregori (Milan: Piccolo Teatro, 2000), 115–5, and Cordelia Dvorak, *Passione teatrale. Giorgio Strehler und das Theater* (Berlin: Henschel, 1994), 127–8. The 'cities' are described in one of the last speeches by Strehler, published under the title 'Les quatre cités du théâtre d'art' in Georges Banu, ed., *Les cités du théâtre d'art de Stanislavskij à Strehler* (Paris: Editions théâtrales, 2000), 9–15.

39 Quoted in Hirst, *Giorgio Strehler*, 18.

40 This was completely different from the author's own, rather naturalistic, production from 1949, repeated in his 1964 television version.

41 Stampalia, *Strehler dirige*, 35–6.

42 Ibid., 11–16.

43 Ibid., 12.

44 Ibid., 14.

45 Ibid., 15.

46 Ibid.

47 Ibid., 15f.

48 Ibid., 125 (emphasis in the original).

49 Ibid., 221 (emphasis in the original). See Wilson's reflections on the continuum quoted in the main body of the text. As for the 'spiritual' aspect, Damiani describes an instinctive reluctance towards more intangible principles in his composition of the stage, cf. Luciano Damiani, *Autoritratto* (Rome: Teatro Documenti, 2001).

50 Strehler and Kessler, *Per un teatro umano*, 136–7.

51 Nanni, *Giorgio Strehler o la passione*, 135.

52 It would be an over-simplification though to suggest that Brecht focused on the second box, and Wilson on the third.

Chapter 4

1 Giorgio Strehler, 'Il teatro nella prospettiva di un'Europa unita', 1993, 1 (Piccolo Teatro Archive). All translations from Italian and French sources are the author's.

2 Matthew J. Goodwin and Oliver Heath, 'The 2016 Referendum, Brexit and the Left Behind: An Aggregate-Level Analysis of the Result', *Political Quarterly* 87, no. 3 (2016): 323–32.

3 Ibid.

4 Some of the most important studies on Strehler are Federica Mazzocchi and Alberto Bentoglio, *Giorgio Strehler e il suo teatro* (Rome: Bulzoni,

1997); Bentoglio, *Invito al teatro*; and Elio Testoni, *Giorgio Strehler: atti del Convegno di studi su Giorgio Strehler e il teatro pubblico* (Catanzaro: Rubbettino, 2009). Many other publications are more celebratory in nature, such as Salvatore Porto, *Strehler e il teatro dell'Europa* (Catania: Edidrama, 1987); Mambrini, *Il giovane Strehler*; and Renzo Tian and Alessandro Martinez, eds, *Giorgio Strehler o la Passione Teatrale: l'opera di un maestro raccontata al Premio Europa per il Teatro* (Milan: Ubulibri, 1998).

5 The Odéon-Théâtre de l'Europe (formerly Théâtre de l'Odéon) is one of Paris's most prominent national theatres, located in the heart of the Latin Quarter on the river Seine's left bank. Its building was first completed in 1782, and it was then known as the Théâtre du Faubourg Saint-Germain. The Union des Théâtres de l'Europe is a network of producing theatres located in Europe who cooperate to exchange expertise and performances.

6 Giorgio Strehler, 'Ci siamo scambiati omicidi ma anche molta cultura', *La Stampa*, 8 June 1979 (Piccolo Teatro Archive).

7 For Strehler, the notion of Europe – and the dream of a united Europe – did not coincide with the political borders of the then European Economic Community. His relationship with Eastern Europe and the Eastern Bloc is evident in his family roots, and in his engagement with Brecht and his fondness for writers from Russia and the former Soviet Union, such as Maxim Gorki. Reflecting Strehler's thinking, in this chapter the term Europe refers to an imaginary place characterized by a shared cultural heritage, rather than a fixed geographical entity.

8 A good source for Strehler's biography is Bentoglio, *Invito al teatro*.

9 Strehler, 'Ci siamo scambiati'.

10 Silvio D'Amico, *Tramonto del grande attore* (Florence: La casa Usher, 1985), 29.

11 Giorgio Strehler and Ugo Ronfani, *Io, Strehler: una vita per il teatro: conversazioni con Ugo Ronfani* (Milan: Rusconi, 1986), 76.

12 See Gianfranco Pedullà, *Il teatro italiano nel tempo del fascismo* (Bologna: Il Mulino, 1994), 211–24, and Luciano Bottoni, *Storia del teatro italiano: 1900–1945* (Bologna: Il Mulino, 1999), 173–96.

13 Pedullà, *Il teatro italiano*, 200–11.

14 Ibid., 38.

15 Ibid., 47–84.

16 Ibid., 75.

17 Alberto Cesare Alberti, *Poetica teatrale e bibliografia di Anton Giulio Bragaglia* (Rome: Bulzoni, 1978).

18 A. Richard Sogliuzzo, *Luigi Pirandello, Director: The Playwright in the Theatre* (Metuchen, NJ: Scarecrow Press, 1982).

19 Pedullà, *Il teatro italiano*, 123–90.

20 Strehler and Kessler, *Per un teatro umano*, 21.

21 Strehler and Ronfani, *Io, Strehler*, 75f.

22 The original manifesto is reprinted in Mazzocchi and Bentoglio, *Giorgio Strehler e il suo teatro,* 34.

23 Hirst calls Strehler's style 'lyrical realism': Hirst, *Giorgio Strehler*, 25.

24 Strehler and Kessler, *Per un teatro umano*, 134.

25 Ibid.

26 Ibid., 135.

27 Reprinted in Mazzocchi and Bentoglio, *Giorgio Strehler e il suo teatro,* 34.

28 Bentoglio, *Invito al teatro,* 33.

29 Ibid., 36–7.

30 Renato Palazzi, 'Le Dimissioni di Strehler dal Piccolo nel 1968 e la contestazione della regia e della politica degli stabili pubblici', in *Giorgio Strehler: Atti del convegno di studi su Giorgio Strehler e il teatro pubblico*, ed. Elio Testoni (Catanzaro: Rubbettino, 2009), 111–21; Strehler and Kessler, *Per un teatro umano*, 51.

31 Strehler and Ronfani, *Io, Strehler*, 303–4; emphasis is in the original.

32 Strehler and Casiraghi, *Lettere sul teatro*, 89.

33 Tobias Theiler, *Political Symbolism and European Integration* (Manchester: Manchester University Press, 2005), 71–3.

34 Giorgio Strehler, *Il Piccolo teatro d'arte: quarant'anni di lavoro teatrale, 1947–1987* (Milan: Electa, 1988), 84.

35 Giorgio Strehler, 'Théâtre de l'Europe, Season 1983–84 Programme Note', 1983.

36 Ibid., emphasis in the original.

37 Strehler and Ronfani, *Io, Strehler*, 307–8.

38 Mariagabriella Cambiaghi, 'L'avventura del teatro dell'Europa', in Mazzocchi and Bentoglio, *Giorgio Strehler e il suo teatro*, 102.

39 Hans van Maanen and S.E. Wilmer, *Theatre Worlds in Motion: Structures, Politics and Developments in the Countries of Western Europe* (Amsterdam: Rodopi, 1998), 31–2.

40 S.E. Wilmer, 'National Theatres and the Construction of Identity in Smaller European Countries', in *Global Changes – Local Stages: How Theatre Functions in Smaller European Countries*, eds Hans van Maanen, Andreas Kotte and Anneli Saro (Amsterdam: Rodopi, 2009), 30.

41 Giorgio Strehler, 'Théâtre de l'Europe, Season 1984–85 Programme Note', 1984.

42 Strehler, 'Il teatro nella prospettiva', 4.

43 Strehler, Season 1984–5, 3.

44 The UTE only started operating in full in 1990. A similar organization, the Informal European Theatre Meeting, had been established before the UTE in 1981 (www.ietm.org) and is still active today, with members from around the world. In 1988, the European Theatre Convention was founded (http://www.etc-cte.org), and is also still active today.

45 The members of the UTE have changed throughout the years and now comprise eighteen theatres in Italy, Germany, France, Romania, Greece, Portugal, Israel, Serbia, the Czech Republic, Russia and Bulgaria; see http://www.union-theatres-europe.eu/.

46 Strehler, *Il Piccolo teatro d'arte*, 85.

47 For instance, Porto, *Strehler e il teatro dell'Europa*; Cambiaghi, 'L'avventura'; and Maria Grazia Gregori, 'Il Teatro d'Europa dall'utopia al progetto', *Teatro in Europa*, no. 3 (1988): 94–100.

48 Strehler, 'Ci siamo scambiati'.

49 John C. Luik, 'Humanism', in *The Routledge Encyclopedia of Philosophy*, ed. John Crane (Abingdon and New York: Routledge, 1998), https://www.rep.routledge.com/articles/thematic/humanism/v-1 (accessed 22 November 2017).

50 Ibid.

51 Alex Callinicos, 'Althusser, Louis Pierre (1918–90)', in Crane, *Routledge Encyclopedia of Philosophy*, https://www.rep.routledge.com/articles/biographical/althusser-louis-pierre-1918-90/v-1 (accessed 22 November 2017).

52 Ibid.

53 Despite their problematic 'appropriation' of non-Western culture, which is criticized by scholars such as Rustom Bharucha, intercultural theatre practitioners of the 1960s and 1970s such as Brook and Mnouchkine did manage to draw spectators' attention to African and Asian theatre traditions and their rich histories. Strehler's interest in Brecht, whose Chinese influences have been amply explored in recent scholarship, never led him to explore theatre traditions beyond those of a narrowly defined Europe.

54 See, for instance, the work of Jean-Marie Serreau, who in the 1950s and 1960s staged Genet as well as a range of francophone Afro-Caribbean authors including Kateb Yacine and Aimé Césaire, and who also incorporated black actors into his ensembles.

55 Strehler, 'Ci siamo scambiati'.

56 Ibid.

57 Strehler and Kessler, *Per un teatro umano*, 51f.

58 Palazzi, 'Le Dimissioni di Strehler', 118–20.

59 Strehler's preferred acting style freely borrowed from both Stanislavskian identification and Brechtian distanciation techniques [**see Volumes 1 and 2**], never really opting for a fully 'epic' actorial delivery despite naming Brecht among his three main 'masters'. Strehler's Enlightenment-derived brand of humanism and approach to actorial work prevented him from experimenting with texts featuring less-than-rounded characters, such as the silhouettes, voices and figures that can be found in the work of Maurice Maeterlinck, Peter Handke or Heiner Müller.

60 See Friedrich Schiller, *Letters upon the Aesthetic Education of Man* (1794), http.//public-library.uk/ebooks/55/76.pdf (accessed 29 August 2017).

61 Strehler and Kessler, *Per un teatro umano*, 37.

62 Strehler, 'Ci siamo scambiati'.

63 Strehler and Kessler, *Per un teatro umano*, 39.

64 Giorgio Strehler, 'Nel teatro si può perdere l'anima', 1985, 10–11 (Piccolo Teatro Archive).

65 Strehler, 'Il teatro nella prospettiva', 2.

66 See Max Horkheimer and Theodor W. Adorno, *Dialectics of Enlightenment: Philosophical Fragments*, trans. Edmund Jephcott (Stanford, CA: Stanford University Press, 2002 [1947]), especially chapter 4 entitled 'The Culture Industry: Enlightenment at Mass Deception', 94–136; and Adorno, *The Culture Industry*.

67 Giorgio Strehler, 'Per un'Europa umana', *Libertà*, 6 June 1979 (Piccolo Teatro Archive), original emphasis.

68 Strehler, 'Il teatro nella prospettiva', 1.

69 Ulrike Hanna Meinhof and Anna Triandafyllidou, eds, *Transcultural Europe: Cultural Policy in a Changing Europe* (Basingstoke and New York: Palgrave Macmillan, 2006), 3f.

70 Joe Kelleher, *Theatre & Politics* (Basingstoke and New York: Palgrave Macmillan, 2009), 15 (original emphasis).

71 Ibid., 23.

72 See their webpages. Prospero Network: www.prospero-theatre.eu/. IYMA: http://iyma.eu. Mitos21: www.mitos21.com. NETA: www.netaart.tv.

73 James Woodall, 'Thomas Ostermeier: On Europe, Theatre, Communication and Exchange', in *Contemporary European Theatre Directors*, ed. Maria M. Delgado and Dan Rebellato (Abingdon and New York: Routledge, 2010), 373.

74 While historic international festivals such as those in Edinburgh and Avignon – both founded in 1947, the same year as the Piccolo in Milan and well before the Théâtre de l'Europe in Paris – led the way in promoting artistic and theatrical exchange with other countries and continents after the Second World War – their mission statements were not openly involved in the European project.

75 Jean-Pierre Han, 'An Unlikely Scene: French Theatre in the New Liberal Economy', in *Contemporary French Theatre and Performance*, ed. Clare Finburgh and Carl Lavery (Basingstoke and New York: Palgrave Macmillan, 2011), 85.

Chapter 5

1 Roger Planchon, conversation with Bernard Villeneuve, recorded July 1985 and held in the Fonds Planchon, Arts du spectacle Collection, Bibliothèque Nationale de France.

2 Translator's note: 'Je me souviens' (I remember) is a French memory game. It evokes Georges Perec's novel, *Je me souviens* (1978).

3 Jean Bouise (1929–89) was a French actor who co-founded the theatre company Théâtre de la Comédie with Planchon, and played in a large number of his productions. He played Falstaff between 1957 and 1961.

4 The Cour d'honneur is the largest and most prestigious performance space at the Avignon Theatre Festival, where some of the world's most renowned directors have been invited to stage productions. It seats 2,000 spectators and is at the heart of the festival.

5 The audio recording of Planchon's *Tartuffe* on tour at the Falkoner Center in 1966 can be found at: https://www.youtube.com/watch?v=JEGoIMAKcUE

(accessed 18 September 2017); and the audio recording of Planchon's *Les Trois mousquetaires* at the Falkoner Center can be found at: https://www.youtube.com/watch?v=B1YQHXQ9Fyo (accessed 18 September 2017).

6 The Branquignols were a group of actors who took cabarets by storm with their sketches, which often contained music and song. The Frères Jacques, also cabaret artists, were four singers and a pianist who combined song and narration, and also adapted literary texts, for example, by the poets Jacques Prévert and Boris Vian. Both acts were formed after the Second World War and disbanded in the 1970s or early 1980s.

7 *Les Rocambolesques aventures de Cartouche* (1953), Lucien Dabril's adaptation of Ponson du Terrail's *Les Aventures de Rocambole* (1953), and *Casque d'or* (1954) are three of Planchon's early productions, which he staged at the Théâtre de la Comédie.

8 The Cartel des quatre, or Cartel, was an association founded in 1927 between four Parisian theatre directors – Louis Jouvet, Charles Dullin, Gaston Baty and Georges Pitoëff – who were committed to making and promoting avant-garde, experimental theatre, in a landscape that had previously been dominated by commercial boulevard shows. The Cartel disbanded shortly before the Second World War, when three of its members, and the like-minded director Jacques Copeau, were invited to modernize France's national theatre, the Comédie-Française. See Gaston Baty, Charles Dullin, Louis Jouvet and Georges Pitoëff, *Le Cartel des quatre* (Arles: Actes Sud-Papiers, 2016).

9 Libertines, contemporary to Molière, and for some critics epitomized by his character Dom Juan, spurned all conventional morality and sexual constraint.

10 *Marivaudage* is a derogatory term attributed to Marivaux' allegedly mannered, over-precious and empty language, and the acting style that can accompany it.

11 Barrault and Renaud were a couple – he was an actor and director and she was an actor – who were prolific in French theatre for much of the twentieth century.

Chapter 6

1 Roger Planchon, 'Entretien avec Jean Mambrino', 17 and 29 June 1979, 2. Unpublished manuscript in Michel Bataillon's possession. The conversation between Planchon and Jean Mambrino was recorded by Planchon's dramaturg, Michel Bataillon. I use the unpublished transcript with Bataillon's permission. Unless otherwise indicated, all translations from French to English are my own. I would like to thank Michel Bataillon at the outset of this article for his invaluable help and advice, especially where it came to identifying the photographers behind images used in my analysis.

2 The personal conversations and tape-recorded interviews I shall refer to in this chapter were conducted with Michel Bataillon on 22 June 1982 in Lyon; Georges Péju, owner of Librairie La Proue, on 24 June 1982 in Lyon; Max Schoendorff, painter, dramaturg, designer, on 25 June 1982 in Lyon; Madeleine Sarrazin, administrator of Planchon's theatre, on 23 June 1982 in Villeurbanne; Claude Lochy, actor and musician, on 25 July 1982 in Paris; Jacques Rosner, actor, director, dramaturg, on 30 June 1982 in Paris; René

Allio, painter and designer, on 16 July 1982 in Paris; Isabelle Sadoyan, actor and costume designer, on 12 July 1982 in Paris; Pierre Meyrand, actor, on 8 July 1982 in Paris; and Roger Planchon on 26 November 2001 in Toronto.

3 For a thorough discussion of the guiding principles of the Cartel as a collective endeavour, see A.C. Gervais, *Propos sur la mise en scène* (Grenoble: Édition Françaises Nouvelles, 1943).

4 Paul-Louis Mignon, 'Roger Planchon', *L'Avant-Scène*, no. 272 (1962): 8.

5 The three scenes were published without an introduction or comment. Abraham published translations of nine scenes from *Fear and Misery of the Third Reich* in three sets of three scenes each, in *La Commune*, no. 66 (1939): 151–63; *Europe*, no. 197 (1939): 14–29; and *La Nouvelle Revue Française*, no. 309 (1939): 924–34.

6 Jacqueline Autrusseau, 'Brecht en France', *Les Lettres Françaises*, no. 828 (9 June 1960), 8. The journal is hereafter referred to as *LLF.*

7 One newspaper carried a pre-production article and three reviewed it after opening: 'Roger Planchon créera "La Bonne âme de Sé-Tchouan", in *Le Progrès*, 23 Jan. 1954; "La Bonne Ame De Se-Tchouan" par le Théâtre de la Comédie', in *L'Echo*, 2 July 1954; 'Le Théâtre de la Comédie crée "La bonne âme de Se-Tchouan" de Bertolt Brecht', in *Le Progrès*, 2 July 1954; 'Le Théâtre de la Comédie présente "La bonne âme de Se-Tchouan"', in *Le Progrès*, 3 July 1954 (newspaper clippings, personal archive Pia Kleber).

8 Autrusseau, 'Brecht en France', 8.

9 Sadoyan, Interview 1982.

10 *Le Progrès*, 3 July 1954.

11 Schoendorff and Rosner, Interviews 1982.

12 Planchon cited in Jacqueline Demornex, '"Le théâtre se meurt? Vive le théâtre!": Portrait d'un fou de théâtre: Roger Planchon', in *Elle* 1637 (23 May 1977), 43.

13 Planchon, 'Entretien avec Mambrino', 1.

14 Planchon, Interview 2001.

15 Planchon, 'Entretien avec Mambrino', 36.

16 Quoted in Michel Bataillon, *Aventures*, a handbook for a 1982 exhibition on Planchon in Lyon, unpaginated.

17 Planchon, Interview 2001.

18 Planchon, 'Entretien avec Mambrino', 17–18.

19 Ibid., 23.

20 Autrusseau, 'Brecht en France', 8.

21 Planchon in *Art et education* no. 22 (March 1968), 20.

22 Autrusseau, 'Brecht en France', 8.

23 Ibid., 8. See also Antonin Artaud, *The Theatre and its Double*, trans. Mary Caroline Richards (New York: Grove Press, 1958), 96.

24 Autrusseau, 'Brecht en France', 8.

25 Bertolt Brecht, *The Good Person of Szechwan*, trans. John Willett (London: Eyre Methuen, 1965), 45.

26 Ibid., 74.

27 Péju, Interview 1982. Péju maintained that he provided Planchon with all of Brecht's writings published in French translation during the five months between the first and second staging of *The Good Person*.

28 Roger Planchon, 'Creating a Theatre of Real Life: Roger Planchon: Actor, Director, Playwright. Interviewed by Michael Kustow', *Theatre Quarterly* 2, no. 5 (1972): 42–57.

29 Autrusseau, 'Brecht en France', 8.

30 Originally, Teo Otto had designed the set for the first performance of the play in Zürich (1943). The same design was used for the 1952 Frankfurt production.

31 Planchon, 'Creating a Theatre of Real Life', 46.

32 Käthe Rülicke, 'Dreizehn Bühnentechniker erzählen', *Sinn und Form* (Special Issue on Bertolt Brecht; 1957), 465–79, here p. 469.

33 Autrusseau, 'Brecht en France', 8.

34 Sadoyan played the sister-in-law in the first and second productions, and Shen Teh/Shui Ta in the third staging.

35 'Au Théâtre de la Comédie "La bonne âme de Sé-Tchouan"', *Le Progrès*, 30 October 1954.

36 Lochy, Interview 1982.

37 Roland Barthes, 'Les maladies du costume de theatre', *Théâtre Populaire* (12 March–April 1955): 68.

38 Bernard Dort, 'Le Lieu de la réprésentation épique', *Travail Théâtral* no. 27 (1977), 35–50, here p. 36.

39 Rosner, Interview 1982.

40 'Au Théâtre de la Comédie'.

41 Wolfgang Gersch, *Film bei Brecht* (Munich: Carl Hanser, 1975), 17.

42 *Cité Panorama* 1 (January 1959), 3; *Lyon-Étudiant* (January 1959) Personal archive Pia Kleber.

43 'Au Théâtre de la Comédie'.

44 Planchon, 'Creating a Theatre of Real Life', 52 (emphasis in the original).

45 'Au Théâtre de la Comédie'.

46 *Cité Panorama* 1 (January 1959).

47 Interview conducted by Claude Sarraute in *Le Monde* (17 October 1956, archive Pia Kleber.

48 *La Vie Lyonnaise* 60 (December 1958), archive Pia Kleber.

49 Allio, Interview 1982.

50 Autrusseau, 'Brecht en France', 8.

51 Ibid., 8.

52 Roger Planchon, 'Note sur le théâtre épique à propos de *La Bonne âme*', *Le Travail au Théâtre de la Cité* no. 1 (1959), 2–3, here p. 2.

53 Hans-Joachim Bunge, 'Notes et reflexions', *Théâtre Populaire* no. 30 (May 1958): 3–18.

54 Arthur Adamov, 'Où en sommes-nous avec Brecht? Entretien avec Roger Planchon et René Allio', in *Ici et maintenant*, ed. Arthur Adamov (Paris: Gallimard, 1964), 212.

55 René Allio, 'Le travail du décorateur', *Théâtre Populaire* no. 28 (January 1958): 25–6.

56 Ibid., 26.

57 Bunge, 'Notes et reflexions', 12–13.

58 Allio, Interview 1982.

59 Gérard Guillot, 'Roger Planchon nous parle *De la bonne âme de Sé-Tchouan*', *LLF* no. 753 (25 December 1958).

60 Ibid.

61 Ibid.

62 Brecht, *The Good Person*, 108.

63 Ibid., 108.

64 Ibid., 6.

65 Ibid., 78.

66 *Le Progrès* (16 December 1958), archive Pia Kleber.

67 Review in *L'Echo* (17 December 1958), archive Pia Kleber.

68 Allio, Interview 1982.

69 *Travail et Culture* (Lyon), December 1958, archive Pia Kleber.

70 Guillot, 'Roger Planchon nous parle'.

71 Ibid.; Gérard Guillot, 'La bonne âme de Sé-Tchouan an Théâtre de la Cité', *LLF* no. 756 (15 January 1959).

72 *Dernière heure lyonnaise*, 16 December 1958, archive Pia Kleber.

73 Jean Beaumont, 'Roger Planchon', in *L'Echo*, 17 December 1958.

74 Sadoyan and Allio, Interviews 1982.

75 Beaumont, 'Roger Planchon'.

76 Guillot, 'Roger Planchon nous parle'.

77 All citations in this paragraph from Allio, Interview 1982.

78 'Note sur le théâtre épique ...', 4.

79 Ibid., 4.

80 Ibid., 4–5.

81 Ibid., 1.

82 Ibid., 2.

83 Rosner, Interview 1982.

84 Dieter Kranz, *Positionen. Strehler, Planchon, Koun, Dario Fo, Långbacka, Stein* (Berlin: Henschel, 1981), 39.

85 Bernard Dort, 'Brecht en France', *Les Temps modernes* no. 171 (1960), 1855–74, here p. 1856ff.

86 Bunge, 'Notes et reflexions', 21.

BIBLIOGRAPHY

General

Adorno, Theodor W. *The Culture Industry: Selected Essays on Mass Culture* [1972/91]. Abingdon and New York: Routledge, 2005.

Althusser, Louis. 'The "Piccolo Teatro": Bertolazzi and Brecht – Notes on a Materialist Theatre' [1962]. In *For Marx*, 129–51. London and New York: Verso, 2005.

Arendt, Hannah. *Eichmann in Jerusalem: A Report on the Banality of the Evil* [1963]. London: Penguin, 2006.

Arendt, Hannah. *The Origins of Totalitarianism*. New edn, with added prefaces. San Diego, CA: Harvest Harcourt Brace, 1973.

Artaud, Antonin. *The Theatre and its Double*. Translated by Mary Caroline Richards. New York: Grove Press, 1958.

Barnett, David. *A History of the Berliner Ensemble*. Cambridge: Cambridge University Press, 2016.

Baty, Gaston, Charles Dullin, Louis Jouvet and Georges Pitoëff. *Le Cartel des quatre*. Arles: Actes Sud-Papiers, 2016.

Bauman, Zygmunt. *Community: Seeking Safety in an Insecure World*. Cambridge: Polity, 2001.

Benjamin, Walter. *Understanding Brecht*. Translated by Anna Bostock. London: New Left Books, 1973.

Bourdieu, Pierre. *Distinction: A Social Critique of the Judgment of Taste*. Translated by Richard Nice. Abingdon and New York: Routledge, 2010 [1984].

Bradby, David. *Modern French Drama*, 2nd edn. Cambridge: Cambridge University Press, 1991.

Bradby, David, and John McCormick. *People's Theatre*. London: Croom Helm, 1978.

Bradby, David, and Annie Sparks. *Mise en Scène: French Theatre Now*. London: Methuen Drama, 1997.

Bradby, David, and David Williams. *Directors' Theatre*. London: Macmillan, 1988.

Brecht, Bertolt. *Brecht on Theatre*. Edited by Marc Silberman, Steve Giles and Tom Kuhn. London: Bloomsbury Methuen, 2015.

Buber, Martin. *Between Man and Man*. London: Fontana, 1961.

Burt, Philippa. 'Punishing the Outsiders: Theatre Workshop and the Arts Council'. *Theatre, Dance and Performance Training* 5, no. 2 (2014): 119–30.

Delgado, Maria, and Paul Heritage, eds. *In Touch with the Gods: Directors Talk Theatre*. Manchester: Manchester University Press, 1996.

Delgado, Maria M., and Dan Rebellato, eds. *Contemporary European Theatre Directors*. Abingdon and New York: Routledge, 2010.

Esslin, Martin. *The Theatre of the Absurd* [1961]. London: Bloomsbury Methuen, 2013.

Fiebach, Joachim. *Von Craig bis Brecht: Studien zu Künstlertheorien des 20. Jahrhunderts*, 3rd rev. edn. Berlin: Henschel, 1991.

Finburgh, Clare, and Carl Lavery, eds. *Contemporary French Theatre and Performance*. Basingstoke and New York: Palgrave Macmillan, 2011.

Forti, Simona. *New Demons: Rethinking Power and Evil Today*. Translated by Zakiya Hanafi. Stanford, CA: Stanford University Press, 2015.

Gervais, A.C. *Propos sur la mise en scène*. Grenoble: Édition Françaises Nouvelles, 1943.

Goodwin, Matthew J., and Oliver Heath. 'The 2016 Referendum, Brexit and the Left Behind: An Aggregate-Level Analysis of the Result'. *Political Quarterly* 87, no. 3 (2016): 323–32.

Gregor, Joseph. *Grosse Regisseure der modernen Bühne*. Vienna: UNESCO Commission, 1958.

Habermas, Jürgen. *The Structural Transformation of the Public Sphere* [1962]. Translated by Thomas McCarthy. Cambridge: Polity, 1992.

Harvie, Jen. *Staging the UK*. Manchester: Manchester University Press, 2005.

Hecht, Werner. *Bert Brecht: Sein Leben in Bildern und Texten*. Frankfurt am Main: Suhrkamp, 1978.

Hobsbawm, Eric. *Age of Extremes: The Short Twentieth Century 1914–91*. London: Abacus, 1995.

Hodge, Alison. *Actor Training*, 2nd edn. Abingdon and New York: Routledge, 2010.

Horkheimer, Max, and Theodor W. Adorno. *Dialectic of Enlightenment: Philosophical Fragments* [1947]. Translated by Edmund Jephcott. Stanford, CA: Stanford University Press, 2002.

Judt, Tony. *Postwar: A History of Europe since 1945*. New York: Penguin, 2005.

Kelleher, Joe. *Theatre and Politics*. Basingstoke and New York: Palgrave Macmillan, 2009.

Lavery, Carl. 'Between Negativity and Resistance: Jean Genet and Committed Theatre'. *Contemporary Theatre Review* 16, no. 2 (2006): 220–34.

Marcuse, Herbert. *The Aesthetic Dimension: Toward a Critique of Marxist Aesthetics*. Boston, MA: Beacon, 1978.

Marcuse, Herbert. *One-Dimensional Man: Studies in the Ideology of Advanced Industrial Society* [1964]. Abingdon and New York: Routledge, 2002.

Martin, Carol, and Henry Bial, eds. *Brecht Sourcebook*. London and New York: Routledge, 2000.

Meinhof, Ulrike Hanna, and Anna Triandafyllidou, eds. *Transcultural Europe: Cultural Policy in a Changing Europe*. Basingstoke and New York: Palgrave Macmillan, 2006.

Pavis, Patrice. *Dictionary of the Theatre*. Toronto: University of Toronto Press, 1998.

Rühle, Günther. 'Die fortschrittliche Revision: Die Bühne als Schauplatz der Kritik'. In *Anarchie der Regie? Theater in unserer Zeit*, vol. 2, 35–52. Frankfurt am Main: Suhrkamp, 1982.

Schumacher, Ernst. *Leben Brechts in Wort und Bild*. Berlin: Henschelverlag, 1978.

Taylor, Diana. *The Archive and the Repertoire: Performing Cultural Memory in the Americas*. Durham, NC, and London: Duke University Press, 2003.

Theiler, Tobias. *Political Symbolism and European Integration*. Manchester: Manchester University Press, 2005.
Thomson, Peter, and Glendwyr Sacks, eds. *The Cambridge Companion to Brecht*. Cambridge: Cambridge University Press, 1994.
Turner, Victor W. *The Ritual Process*. Harmondsworth: Penguin, 1974.
Tynan, Kenneth. *Tynan on Theatre*. Harmondsworth: Penguin, 1964.
Tynan, Kenneth. *Tynan Right and Left*. London: Longmans, 1967.
Van Maanen, Hans, and S.E. Wilmer. *Theatre Worlds in Motion: Structures, Politics and Developments in the Countries of Western Europe*. Amsterdam: Rodopi, 1998.
Van Maanen, Hans, Andreas Kotte and Anneli Saro, eds. *Global Changes – Local Stages: How Theatre Functions in Smaller European Countries*. Amsterdam: Rodopi, 2009.
Vilar, Jean. 'The T.N.P. – Public Service' [1953]. In *Twentieth-Century Theatre: A Sourcebook*, edited by Richard Drain, 193. London and New York: Routledge, 1995.
Weimann, Robert. *Shakespeare and Popular Tradition in the Theatre: Studies in the Social Dimension of the Dramatic Form and Function*. Baltimore, MD: Johns Hopkins University Press, 1978.

Joan Littlewood

Arden, John. *Plays: One*. London: Eyre Methuen, 1977.
Arditti, Michael. 'Joan Littlewood is Making a Scene, Interview'. *The Independent Magazine*, 26 March 1994. http://www.michaelarditti.com/non-fiction/joan-littlewood-making-a-scene/. Accessed 22 November 2017.
Barker, Clive. *Theatre Games: A New Approach to Drama Training*. London: Methuen, 1977.
Behan, Brendan. *The Hostage*. London: Methuen Drama, 1970.
Bridson, Douglas Geoffrey. *Prospero and Ariel: A Personal Recollection*. London: Golancz, 1971.
Callow, Simon. 'Character Building Stuff'. *The Guardian Review*, 13 March 2013.
Chambers, Colin. *The Story of Unity Theatre*. London: Lawrence and Wishart, 1989.
Delaney, Shelagh. *A Taste of Honey*. London: Methuen, 2000.
Edwards, Ness. *The Workers Theatre*. Cardiff: Cymric Federation Press, 1930.
Goorney, Howard. *The Theatre Workshop Story*. London: Methuen, 1981.
Goorney, Howard, and Ewan MacColl, eds. *Agit-Prop to Theatre Workshop: Political Playscripts 1930–50*. Manchester: Manchester University Press, 1986.
Hawthorne, Nigel. *Straight Face*. London: BBC Audiobooks, 2004.
Holdsworth, Nadine. *Joan Littlewood's Theatre*. Cambridge: Cambridge University Press, 2011.
Holdsworth, Nadine. '"They'd Have Pissed on My Grave": The Arts Council and Theatre Workshop'. *New Theatre Quarterly* 15, no. 1 (1999): 3–16.
Kennedy, Dennis. 'Shakespeare and the Cold War'. In *400 Hundred Years of Shakespeare in Europe*, edited by Angel Luis Pujante and Ton Hoenselaars, 163–79. Newark, NJ: Delaware University Press, 2003.
Kourilsky, Françoise. 'La Nouvelle Compagnie d'Avignon'. *Travail Théâtral*, no. 5 (1971): 3–26.

Kuhns, David F. *German Expressionist Theatre: The Actor and the Stage*. Cambridge: Cambridge University Press, 1997.

Leach, Robert. *Theatre Workshop: Joan Littlewood and the Making of Modern British Theatre*. Exeter: Exeter University Press, 2006.

Littlewood, Joan. *Joan's Book*. London: Methuen, 1994.

Littlewood, Joan. *Notes*. *Joan Littlewood and the Theatre Workshop Collection*. Harry Ransom Humanities Research Center, University of Texas, Austin.

MacColl, Ewan. *Journeyman*. London: Sidgwick and Jackson, 1990.

MacColl, Ewan. (Typescript 2) *Landscape with Chimneys*. Oxford: Ruskin College Library.

MacColl, Ewan. (Typescript 1) *The Good Soldier Schweik*. Oxford: Ruskin College Library.

MacColl, Ewan. *Uranium 235*. Glasgow: William MacLellan, 1946.

Marowitz, Charles, Tom Milne and Owen Hale, eds. *The Encore Reader*. London: Methuen, 1965.

Melvin, Murray. *Interview*. BBC 4, 9 February 2004. Transcript.

Melvin, Murray. *Interview with Danielle Mérahi*. 5 June 2000. Transcript.

Mérahi, Danielle. *Joan Littlewood l'insoumise et le Theatre Workshop*. Paris: L'Entretemps, 2010.

Milne, Tom. 'Art in Angel Lane'. In *The Encore Reader*, edited by Charles Marowitz, Tom Milne and Owen Hale, 80–6 London: Methuen, 1965.

Morgan, Kevin, Gideon Cohen and Andrew Flinn. *Communism and British Society*. London: Rivers Oram Press, 2007.

Moussinac, Léon. *Tendances Nouvelles du Théâtre*. Paris: Ed. Albert Lévy, 1931.

Moussinac, Léon. *The New Movement in Theatre: A Survey of Recent Developments in Europe and America*. Translated by R.H. Packman. London: Batsford, 1931.

Moussinac, Léon. *Traité de la Mise en Scène*. Paris: Ed. d'Aujourd'hui, 1948.

Newlove, Jean. *Laban for Actors and Dancers*. London: Nick Hern Books, 1993.

Norman, Frank. *Fings Ain't Wot They Used T'Be*. New York: Grove Press, 1962.

Paget, Derek. *True Stories? Documentary Drama on Radio, Screen and Stage*. Manchester: Manchester University Press, 1990.

Piscator, Erwin. *The Political Theatre*. London: Eyre Methuen, 1980.

Pitches, Jonathan. *Russians in Britain*. Abingdon and New York: Routledge, 2012.

Planson, Claude. *Il était une fois le théâtre des Nations*. Paris: Maison des Cultures du Monde, 1984.

Rivier, Estelle. *La scène de Richard II*. Rennes: Presses Universitaires de Rennes, 2007.

Rufford, Juliet. '"What Have We Got to Do with Fun?": Littlewood, Price, and the Policy Makers'. *New Theatre Quarterly* 27, no. 4 (2011): 313–28.

Runkel, Richard. 'Theatre Workshop: Its Philosophy, Plays, Process and Productions.' PhD thesis, University of Texas Austin, 1987.

Samuel, Raphael, Ewan MacColl and Stuart Cosgrave. *Theatres of the Left, 1880–1935*. London: Routledge and Kegan Paul, 1985.

Schwaiger, Michael. *Bertolt Brecht und Erwin Piscator*. Vienna: Verlag Christian Brandstätter, 2004.

Theatre Workshop. *Oh What a Lovely War*, rev. edn. London: Methuen, 2000.

Van Gyseghem, André. *Theatre in Soviet Russia*. London: Faber & Faber, 1943.

Giorgio Strehler

Alberti, Alberto Cesare. *Poetica teatrale e bibliografia di Anton Giulio Bragaglia*. Rome: Bulzoni, 1978.
Banu, Georges, ed. *Les cités du théâtre d'art de Stanislavskij à Strehler*. Paris: Editions théâtrales, 2000.
Battistini, Fabio. *Giorgio Strehler*. Rome: Gremese, 1980.
Benedetto, Alberto. *Brecht e il Piccolo Teatro. Una questione di diritti*. Milan: Mimesis, 2016.
Bentoglio, Alberto. *Invito al teatro di Giorgio Strehler*. Milan: Mursia, 2002.
Bottoni, Luciano. *Storia del teatro italiano: 1900–1945*. Bologna: Il Mulino, 1999.
Bucciantini, Massimo. *Un Galileo a Milano*. Torino: Einaudi, 2017
Cambiaghi, Mariagabriella. 'L'avventura del teatro dell'Europa'. In *Giorgio Strehler e il suo teatro*, edited by Federica Mazzocchi and Alberto Bentoglio, 101–17. Rome: Bulzoni, 1997.
Damiani, Luciano. Autoritratto. Rome: Teatro Documenti, 2001. Unpublished MS.
D'Amico, Silvio. *Tramonto del grande attore*. Florence: La casa Uscher, 1985.
Douël Dell'Agnola, Catherine. *Gli spettacolo goldoniani di Giorgio Strehler (1947–1991)*. Rome: Bulzoni, 1992.
Douël Dell'Agnola, Catherine. *Strehler e Brecht*. Rome: Bulzoni, 1994.
Dvorak, Cordelia. *Passione teatrale. Giorgio Strehler und das Theater*. Berlin: Henschel, 1994.
Farrell, Joseph, and Paolo Puppa, eds. *A History of Italian Theatre*. Cambridge: Cambridge University Press, 2006.
Fechner, Eberhard. *Giorgio Strehler inszeniert*. Hanover: Friedrichs, 1963.
Gaipa, Ettore. *Giorgio Strehler*. Berlin: Henschelverlag, 1963.
Grassi, Paolo, and Giorgio Strehler. *I primi dieci anni del Piccolo Teatro*. Milan: Electra, 1982.
Gregori, Maria Grazia, ed. *Piccolo Teatro di Milano*. Milan: Piccolo Teatro, 2000.
Gregori, Maria Grazia. 'Il Teatro d'Europa dall'utopia al progetto'. *Teatro in Europa*, no. 3 (1988): 94–100.
Guazzotti, Giorgio. *Teoria e realtà del Piccolo Teatro di Milano*. Turin: Einaudi, 1965.
Hirst, David L. *Giorgio Strehler*. Cambridge: Cambridge University Press, 1993.
Holm, Bent. 'Dario Fo's bourgeois Period: Carnival and Criticism'. In *Dario Fo: Stage, Text and Tradition*, edited by Joseph Farrell and Antonio Scuderi, 122–42. Carbondale and Edwardsville: Southern Illinois University Press, 2000.
Holm, Bent. 'Sogno del teatro. Teatro del sogno'. In *In Ombra delle Muse: Spettacoli e arti visive*, edited by Paolo Puppa, 54–60. Reggio Emilia: Tecnostampa, 1994.
Kranz, Dieter. *Positionen: Strehler, Planchon, Koun, Dario Fo, Långbacka, Stein*. Berlin: Henschel, 1981.
Mainusch, Herbert. '"Kunst ist die wirklich aktive Seite des Menschen": Gespräch mit Giorgio Strehler'. In *Regie und Interpretation: Gespärche mit Regisseuren*, 119–30. Munich: Wilhelm Fink, 1985.
Mambrini, Clarissa Egle. *Il giovane Strehler: Da Novara al Piccolo Teatro di Milano*. Milan: Lampi di stampa, 2013.
Mazzocchi, Federica and Alberto Bentoglio. *Giorgio Strehler e il suo teatro*. Rome: Bulzoni, 1997.

Nanni, Andrea, ed. *Giorgio Strehler o la passione teatrale*. Milan: Ubulibri, 1998.

Palazzi, Renato. 'Le Dimissioni di Strehler dal Piccolo nel 1968 e la contestazione della regia e della politica degli stabili pubblici'. In *Giorgio Strehler: Atti del convegno di studi su Giorgio Strehler e il teatro pubblico*, edited by Elio Testoni, 111–21. Catanzaro: Rubbettino, 2009.

Pedullà, Gianfranco. *Il teatro italiano nel tempo del fascismo*. Bologna: Il Mulino, 1994.

Porto, Salvatore. *Strehler e il teatro dell'Europa*. Catania: Edidrama, 1987.

Quadri, Franco. *Il teatro del regime*. Milan: Mazzotta, 1976.

Sogliuzzo, A. Richard. *Luigi Pirandello, Director: The Playwright in the Theatre*. Metuchen, NJ: Scarecrow Press, 1982.

Stampalia, Giancarlo. *Strehler dirige. Le fasi di un allestimento e l'impulso musicale nel teatro*. Venezia: Marsilio, 1997.

Strehler, Giorgio. 'Ci siamo scambiati omicidi ma anche molta cultura'. *La Stampa*, 8 June 1979 (Piccolo Teatro Archive).

Strehler, Giorgio. 'Il teatro nella prospettiva di un'Europa unita', 1993 (Piccolo Teatro Archive).

Strehler, Giorgio. *Il Piccolo teatro d'arte: quarant'anni di lavoro teatrale, 1947–1987*. Milan: Electa, 1988.

Strehler, Giorgio. 'Nel teatro si può perdere l'anima', 1985 (Piccolo Teatro Archive).

Strehler, Giorgio. 'Per un'Europa umana'. *Libertà*, 6 June 1979 (Piccolo Teatro Archive).

Strehler, Giorgio. *Théâtre de l'Europe, Season 1983–84, Programme Note*, 1983.

Strehler, Giorgio. *Théâtre de l'Europe, Season 1984–85 Programme Note*, 1984.

Strehler, Giorgio, and Stella Casiraghi. *Lettere sul teatro*. Milan: Archinto, 2000.

Strehler, Giorgio, and Stella Casiraghi. *Nessuno è incolpevole: scritti politici e civili*. Milan: Melampo, 2007.

Strehler, Giorgio, and Sinah Kessler. *Per un teatro umano: pensieri scritti, parlati e attuati*. Milan: Feltrinelli, 1974.

Strehler, Giorgio, and Sinah Kessler. *Für ein menschlicheres Theater*. Frankfurt am Main: Suhrkamp, 1975.

Strehler, Giorgio, and Ugo Ronfani. *Io, Strehler: una vita per il teatro: conversazioni con Ugo Ronfani*. Milan: Rusconi, 1986.

Testoni, Elio. *Giorgio Strehler: atti del Convegno di studi su Giorgio Strehler e il teatro pubblico*. Catanzaro: Rubbettino, 2009.

Tian, Renzo, and Alessandro Martinez, eds. *Giorgio Strehler o la Passione Teatrale: l'opera di un maestro raccontata al Premio Europa per il Teatro*. Milan: Ubulibri, 1998.

Unseld, Siegfried, ed. *Bertolt Brechts Dreigroschenbuch: Texte Materialien Dokumente*. Frankfurt am Main: Suhrkamp, 1960.

Roger Planchon

Adamov, Arthur. 'Où en sommes-nous avec Brecht? Entretien avec Roger Planchon et René Allio'. In *Ici et maintenant*, edited by Arthur Adamov, 208–20. Paris: Gallimard, 1964.

Allio, René. 'Le travail du décorateur'. *Théâtre Populaire*, 28 January 1958, 25–6.

Autrusseau, Jacqueline. 'Brecht en France'. *Les Lettres Françaises*, 9 June 1960.

Bataillon, Michel. *Aventures: Expoplanchon*. Exhibition Catalogue. Vénissieux: Centre Culturel, 1982.

Beaumont, Jean. 'Roger Planchon'. *L'Echo*, 17 December 1958.

Brecht, Bertolt. 'Essai Numero 3'. Translated by Claude Vernier and Joan Rougeul. *K. Revue de la poésie*, no. 3 (1949): 23–5.

Brecht, Bertolt. *La Bonne âme de Sé-Tchouan*. Translated by Jeanne Stern. *Botteghe Oscuro*, no. 6 (1950): 199–312.

Bunge, Hans-Joachim. 'Notes et reflexions'. *Théâtre Populaire* 30 (May 1958): 3–18.

Daoust, Yvette. *Roger Planchon: Director and Playwright*. Cambridge: Cambridge University Press, 1981.

Guillot, Gérard. 'Roger Planchon nous parle *De la bonne âme de Sé-Tchouan*'. *Les Lettres Françaises*, 25 December 1958.

Kranz, Dieter. *Positionen: Strehler, Planchon, Koun, Dario Fo, Långbacka, Stein*. Berlin: Henschel, 1981.

Mignon, Paul-Louis. 'Roger Planchon'. *L'Avant-Scène*, no. 272 (1962): 8.

Planchon, Roger. '"Creating a Theatre of Real Life": Roger Planchon: Actor, Director, Playwright: Interviewed by Michael Kustow'. *Theatre Quarterly* 2, no. 5 (1972): 42–57.

Planchon, Roger. 'Entretien avec Jean Mambrino', 17 and 29 June 1979. Transcript. Unpublished MS.

Planchon, Roger. 'Note sur le théâtre épique à propos de *La Bonne âme*'. *Le Travail au Théâtre de la Cité*, 1. Paris: L' Arche, 1959.

INDEX